100 BULLETS: THE COUNTERFIFTH DETECTIVE

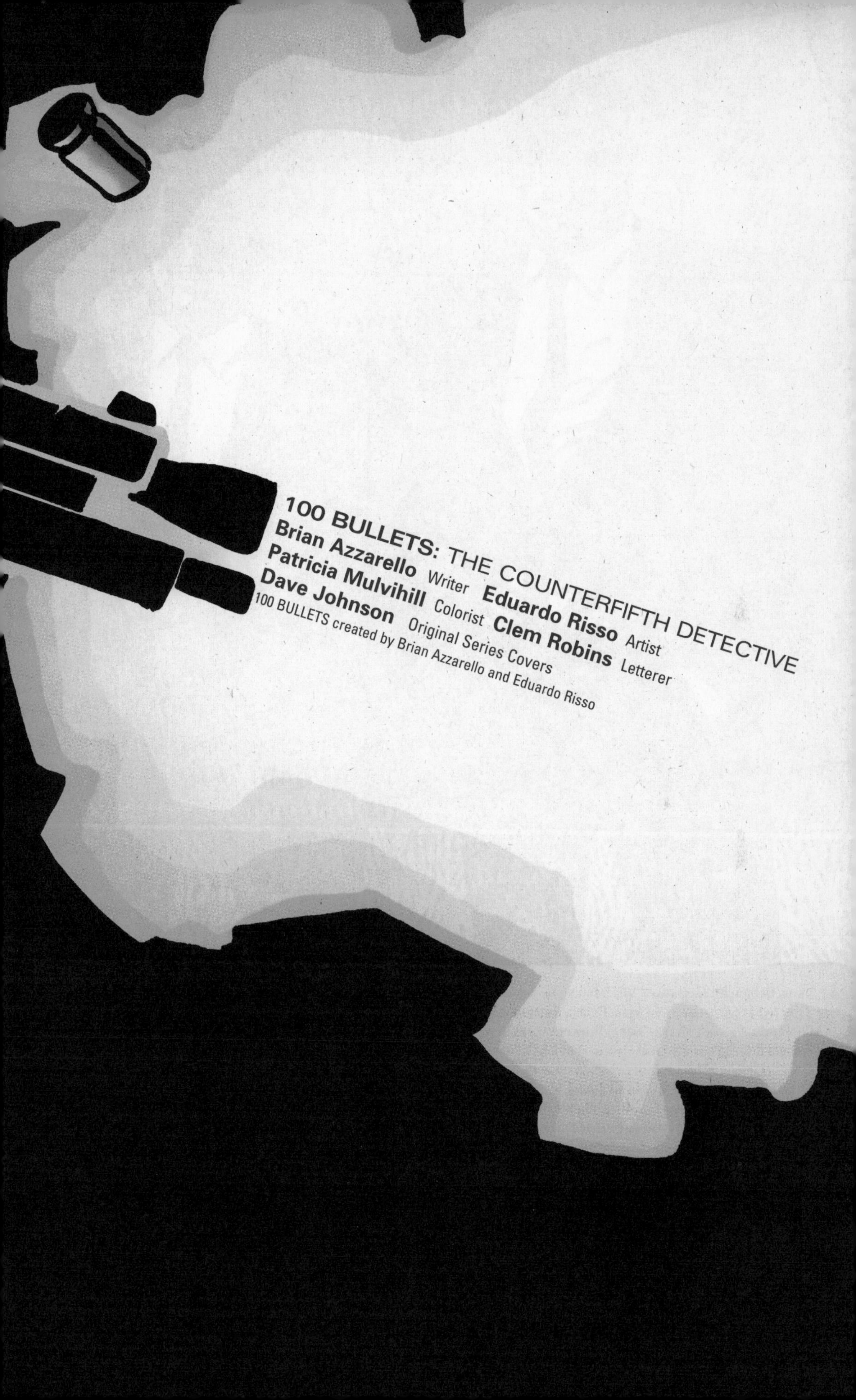

100 BULLETS: THE COUNTERFIFTH DETECTIVE

Brian Azzarello Writer **Eduardo Risso** Artist
Patricia Mulvihill Colorist **Clem Robins** Letterer
Dave Johnson Original Series Covers
100 BULLETS created by Brian Azzarello and Eduardo Risso

Karen Berger VP-Executive Editor Will Dennis Editor-original series
Scott Nybakken Editor-collected edition Robbin Brosterman Senior Art Director
Paul Levitz President & Publisher Georg Brewer VP-Design & Retail Product Development
Richard Bruning Senior VP-Creative Director Patrick Caldon Senior VP-Finance & Operations
Chris Caramalis VP-Finance Terri Cunningham VP-Managing Editor
Stephanie Fierman Senior VP-Sales & Marketing Alison Gill VP-Manufacturing
Rich Johnson VP-Book Trade Sales Hank Kanalz VP-General Manager, WildStorm
Lillian Laserson Senior VP & General Counsel Jim Lee Editorial Director-WildStorm
Paula Lowitt Senior VP-Business & Legal Affairs David McKillips VP-Advertising & Custom Publishing
John Nee VP-Business Development Gregory Noveck Senior VP-Creative Affairs
Cheryl Rubin Senior VP-Brand Management Bob Wayne VP-Sales

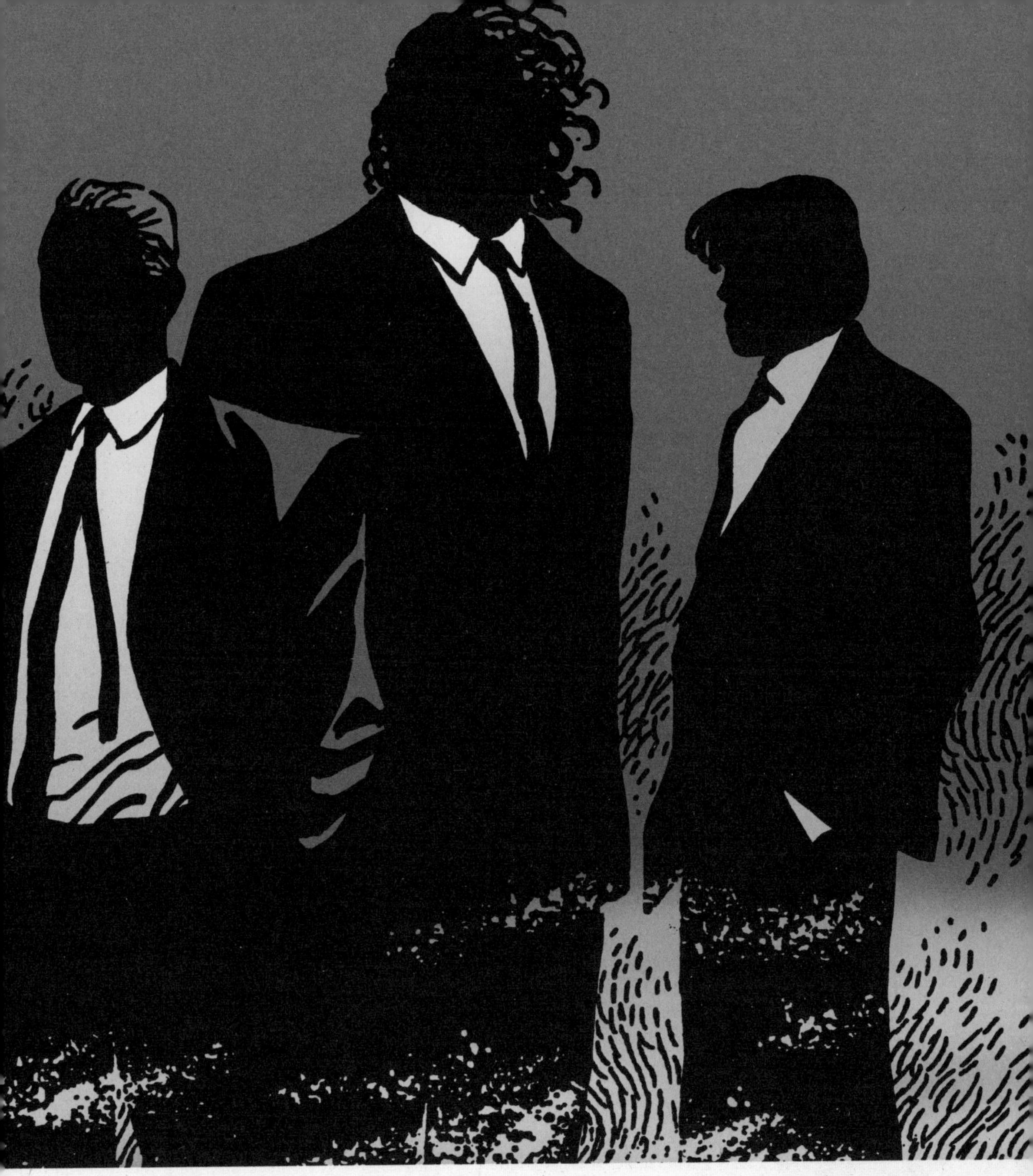

Introduction by Rob Elder

Hey.

Sit down.

No, I don't read introductions either. Sit the fuck down.

Thank you.

Cigarette?

No? There are other things that will kill you quicker.

[Pause]

You know what you're getting yourself into? What you have in your hand?

Didn't think so. That's a dangerous package you're carrying. You'd be wise to ask yourself what you know about the attaché case and the man who gave it to you. Yes, yes. One hundred bullets, airtight proof that you've been wronged and a bull's-eye on the bastards responsible. The enclosed gun, a license to set things right. *Carte blanche* to commit murder and get away with it from a kindly old man calling himself Agent Graves.

He's handed out other attaché cases, y'know.

We've assembled four previous casebooks on him. You'll find the fifth volume on the seat next to you. In each one, we've uncovered a little bit more about Agent Graves, his Minutemen, and their thus far undefined goals. We still don't know everything. Mostly blind guesses at a puzzle with pieces missing. Rumor has it they were enforcers, assassin Reservoir Dogs meant to keep The Trust — an underworld association of family cartels — honest, to settle disputes swiftly and without prejudice. But whatever they were, they're rogues now.

The Trust tried to wipe them out. So now they are *ronin*, samurai without masters, but not without honor. Honor is

the little game Graves plays. Graves is waking up his sleeper Minutemen, some retired, and making himself and his crusade even more powerful.

But more dangerous are the men above Graves — Brian Azzarello and Eduardo Risso. Azz is a chain smoker, a literary type. Quiet. Doesn't like his picture taken. His co-conspirator is an Argentinean cat named Risso, shadowy character with ink stains on his hands.

Ever met them? No?

I have, but only Azzarello. The first time was in a little hole in the wall in Chicago called the Half Shell. One of us barely got out alive. Never mind which one.

Together, the pair are lethal. They're men of letters now, award winners. Taught in college for chrissake. To paraphrase a former Corleone, now that they're respectable, they're even more dangerous.

This two-man syndicate deals in *noir*, what's been called "Greek tragedy for the underclass." Translated: The little guy gets stepped on. Sometimes the little guy gets a bit of power, a chance to make things right, to quit the grift, to make his mama proud, etc. Maybe even bed a dame so far out of his league she's playing a different game. (But then again, skirts are always playing a different game for different stakes, aren't they?)

Usually, these guys are thugs, suckers, and losers who think life can't get any worse. Until it does, of course.

Any of this sounding familiar?

This latest gambit is Azzarello and Risso's tip of the hat to Raymond Chandler, wordsmith and paperback peddler of bullet-ridden morality tales. He gave us Philip Marlowe, private dick in the center of *The Big Sleep* and *The Long Goodbye*. Since, there's been Jim Thompson, Elmore Leonard, a few in between. Hell, even dames are getting into it now. Janet Evanovich is a heavy, but few have come close to Chandler's sinister wit, his blood-smeared unpredictability.

Instead of Marlowe, they give us Milo Garret, "The Counterfifth Detective," another faceless gutter-level private eye. 'Cept he's got no face, literally. Seems his mug was introduced to a windshield at high velocity. It didn't improve Milo's demeanor none.

And guess what? Milo got a hospit room visit, not long after his "accident from a craggy silver-haired codger wi an attaché case. He wasn't there for th Jell-O.

Milo carted off the briefcase, b maybe he's smarter. True, there's th drinking problem. He likes to fight ar fuck, and is prone to poetic pontificatio in voiceover form. We all have o quirks.

Aside from looking like The Mumm Milo is the perfect protagonist, a mar you can love. That's one of the insidiou things about the *noir* game — just whe you get to like a guy, they take away h dignity, a couple of his teeth, and som times his life. That's part of *noir*'s charm you fall in love with the doomed. It's se dom pretty.

You know what Chandler onc wrote?

"There are two kinds of truth: th truth that lights the way and the tru that warms the heart. The first of these is science, and the second is art. Neithe is independent of the other or mor important than the other... The truth o art keeps science from becoming inhu man, and the truth of science keeps a from becoming ridiculous."

100 BULLETS doesn't exactly warr the heart, does it? Forget about findin your way around. You'll end up mor lost, even if you think you're on the righ path.

Yet 100 BULLETS is art, the most vita compelling kind — the kind that defie definition. It's neither this thing, nor that It's noisy, bloody, white-knuckled stuf that challenges the boundaries of it predecessors. It's part conspiracy theo ry playground, part gangster tome, an part ghetto justice.

Still a question mark hanging ove your head? Well then, by all means, con tinue on your current course.

Happy hunting. It's your funeral.

ROB ELDER, if indeed that is his rea name, writes about film, comics, an pop culture for The Chicago Tribune. *Hi work has also appeared in* The New York Times, Premiere, Gear, Salon.com, The Los Angeles Times, *and* The Bostor Globe. *A Montana native, Elder hangs his hat in Chicago.*

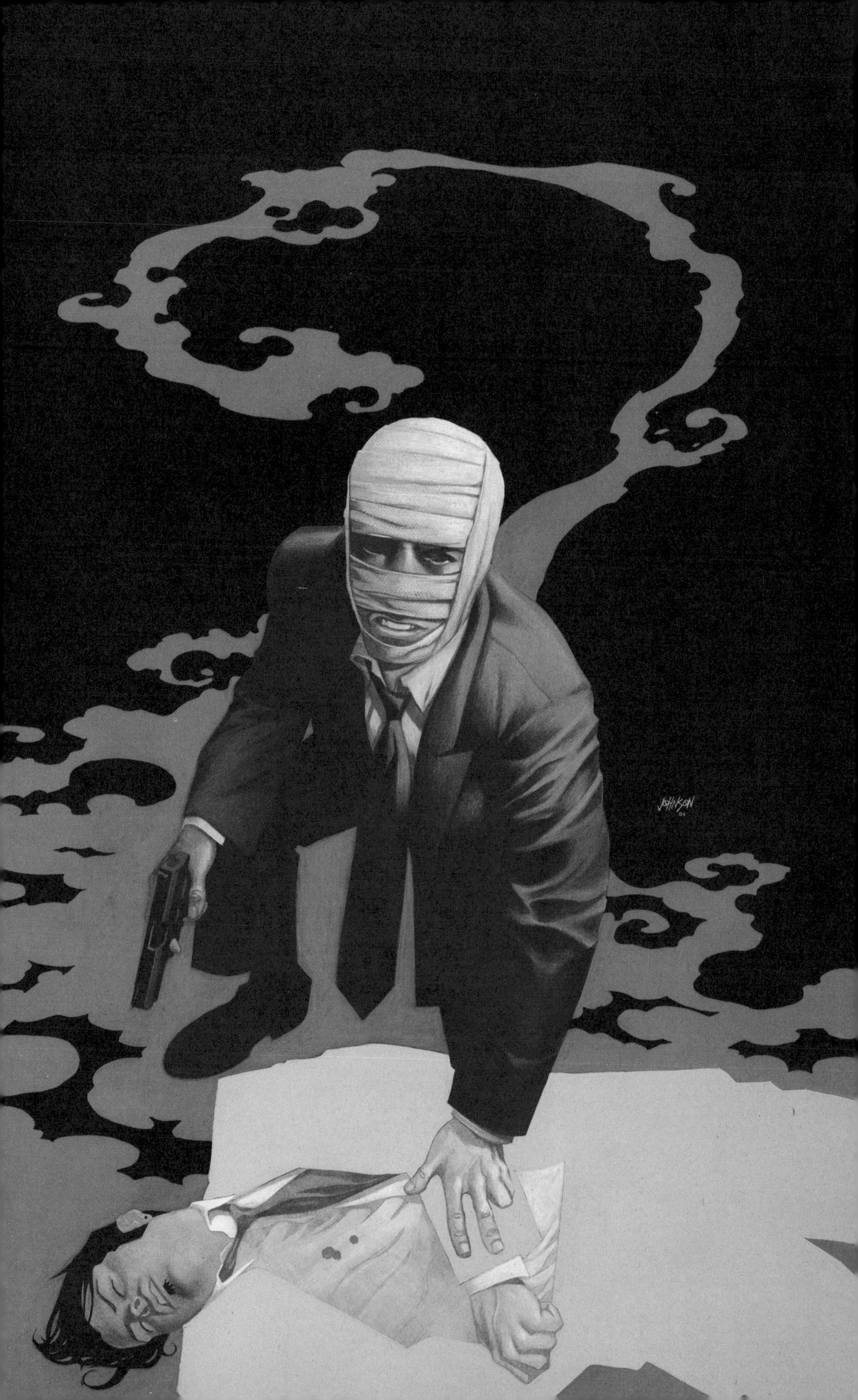
JOHNSON '01

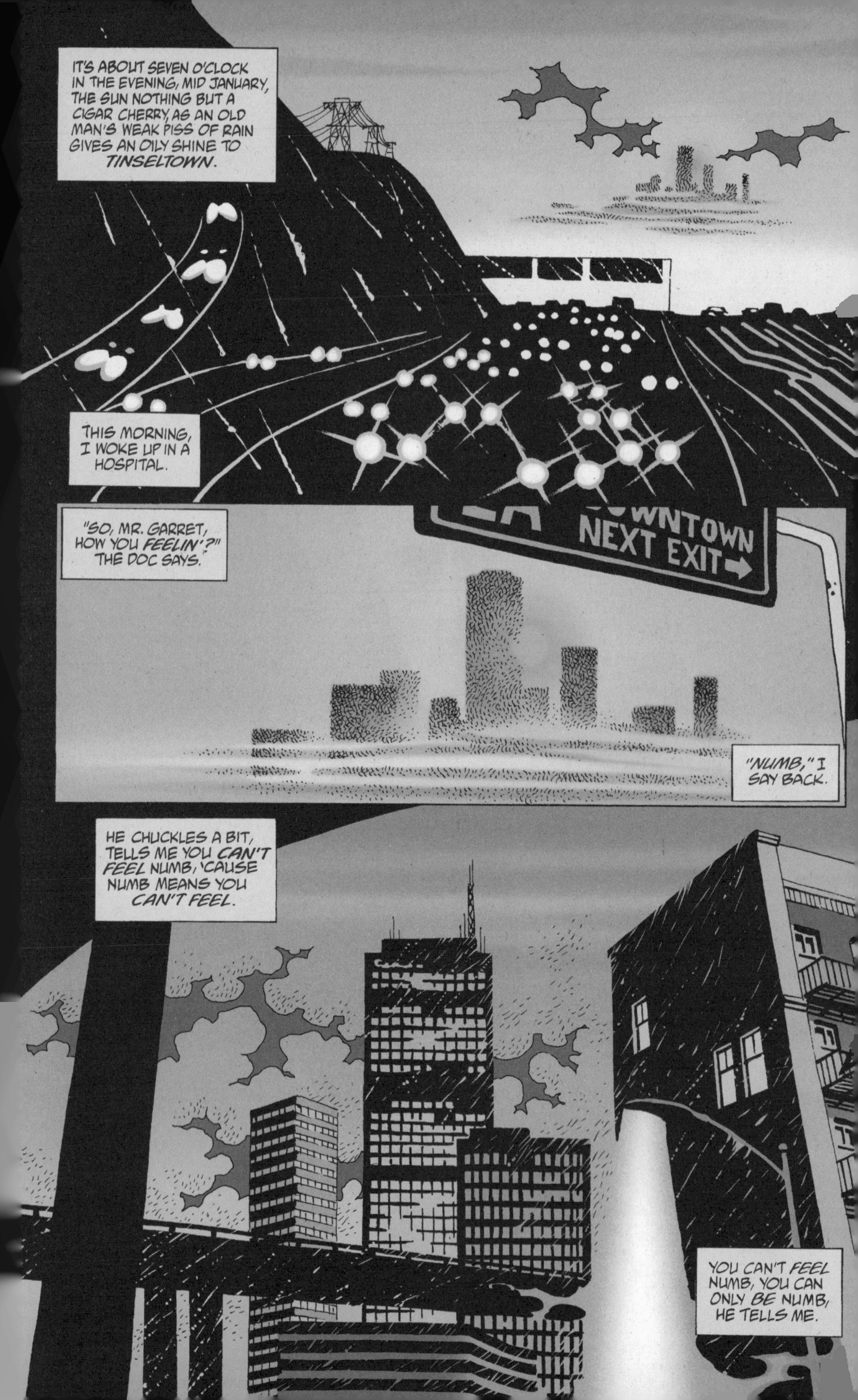
IT'S ABOUT SEVEN O'CLOCK IN THE EVENING, MID JANUARY, THE SUN NOTHING BUT A CIGAR CHERRY, AS AN OLD MAN'S WEAK PISS OF RAIN GIVES AN OILY SHINE TO TINSELTOWN.
THIS MORNING, I WOKE UP IN A HOSPITAL.
"SO, MR. GARRET, HOW YOU FEELIN'?" THE DOC SAYS.
NEXT EXIT
"NUMB," I SAY BACK.
HE CHUCKLES A BIT, TELLS ME YOU CAN'T FEEL NUMB, 'CAUSE NUMB MEANS YOU CAN'T FEEL.
YOU CAN'T FEEL NUMB, YOU CAN ONLY BE NUMB, HE TELLS ME.

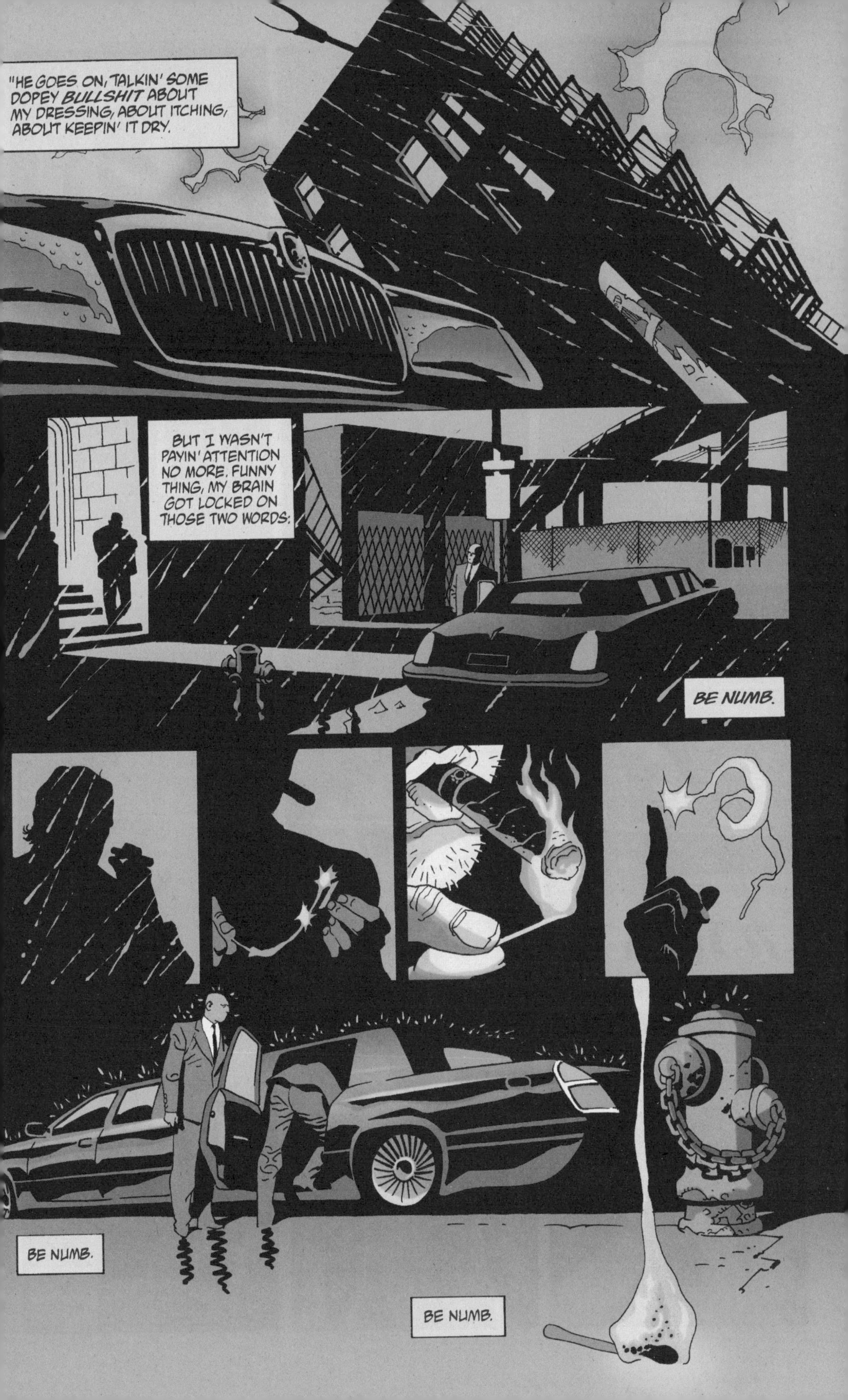
"HE GOES ON, TALKIN' SOME DOPEY BULLSHIT ABOUT MY DRESSING, ABOUT ITCHING, ABOUT KEEPIN' IT DRY.
BUT I WASN'T PAYIN' ATTENTION NO MORE. FUNNY THING, MY BRAIN GOT LOCKED ON THOSE TWO WORDS:
BE NUMB.
BE NUMB.
BE NUMB.

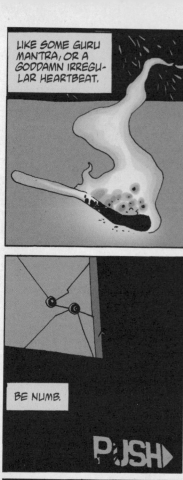

LIKE SOME GURU MANTRA, OR A GODDAMN IRREGULAR HEARTBEAT.

GOODIS Piano bar

BE NUMB.

PUSH►

HUNNER 1885

BE NUMB.

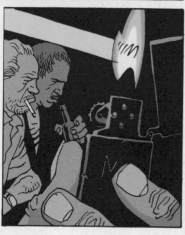

BE NUMB.

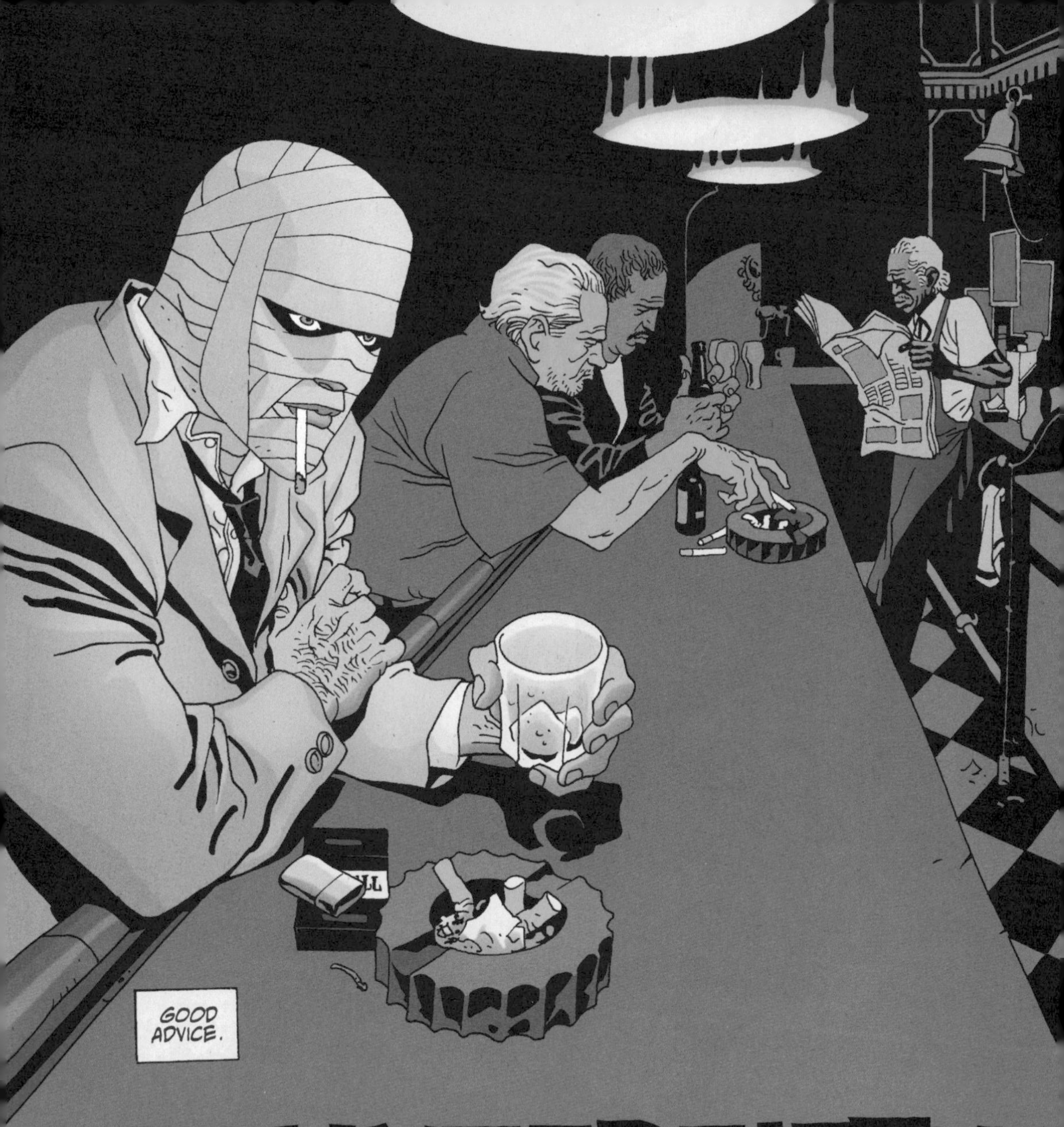
GOOD ADVICE.

THE COUNTERFIFTH DETECTIVE PART ONE

BRIAN AZZARELLO writer
EDUARDO RISSO artist
PATRICIA MULVIHILL colorist
CLEM ROBINS letterer
DIGITAL CHAMELEON separations
DAVE JOHNSON cover artist
ZACHARY RAU ass't ed.
WILL DENNIS editor

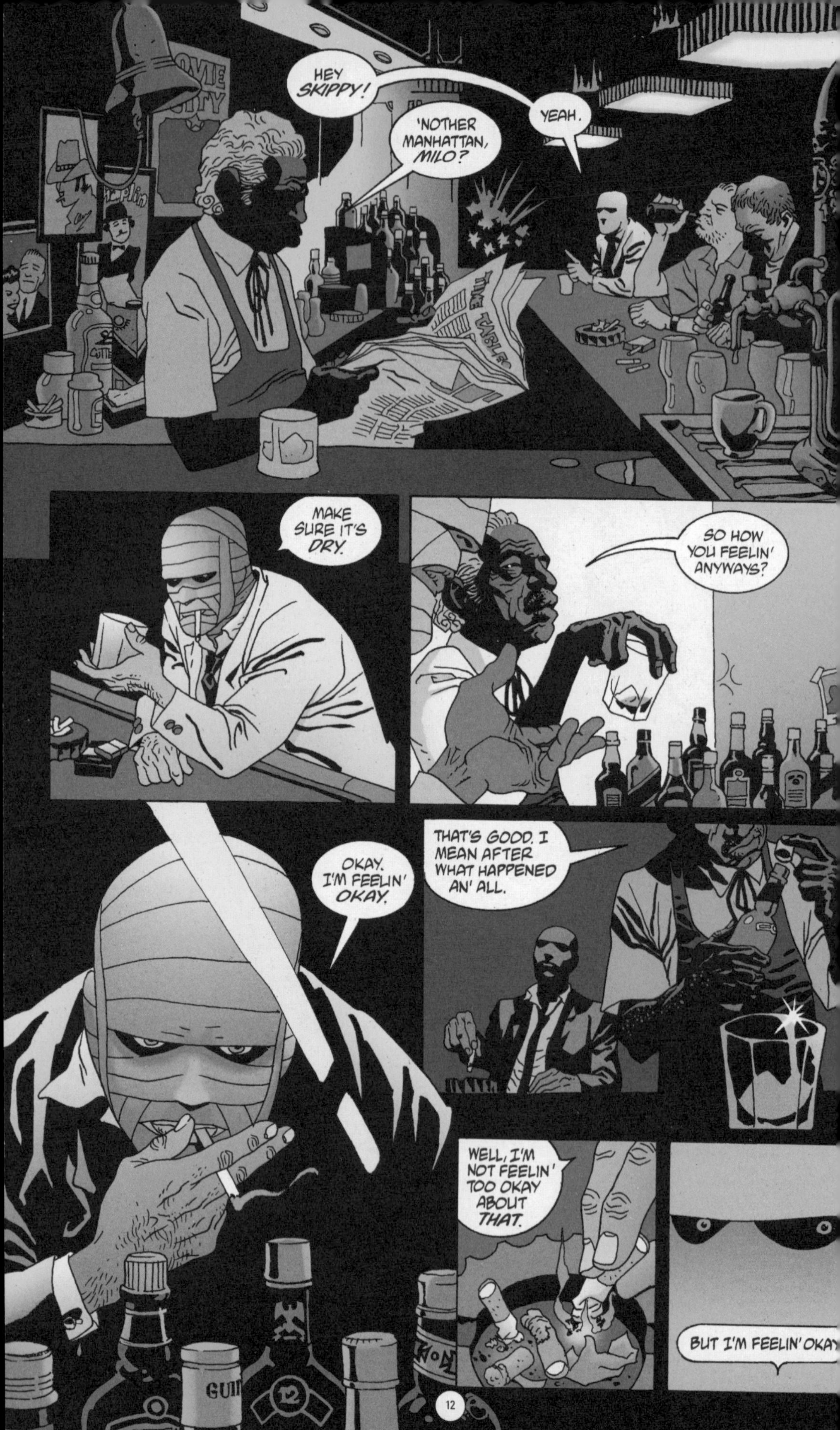
HEY SKIPPY!
'NOTHER MANHATTAN, MILO?
YEAH.
MAKE SURE IT'S DRY.
SO HOW YOU FEELIN' ANYWAYS?
OKAY. I'M FEELIN' OKAY.
THAT'S GOOD. I MEAN AFTER WHAT HAPPENED AN' ALL.
WELL, I'M NOT FEELIN' TOO OKAY ABOUT THAT.
BUT I'M FEELIN' OKAY.

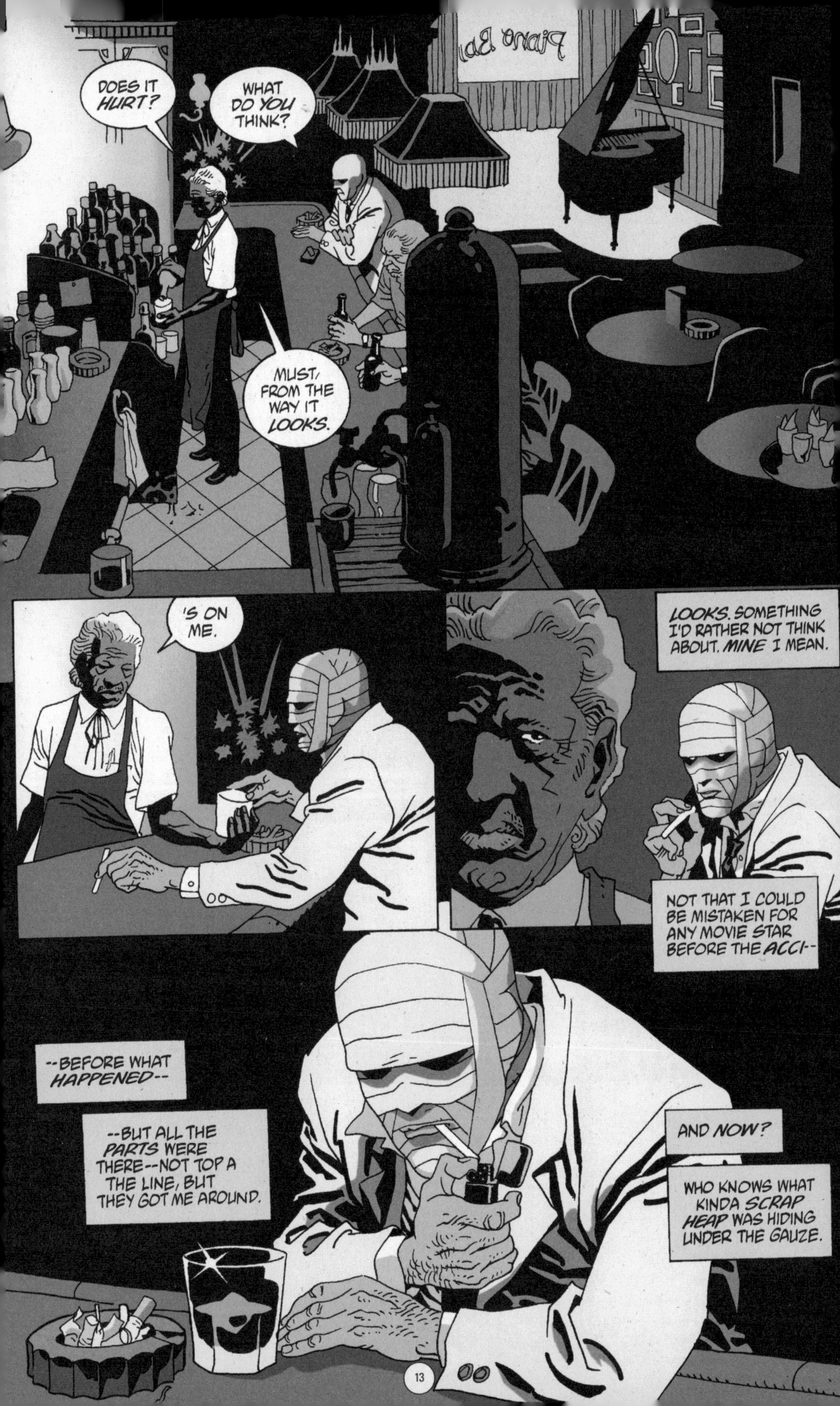
DOES IT *HURT?*
WHAT DO *YOU* THINK?
MUST, FROM THE WAY IT *LOOKS.*
'S ON ME.
LOOKS. SOMETHING I'D RATHER NOT THINK ABOUT. *MINE* I MEAN.
NOT THAT I COULD BE MISTAKEN FOR ANY MOVIE STAR BEFORE THE *ACCI*-
--BEFORE WHAT *HAPPENED*--
--BUT ALL THE *PARTS* WERE THERE--NOT TOP A THE LINE, BUT THEY GOT ME AROUND.
AND *NOW?*
WHO KNOWS WHAT KINDA *SCRAP HEAP* WAS HIDING UNDER THE GAUZE.

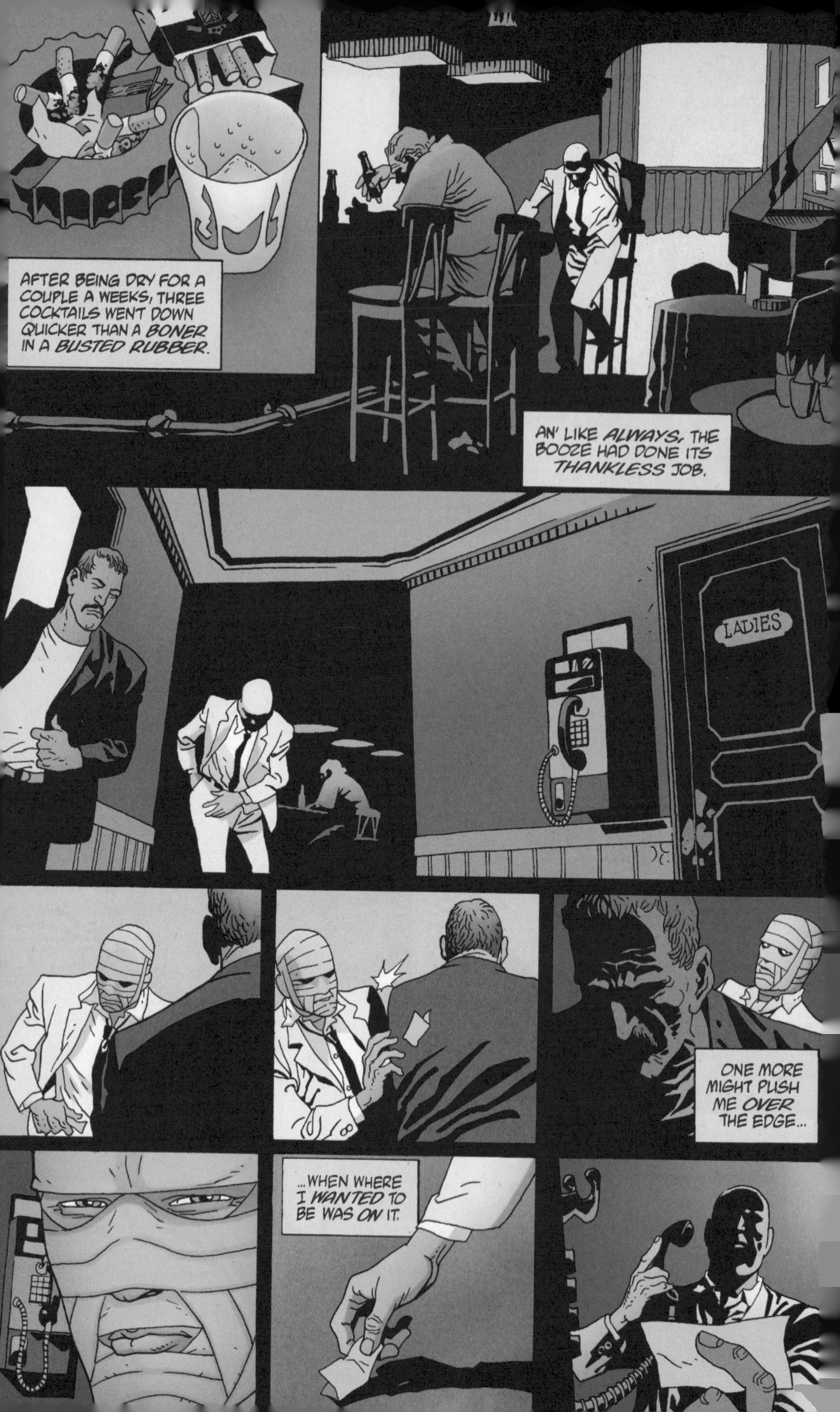
AFTER BEING DRY FOR A COUPLE A WEEKS, THREE COCKTAILS WENT DOWN QUICKER THAN A BONER IN A BUSTED RUBBER.
AN' LIKE ALWAYS, THE BOOZE HAD DONE ITS THANKLESS JOB.
LADIES
ONE MORE MIGHT PUSH ME OVER THE EDGE...
...WHEN WHERE I WANTED TO BE WAS ON IT.

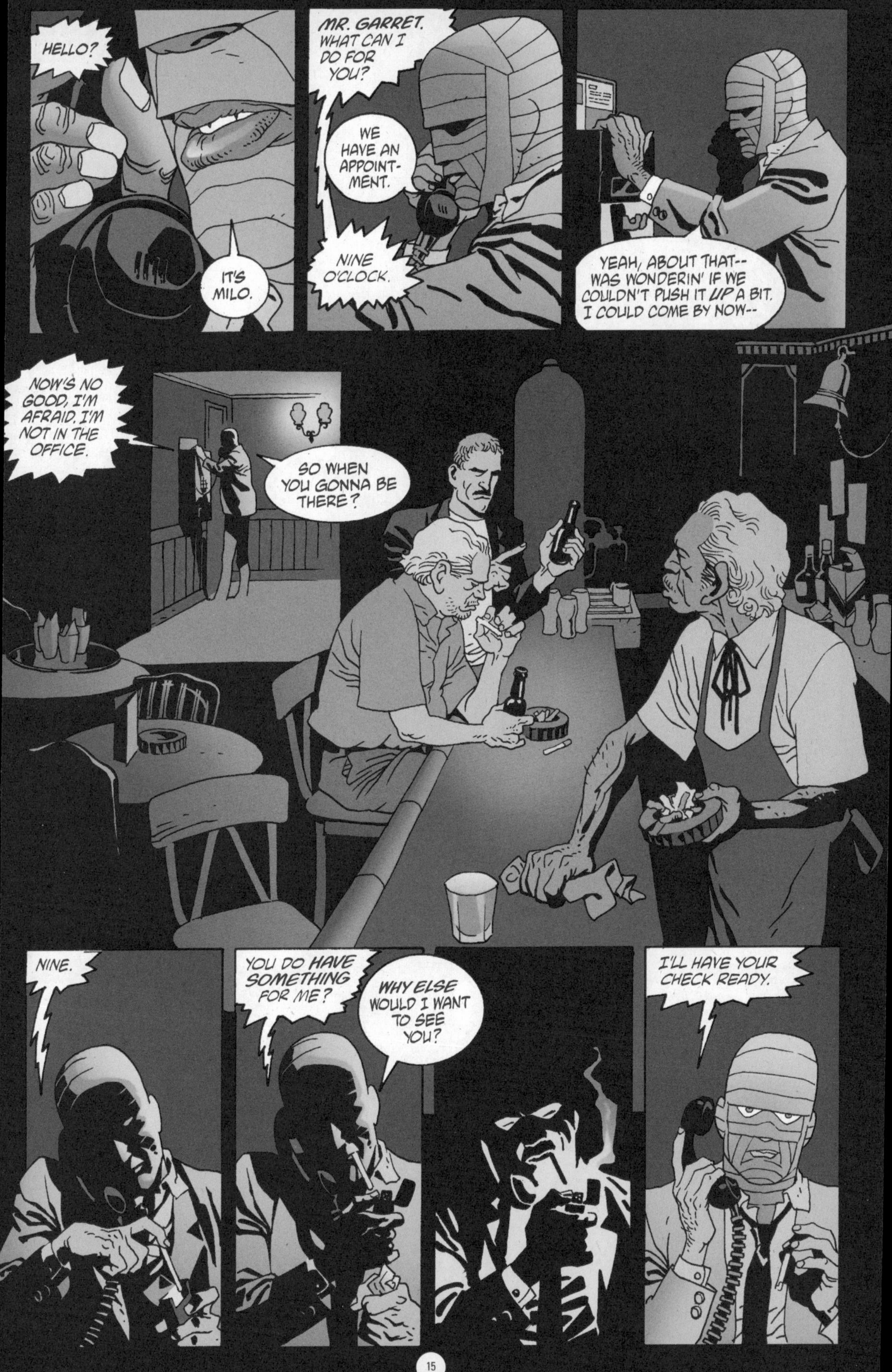
HELLO?
IT'S MILO.
MR. GARRET. WHAT CAN I DO FOR YOU?
WE HAVE AN APPOINT-MENT.
NINE O'CLOCK.
YEAH, ABOUT THAT-- WAS WONDERIN' IF WE COULDN'T PUSH IT UP A BIT. I COULD COME BY NOW--
NOW'S NO GOOD, I'M AFRAID. I'M NOT IN THE OFFICE.
SO WHEN YOU GONNA BE THERE?
NINE.
YOU DO HAVE SOMETHING FOR ME?
WHY ELSE WOULD I WANT TO SEE YOU?
I'LL HAVE YOUR CHECK READY.

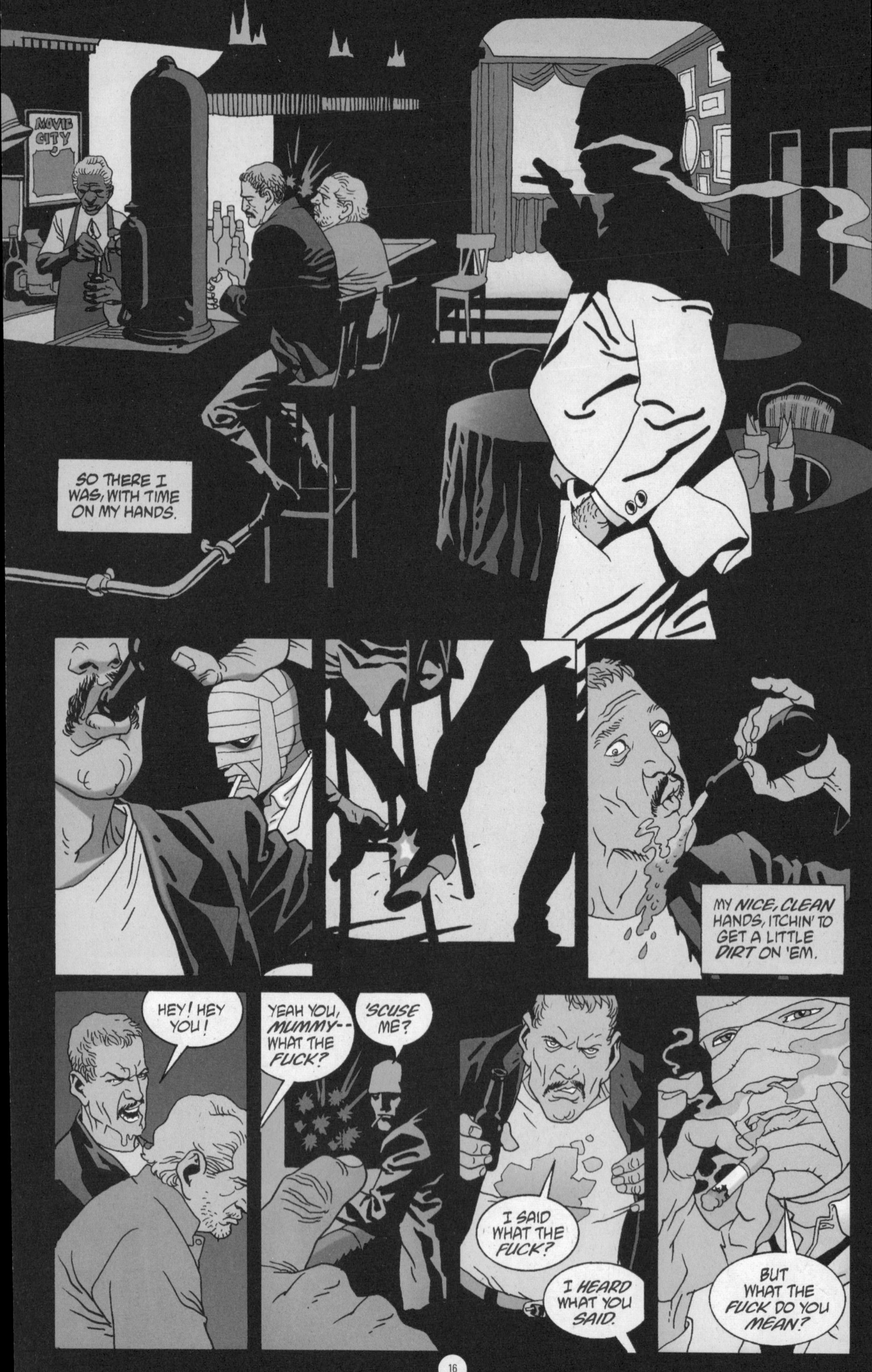
MOVIE CITY
SO THERE I WAS, WITH TIME ON MY HANDS.
MY NICE, CLEAN HANDS, ITCHIN' TO GET A LITTLE DIRT ON 'EM.
HEY! HEY YOU!
YEAH YOU, MUMMY-- WHAT THE FUCK?
'SCUSE ME?
I SAID WHAT THE FUCK?
I HEARD WHAT YOU SAID.
BUT WHAT THE FUCK DO YOU MEAN?

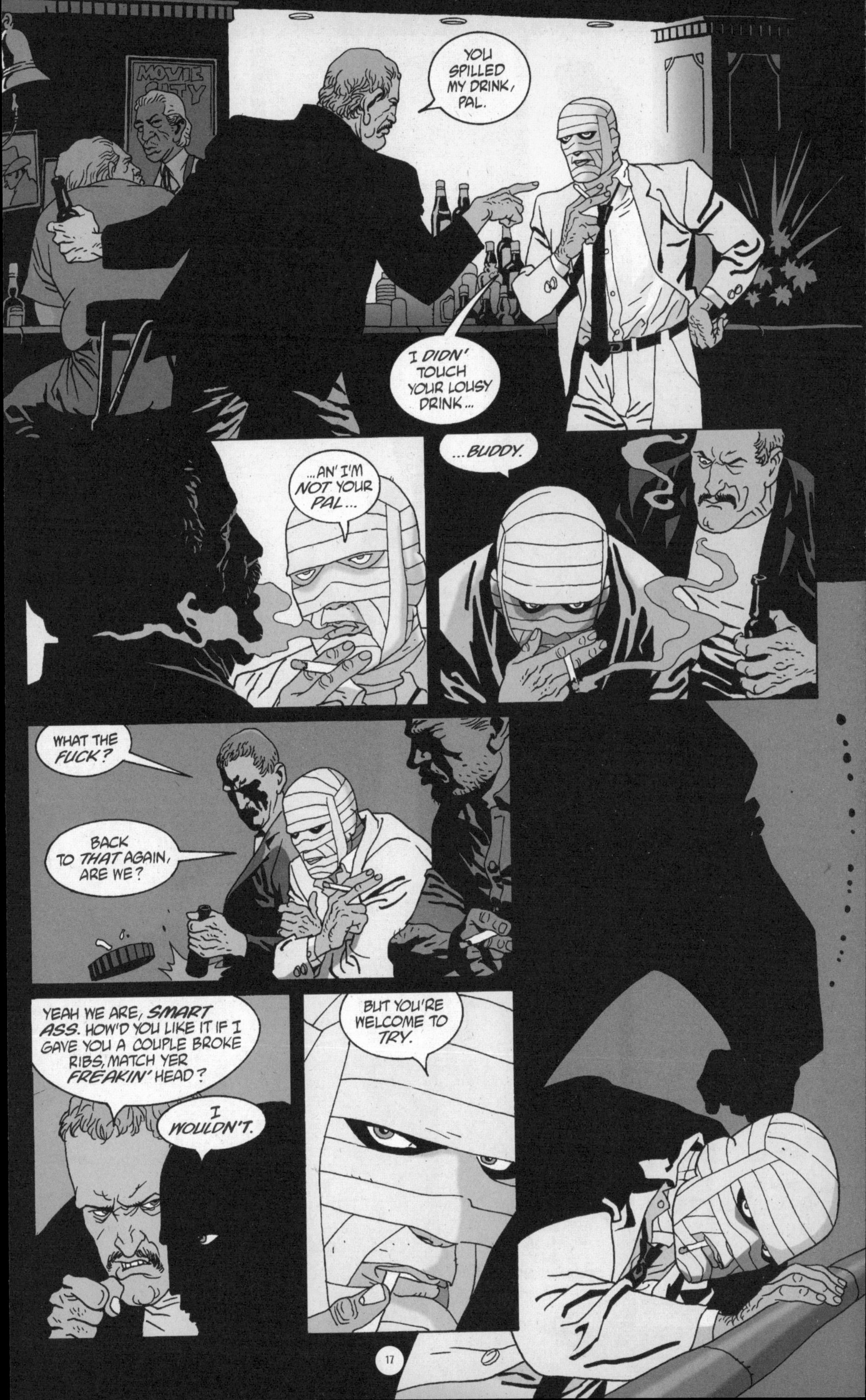
MOVIE CITY
YOU SPILLED MY DRINK, PAL.
I DIDN' TOUCH YOUR LOUSY DRINK...
...AN' I'M NOT YOUR PAL...
...BUDDY.
WHAT THE FUCK?
BACK TO THAT AGAIN, ARE WE?
YEAH WE ARE, SMART ASS. HOW'D YOU LIKE IT IF I GAVE YOU A COUPLE BROKE RIBS, MATCH YER FREAKIN' HEAD?
I WOULDN'T.
BUT YOU'RE WELCOME TO TRY.

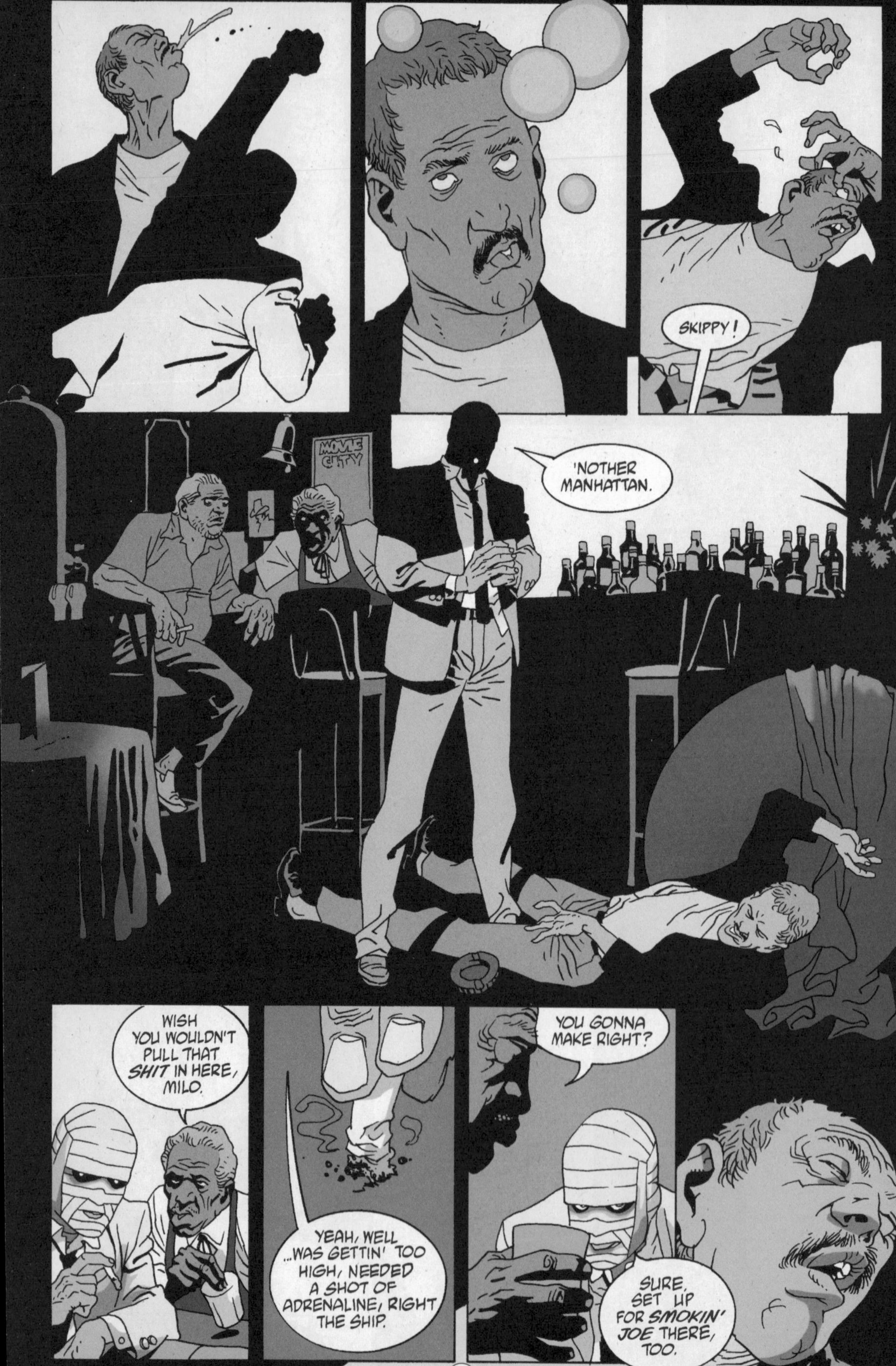
SKIPPY!
'NOTHER MANHATTAN.
MOVIE CITY
WISH YOU WOULDN'T PULL THAT *SHIT* IN HERE, MILO.
YEAH, WELL ...WAS GETTIN' TOO HIGH, NEEDED A SHOT OF ADRENALINE, RIGHT THE SHIP.
YOU GONNA MAKE RIGHT?
SURE, SET UP FOR *SMOKIN'* JOE THERE, TOO.

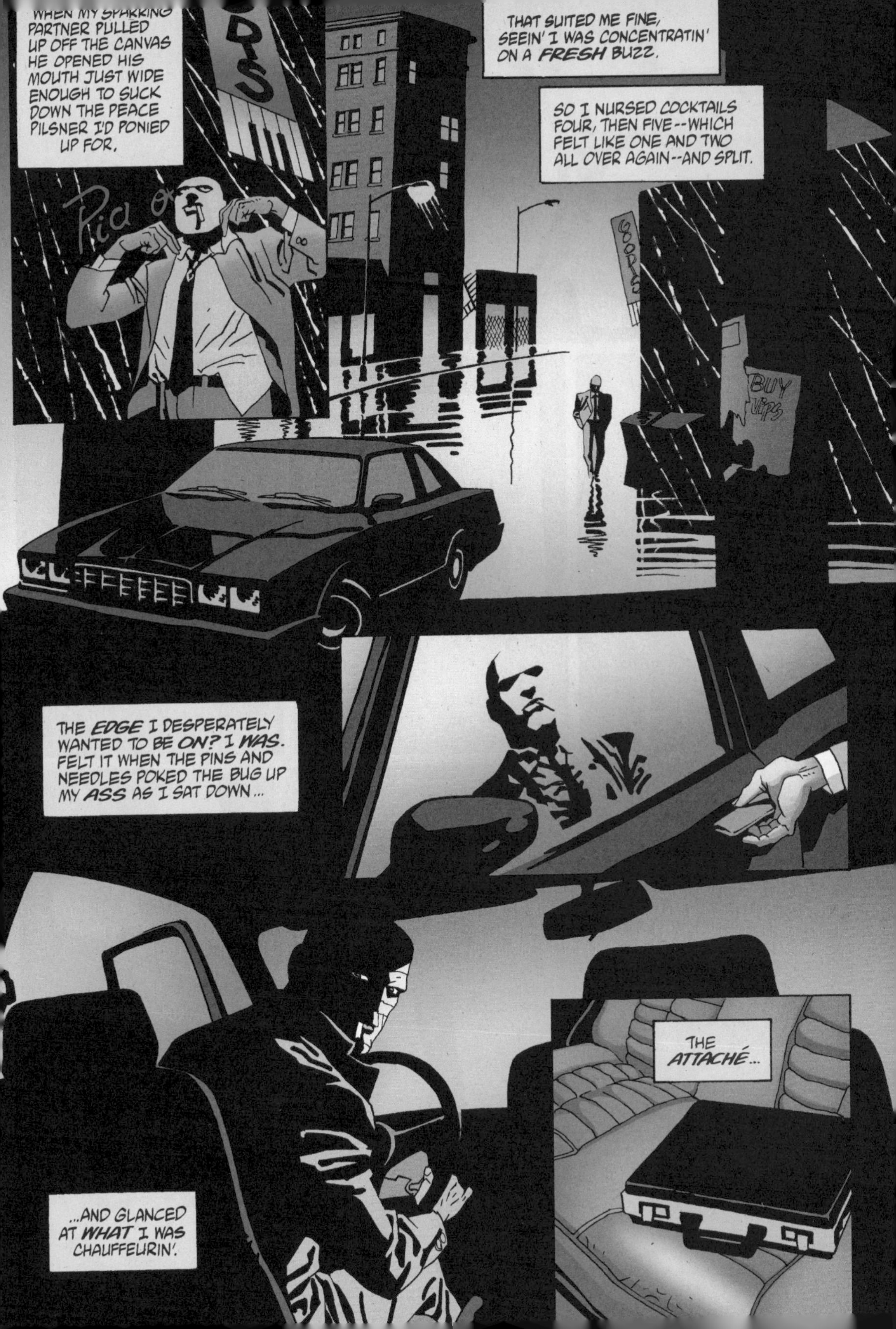
WHEN MY SPARRING PARTNER PULLED UP OFF THE CANVAS HE OPENED HIS MOUTH JUST WIDE ENOUGH TO SUCK DOWN THE PEACE PILSNER I'D PONIED UP FOR.
THAT SUITED ME FINE, SEEIN' I WAS CONCENTRATIN' ON A FRESH BUZZ.
SO I NURSED COCKTAILS FOUR, THEN FIVE--WHICH FELT LIKE ONE AND TWO ALL OVER AGAIN--AND SPLIT.
BUY
THE EDGE I DESPERATELY WANTED TO BE ON? I WAS. FELT IT WHEN THE PINS AND NEEDLES POKED THE BUG UP MY ASS AS I SAT DOWN...
...AND GLANCED AT WHAT I WAS CHAUFFEURIN'.
THE ATTACHÉ...

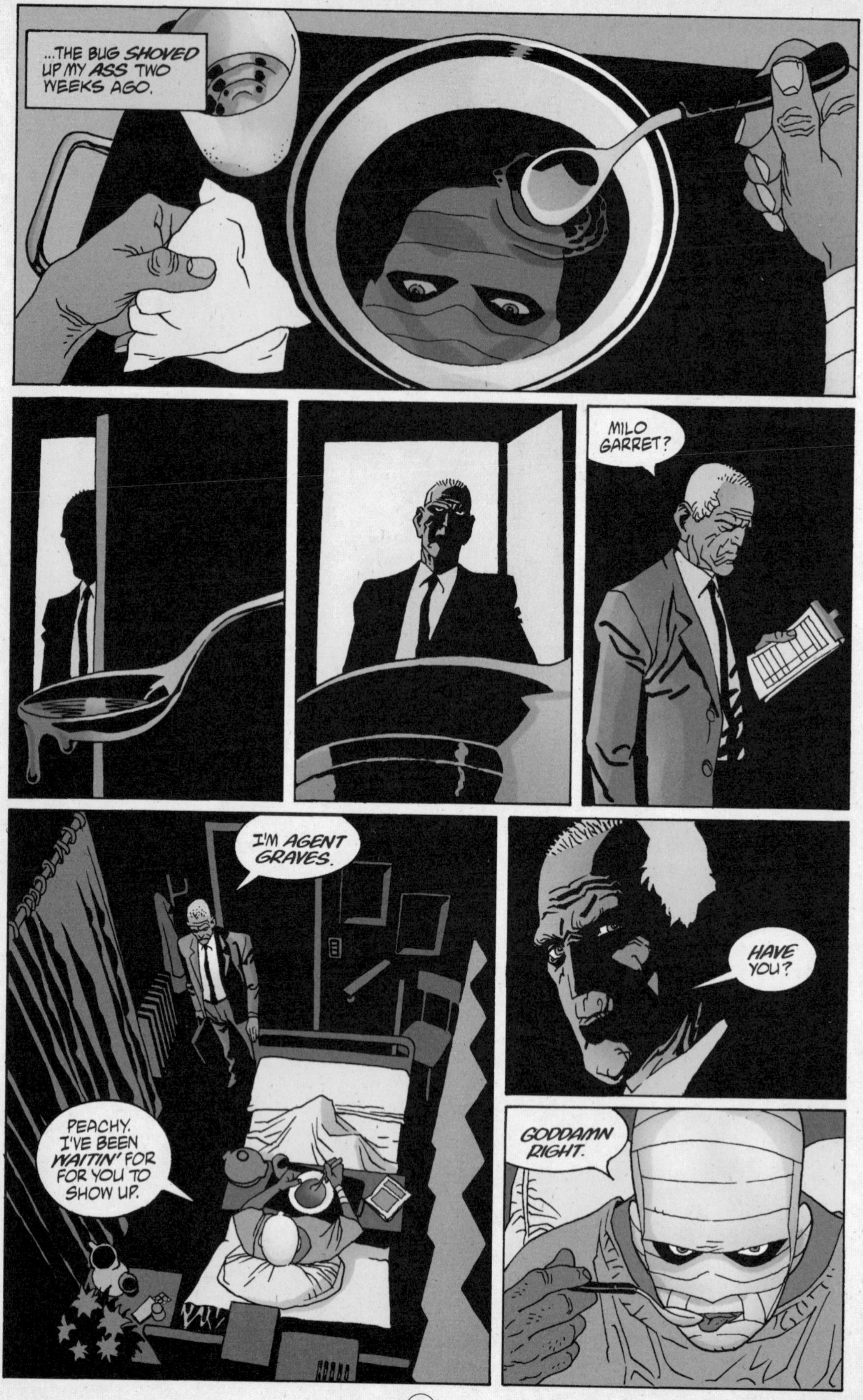
...THE BUG SHOVED UP MY ASS TWO WEEKS AGO.
MILO GARRET?
I'M AGENT GRAVES.
PEACHY. I'VE BEEN WAITIN' FOR FOR YOU TO SHOW UP.
HAVE YOU?
GODDAMN RIGHT.

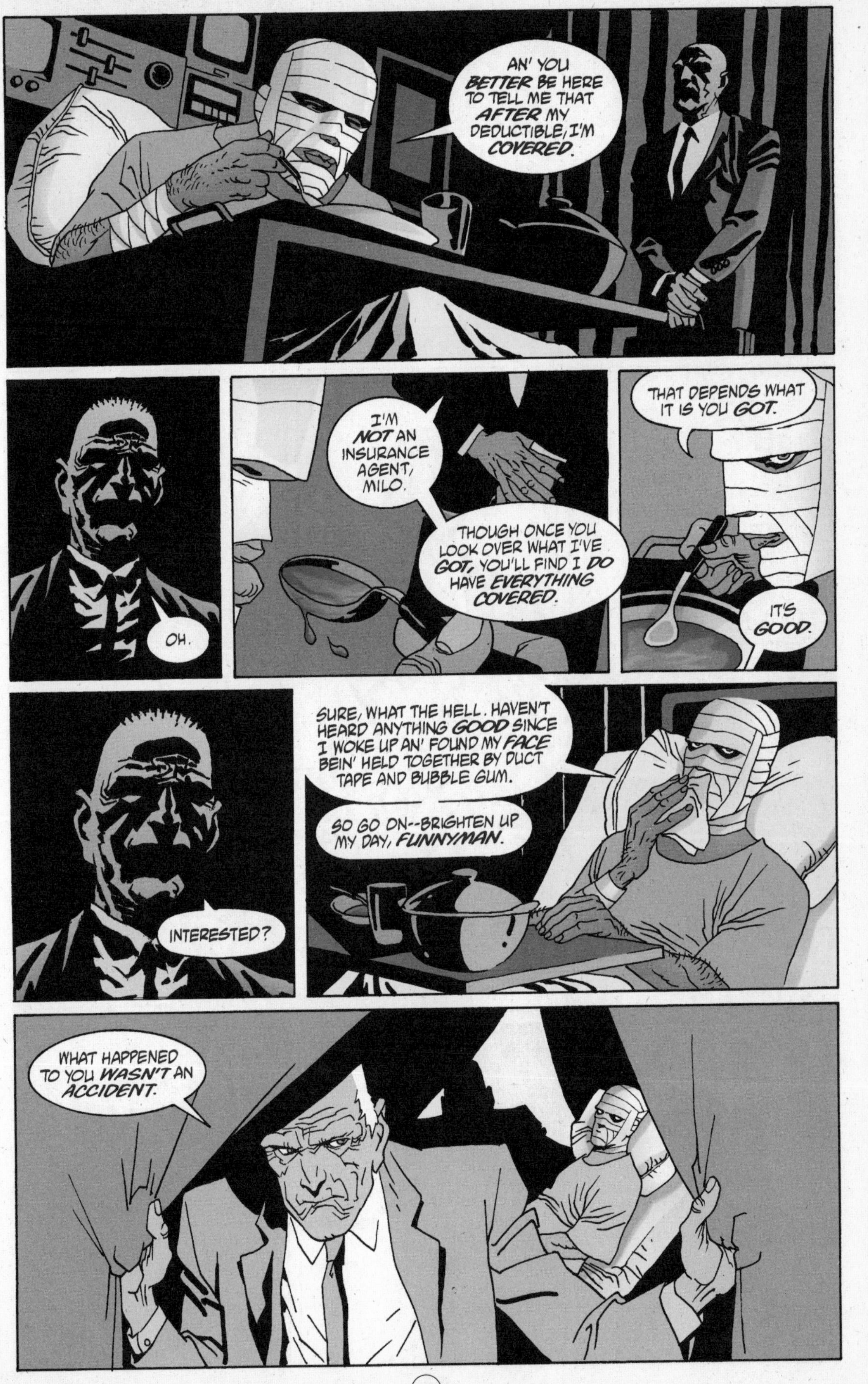
AN' YOU BETTER BE HERE TO TELL ME THAT AFTER MY DEDUCTIBLE, I'M COVERED.
OH.
I'M NOT AN INSURANCE AGENT, MILO.
THOUGH ONCE YOU LOOK OVER WHAT I'VE GOT, YOU'LL FIND I DO HAVE EVERYTHING COVERED.
THAT DEPENDS WHAT IT IS YOU GOT.
IT'S GOOD.
INTERESTED?
SURE, WHAT THE HELL. HAVEN'T HEARD ANYTHING GOOD SINCE I WOKE UP AN' FOUND MY FACE BEIN' HELD TOGETHER BY DUCT TAPE AND BUBBLE GUM.
SO GO ON--BRIGHTEN UP MY DAY, FUNNYMAN.
WHAT HAPPENED TO YOU WASN'T AN ACCIDENT.

HAH! THAT *IS* A GOOD ONE.

WAIT'LL YOU HEAR THE *PUNCH* LINE.

HIT ME.

--NO ACCIDENT, BUT A *MESSAGE.*

"YEAH? CALL ME SLOW ON THE UPTAKE, BUT I DON'T GET WHAT MAKIN' MY MUG *DOGFOOD'S* S'POSED TO MEAN."

ANTA MONICA MASONIC HOSPITAL 4-

"THAT'S BECAUSE THE *MESSAGE* WASN'T INTENDED FOR *YOU.* SADLY...

"...YOU'RE JUST THE *MESSENGER.*"

AND A *MESS* OF ONE NOW, AT THAT."

BUT *TRUST* ME, THE MESSAGE WAS *RECEIVED.*

BY *WHO?*

LIKE I SAID, WHAT HAPPENED TO YOU WAS *NO ACCIDENT.*

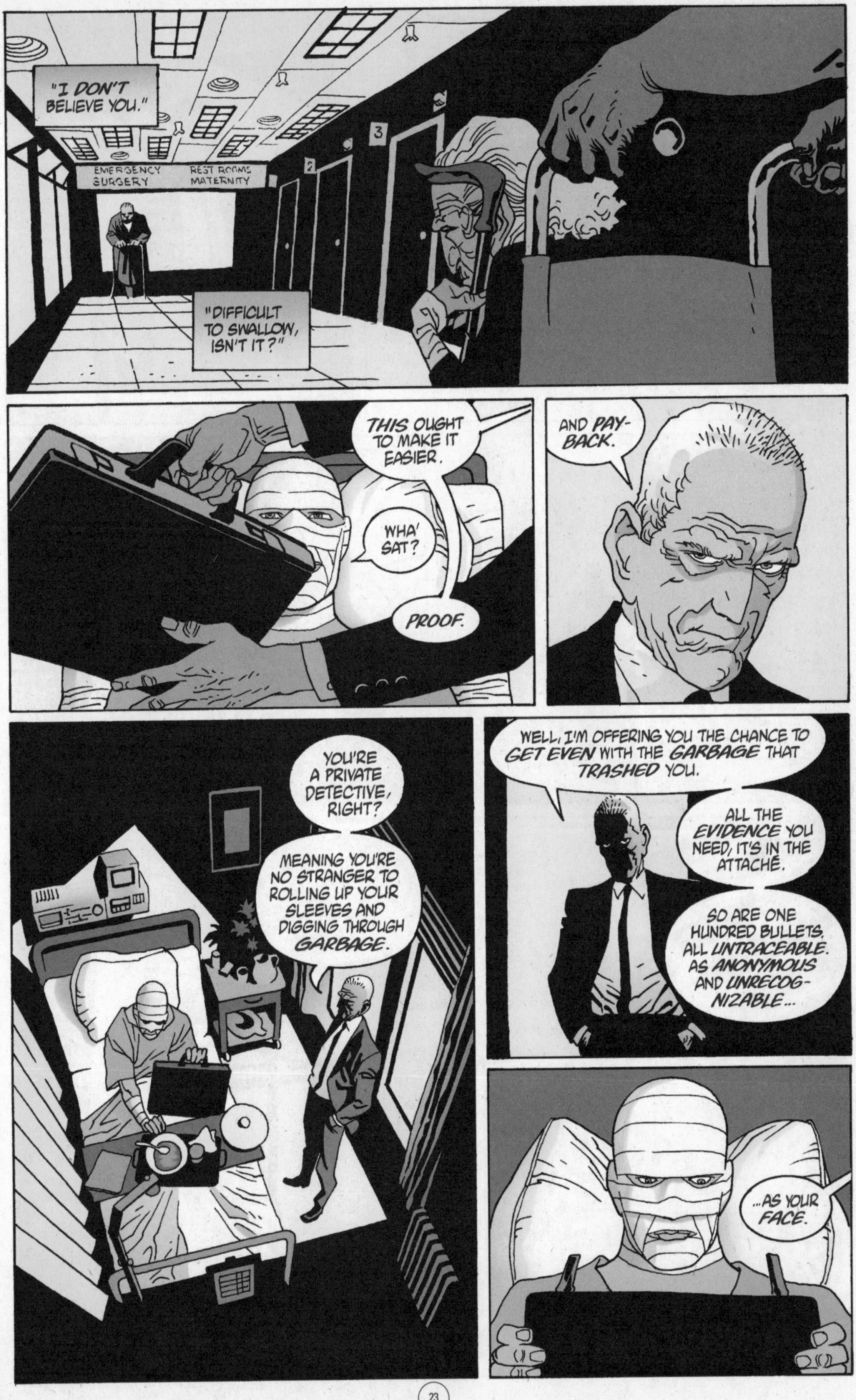
"I DON'T BELIEVE YOU."
EMERGENCY SURGERY
REST ROOMS MATERNITY
"DIFFICULT TO SWALLOW, ISN'T IT?"
THIS OUGHT TO MAKE IT EASIER.
WHA' SAT?
PROOF.
AND PAY-BACK.
YOU'RE A PRIVATE DETECTIVE, RIGHT?
MEANING YOU'RE NO STRANGER TO ROLLING UP YOUR SLEEVES AND DIGGING THROUGH GARBAGE.
WELL, I'M OFFERING YOU THE CHANCE TO GET EVEN WITH THE GARBAGE THAT TRASHED YOU.
ALL THE EVIDENCE YOU NEED, IT'S IN THE ATTACHÉ.
SO ARE ONE HUNDRED BULLETS. ALL UNTRACEABLE. AS ANONYMOUS AND UNRECOG-NIZABLE...
...AS YOUR FACE.

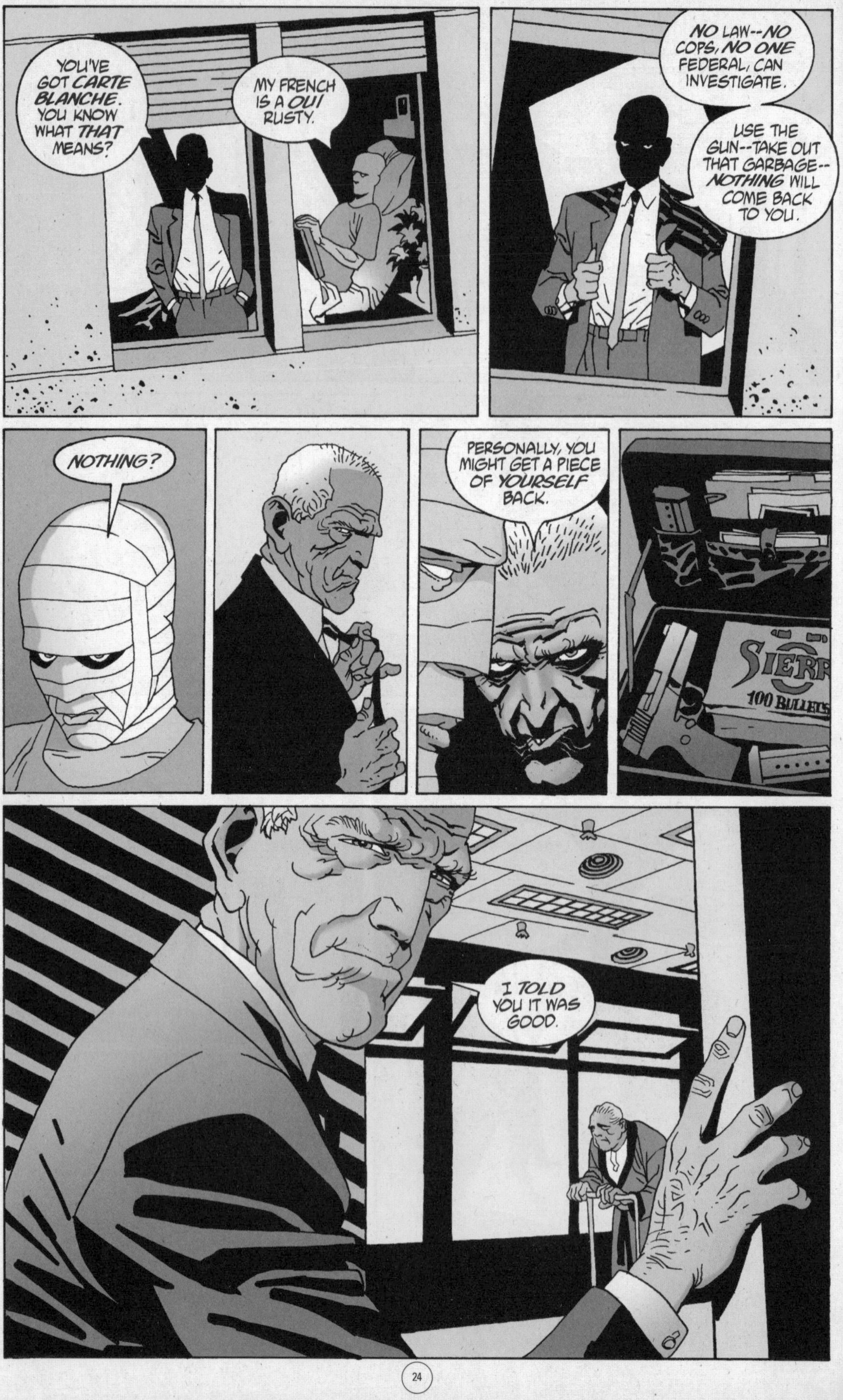
YOU'VE GOT CARTE BLANCHE. YOU KNOW WHAT THAT MEANS?
MY FRENCH IS A OUI RUSTY.
NO LAW--NO COPS, NO ONE FEDERAL, CAN INVESTIGATE.
USE THE GUN--TAKE OUT THAT GARBAGE--NOTHING WILL COME BACK TO YOU.
NOTHING?
PERSONALLY, YOU MIGHT GET A PIECE OF YOURSELF BACK.
SIERR
100 BULLETS
I TOLD YOU IT WAS GOOD.

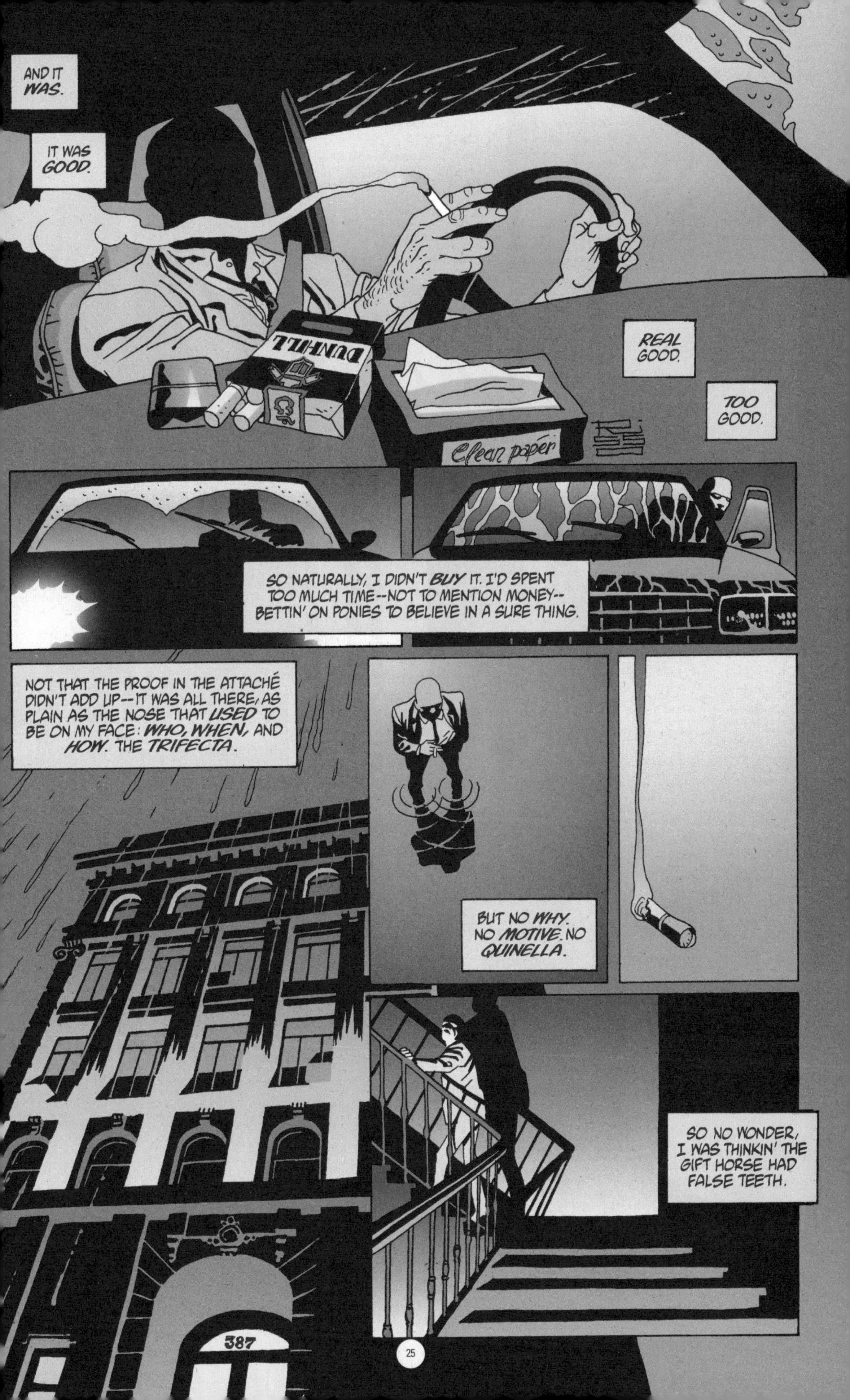
AND IT WAS.
IT WAS GOOD.
DUNHILL
REAL GOOD.
TOO GOOD.
Clean paper
SO NATURALLY, I DIDN'T BUY IT. I'D SPENT TOO MUCH TIME--NOT TO MENTION MONEY--BETTIN' ON PONIES TO BELIEVE IN A SURE THING.
NOT THAT THE PROOF IN THE ATTACHÉ DIDN'T ADD UP--IT WAS ALL THERE, AS PLAIN AS THE NOSE THAT USED TO BE ON MY FACE: WHO, WHEN, AND HOW. THE TRIFECTA.
BUT NO WHY. NO MOTIVE. NO QUINELLA.
SO NO WONDER, I WAS THINKIN' THE GIFT HORSE HAD FALSE TEETH.
387

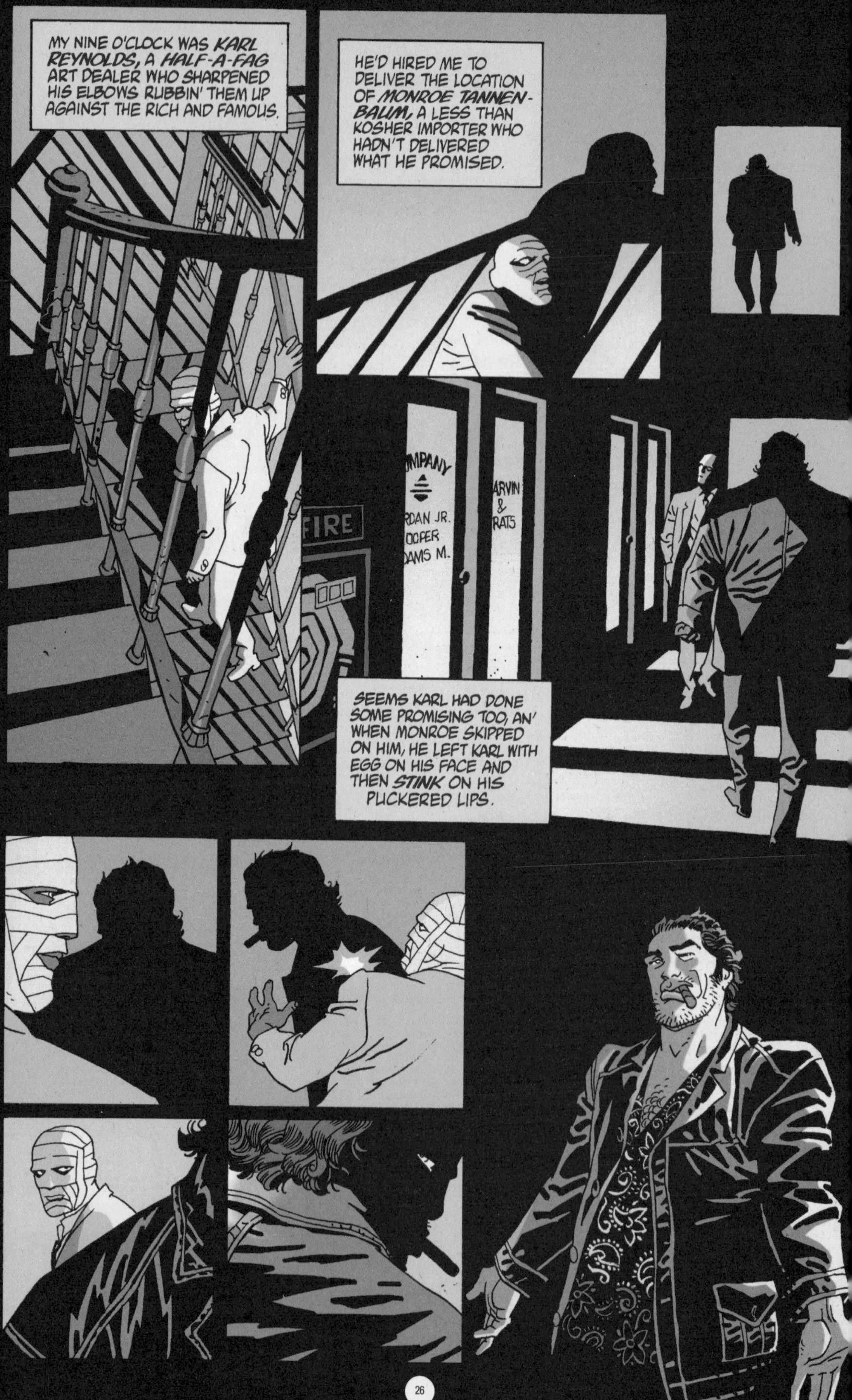
MY NINE O'CLOCK WAS KARL REYNOLDS, A HALF-A-FAG ART DEALER WHO SHARPENED HIS ELBOWS RUBBIN' THEM UP AGAINST THE RICH AND FAMOUS.
HE'D HIRED ME TO DELIVER THE LOCATION OF MONROE TANNEN-BAUM, A LESS THAN KOSHER IMPORTER WHO HADN'T DELIVERED WHAT HE PROMISED.
FIRE
SEEMS KARL HAD DONE SOME PROMISING TOO, AN' WHEN MONROE SKIPPED ON HIM, HE LEFT KARL WITH EGG ON HIS FACE AND THEN STINK ON HIS PUCKERED LIPS.

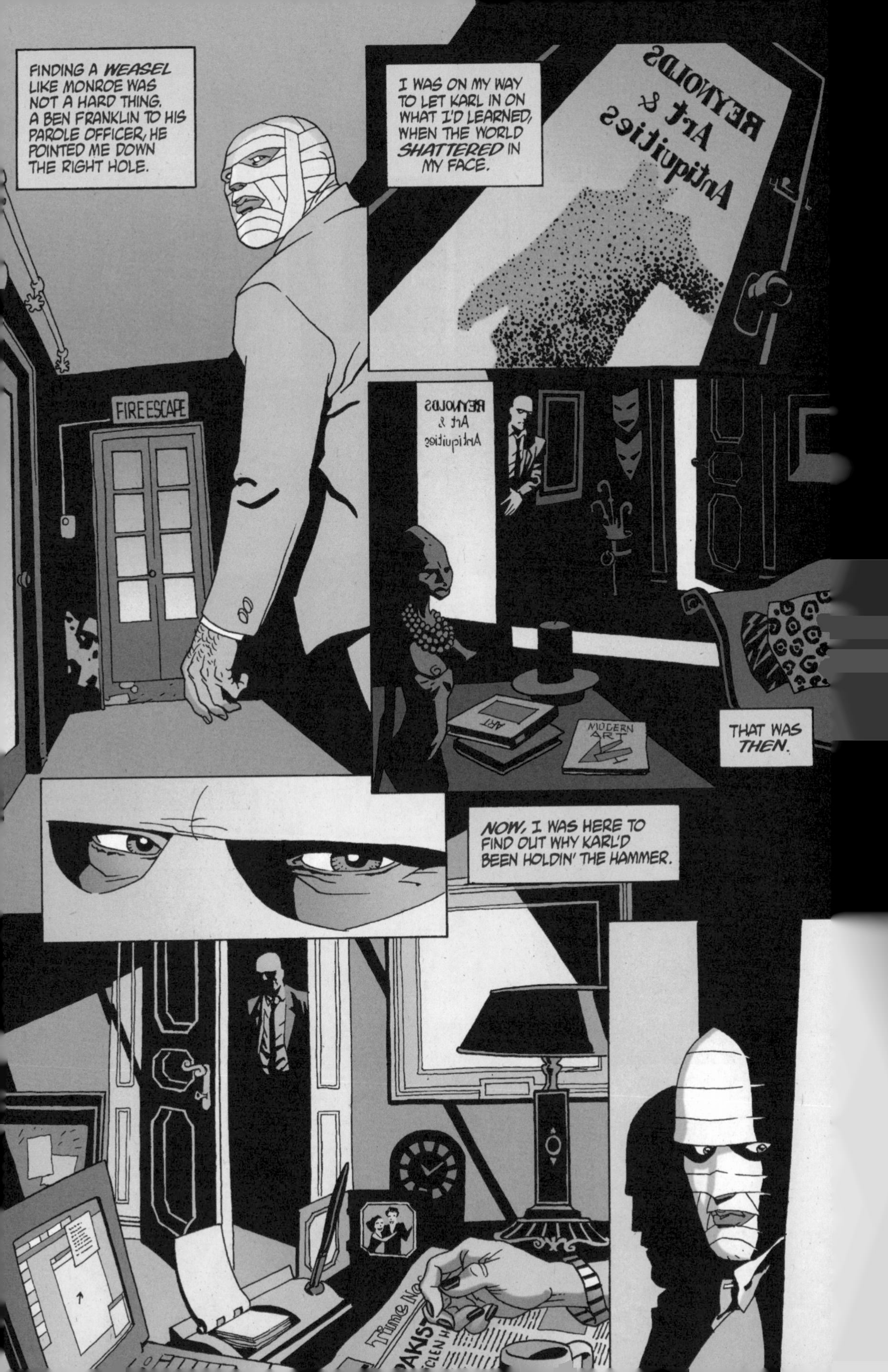
FINDING A *WEASEL* LIKE MONROE WAS NOT A HARD THING. A BEN FRANKLIN TO HIS PAROLE OFFICER, HE POINTED ME DOWN THE RIGHT HOLE.
FIRE ESCAPE
I WAS ON MY WAY TO LET KARL IN ON WHAT I'D LEARNED, WHEN THE WORLD *SHATTERED* IN MY FACE.
REYNOLDS
Art &
Antiquities
ART
MODERN ART
THAT WAS *THEN*.
NOW, I WAS HERE TO FIND OUT WHY KARL'D BEEN HOLDIN' THE HAMMER.

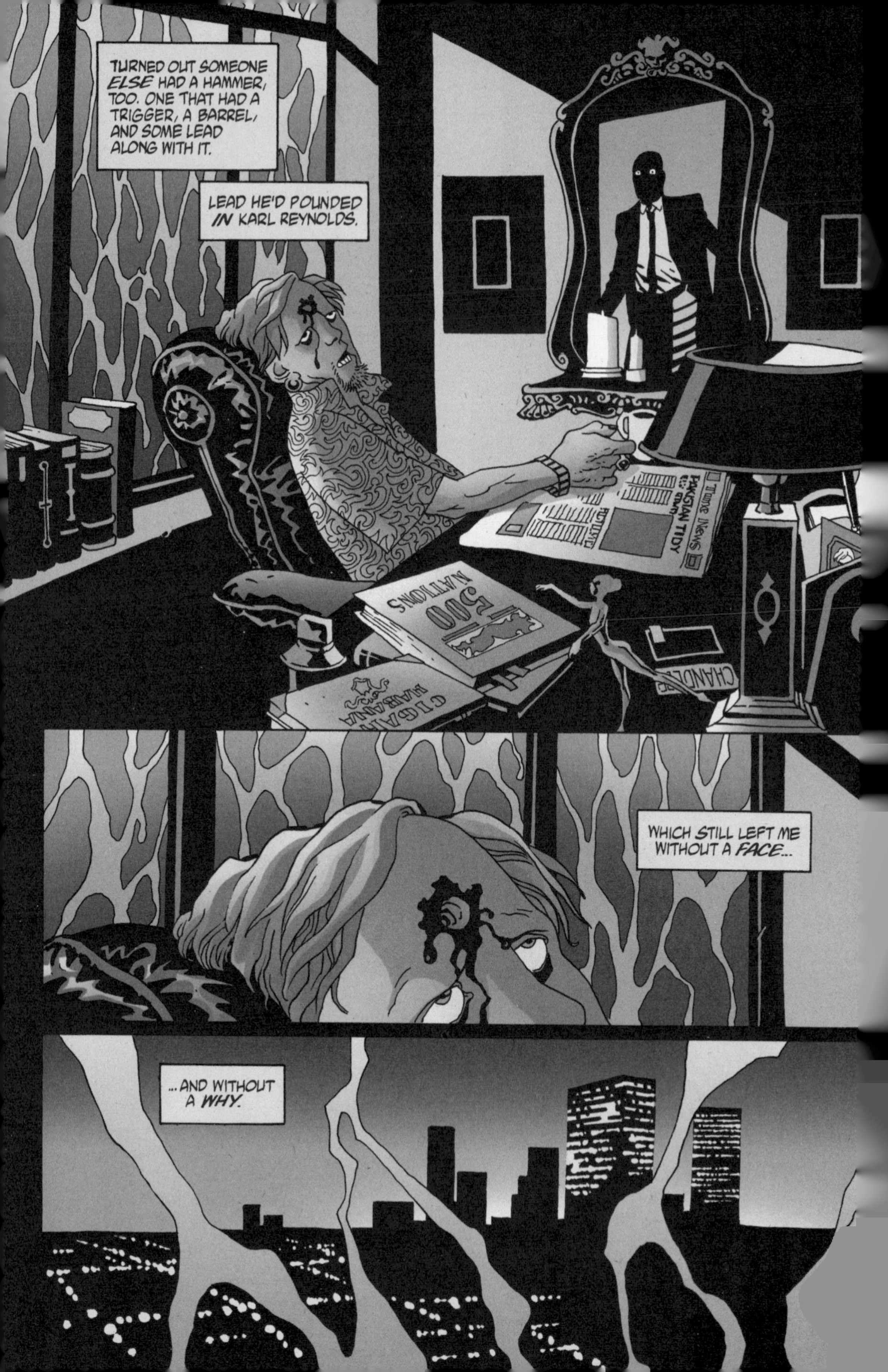
TURNED OUT SOMEONE ELSE HAD A HAMMER, TOO. ONE THAT HAD A TRIGGER, A BARREL, AND SOME LEAD ALONG WITH IT.
LEAD HE'D POUNDED IN KARL REYNOLDS.
500 NATIONS
CIGAR HABANA
WHICH STILL LEFT ME WITHOUT A FACE...
...AND WITHOUT A WHY.

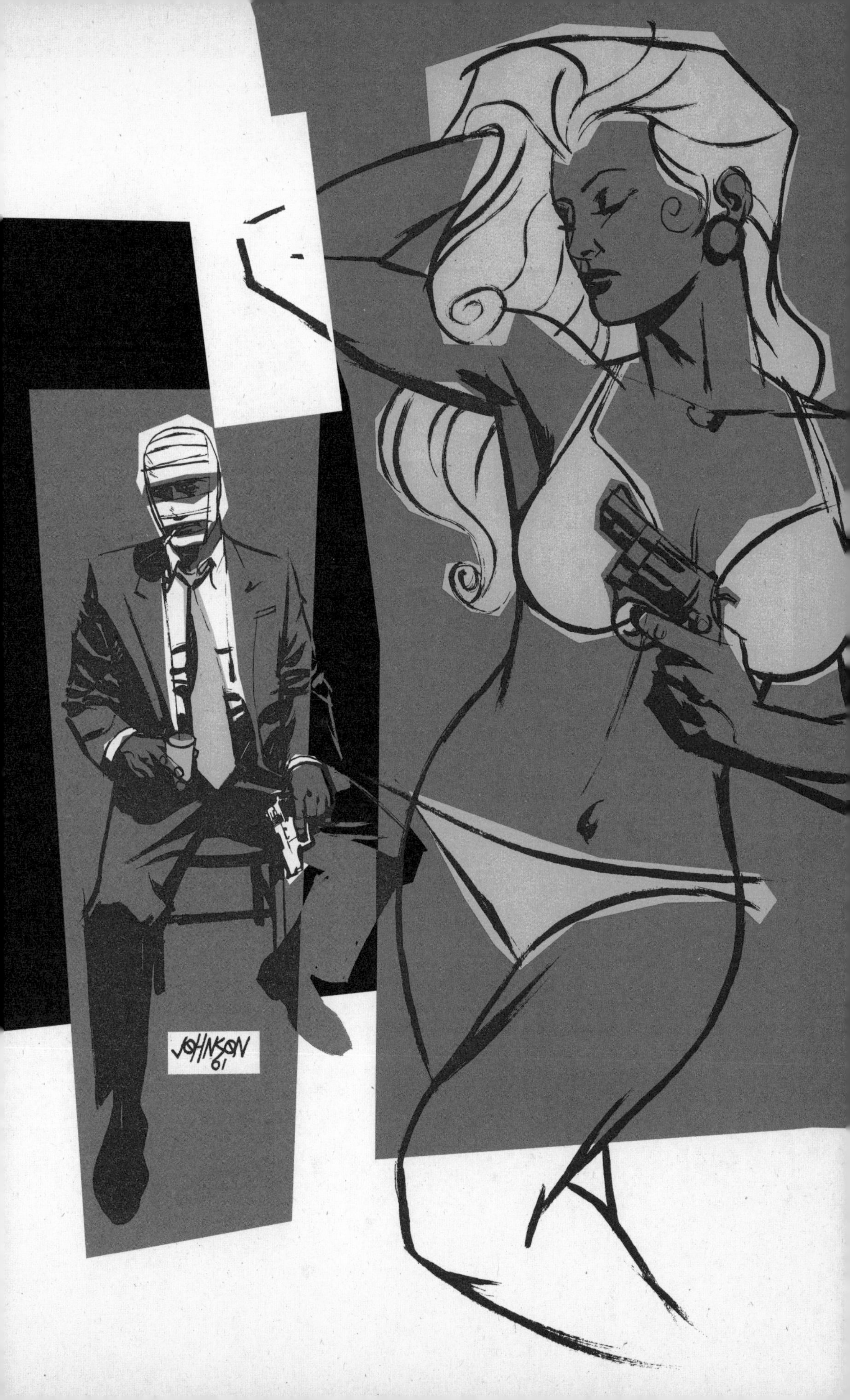
JOHNSON
61

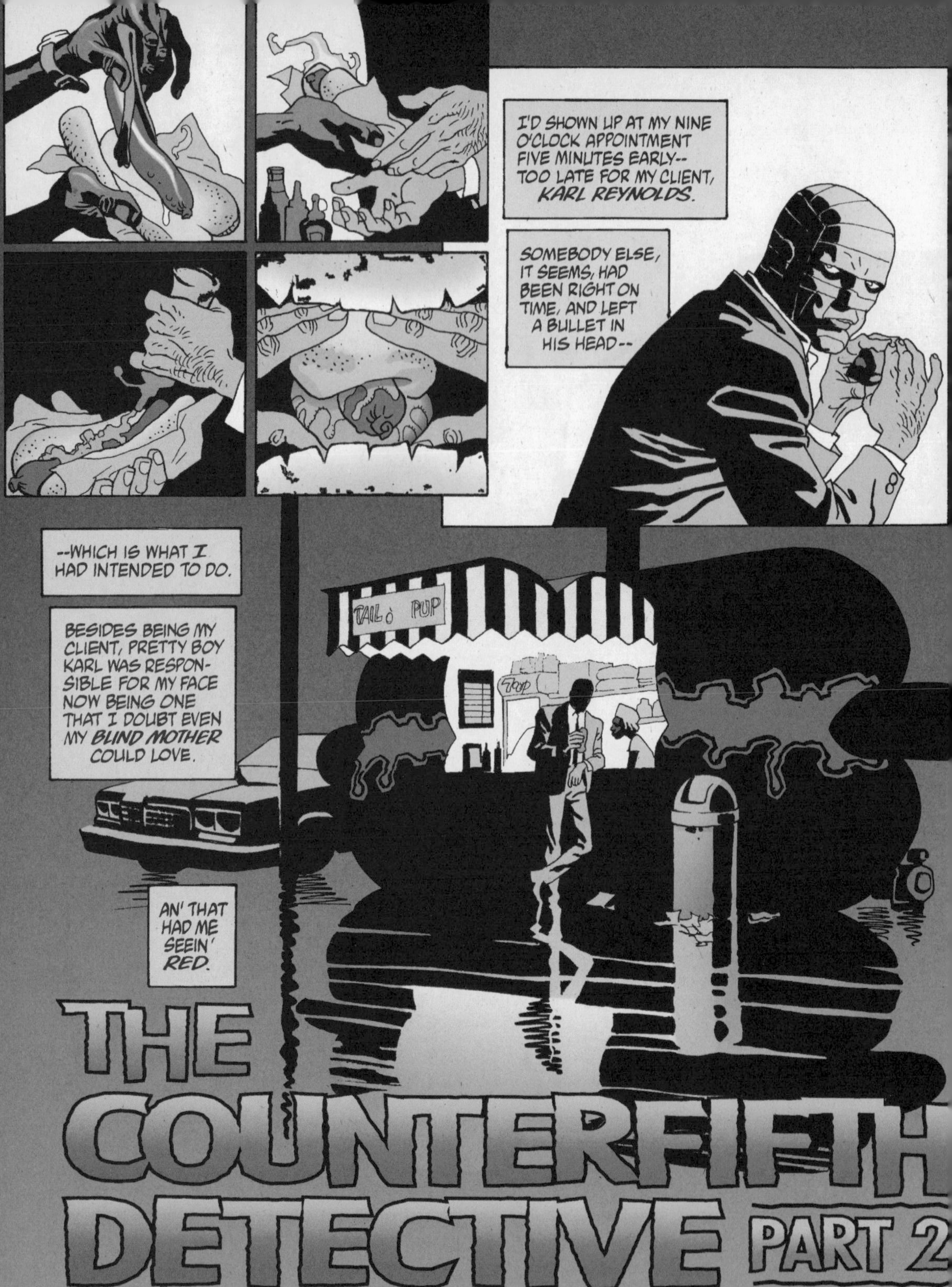
I'D SHOWN UP AT MY NINE O'CLOCK APPOINTMENT FIVE MINUTES EARLY-- TOO LATE FOR MY CLIENT, KARL REYNOLDS.
SOMEBODY ELSE, IT SEEMS, HAD BEEN RIGHT ON TIME, AND LEFT A BULLET IN HIS HEAD--
--WHICH IS WHAT I HAD INTENDED TO DO.
BESIDES BEING MY CLIENT, PRETTY BOY KARL WAS RESPONSIBLE FOR MY FACE NOW BEING ONE THAT I DOUBT EVEN MY BLIND MOTHER COULD LOVE.
TAIL o' PUP
AN' THAT HAD ME SEEIN' RED.

THE COUNTERFIFTH DETECTIVE PART 2

BRIAN AZZARELLO writer · EDUARDO RISSO artist · PATRICIA MULVIHILL colorist · CLEM ROBINS letterer · DIGITAL CHAMELEON separations · DAVE JOHNSON cover artist · ZACHARY RAU ass't ed. · WILL DENNIS editor

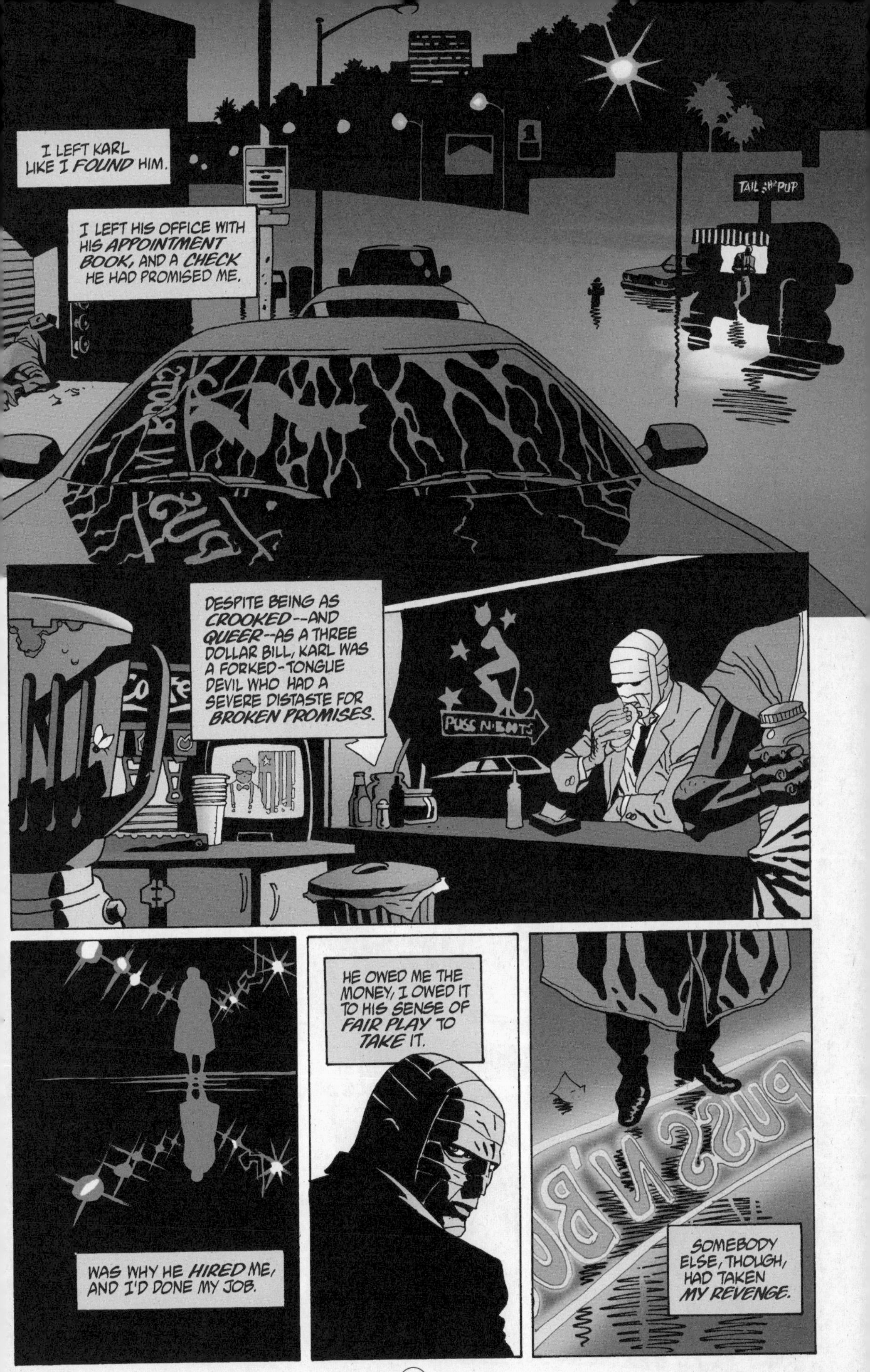
I LEFT KARL LIKE I FOUND HIM.
I LEFT HIS OFFICE WITH HIS APPOINTMENT BOOK, AND A CHECK HE HAD PROMISED ME.
TAIL O' THE PUP
DESPITE BEING AS CROOKED--AND QUEER--AS A THREE DOLLAR BILL, KARL WAS A FORKED-TONGUE DEVIL WHO HAD A SEVERE DISTASTE FOR BROKEN PROMISES.
PUSS N' BOOTS
WAS WHY HE HIRED ME, AND I'D DONE MY JOB.
HE OWED ME THE MONEY, I OWED IT TO HIS SENSE OF FAIR PLAY TO TAKE IT.
SOMEBODY ELSE, THOUGH, HAD TAKEN MY REVENGE.

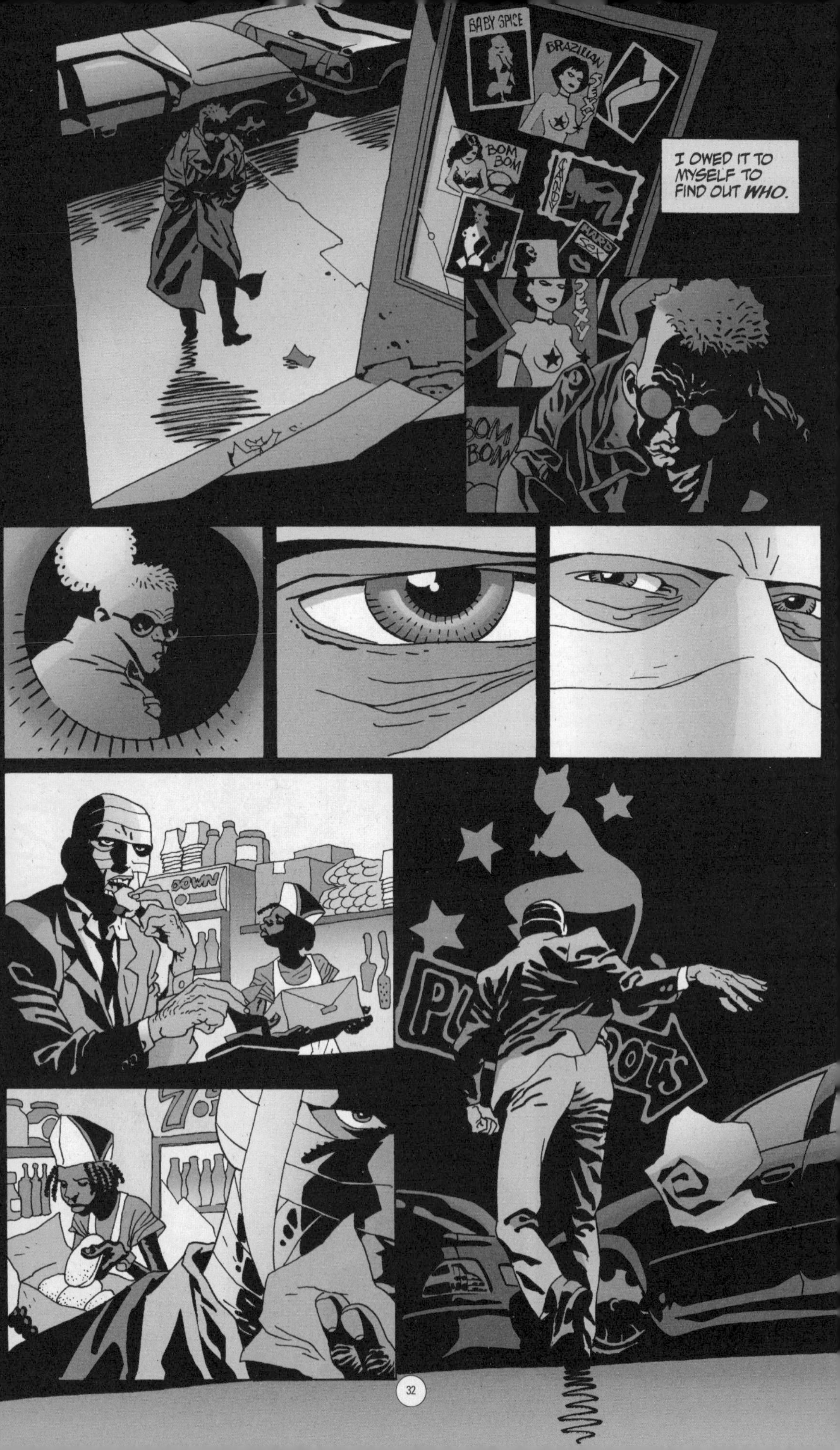
I OWED IT TO MYSELF TO FIND OUT WHO.
BABY SPICE
BRAZILIAN
SEXY
BOM BOM
CANDY
HARD SEX
DOWN

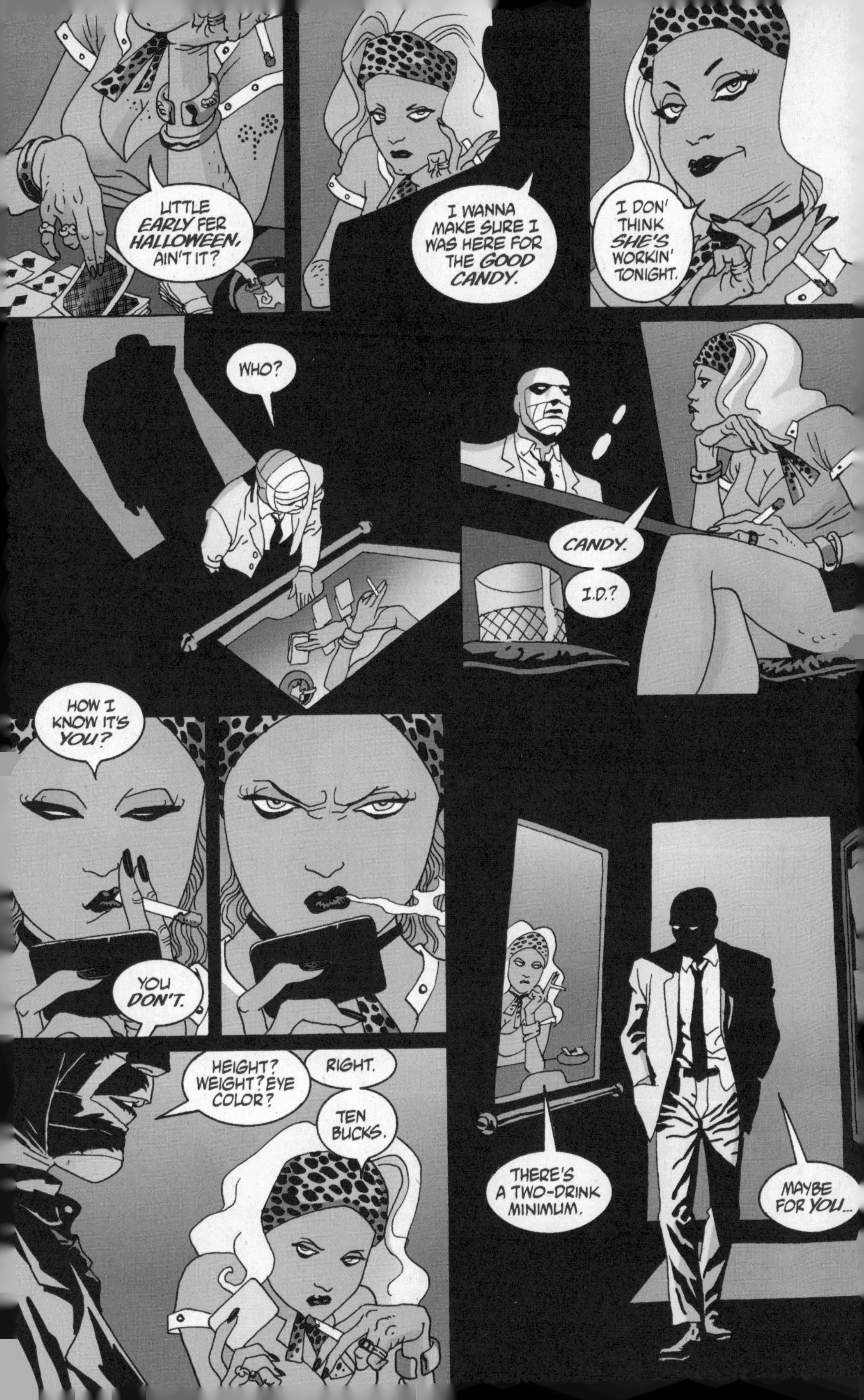

LITTLE EARLY FER HALLOWEEN, AIN'T IT?
I WANNA MAKE SURE I WAS HERE FOR THE GOOD CANDY.
I DON' THINK SHE'S WORKIN' TONIGHT.
WHO?
CANDY.
I.D.?
HOW I KNOW IT'S YOU?
YOU DON'T.
HEIGHT? WEIGHT? EYE COLOR?
RIGHT.
TEN BUCKS.
THERE'S A TWO-DRINK MINIMUM.
MAYBE FOR YOU...

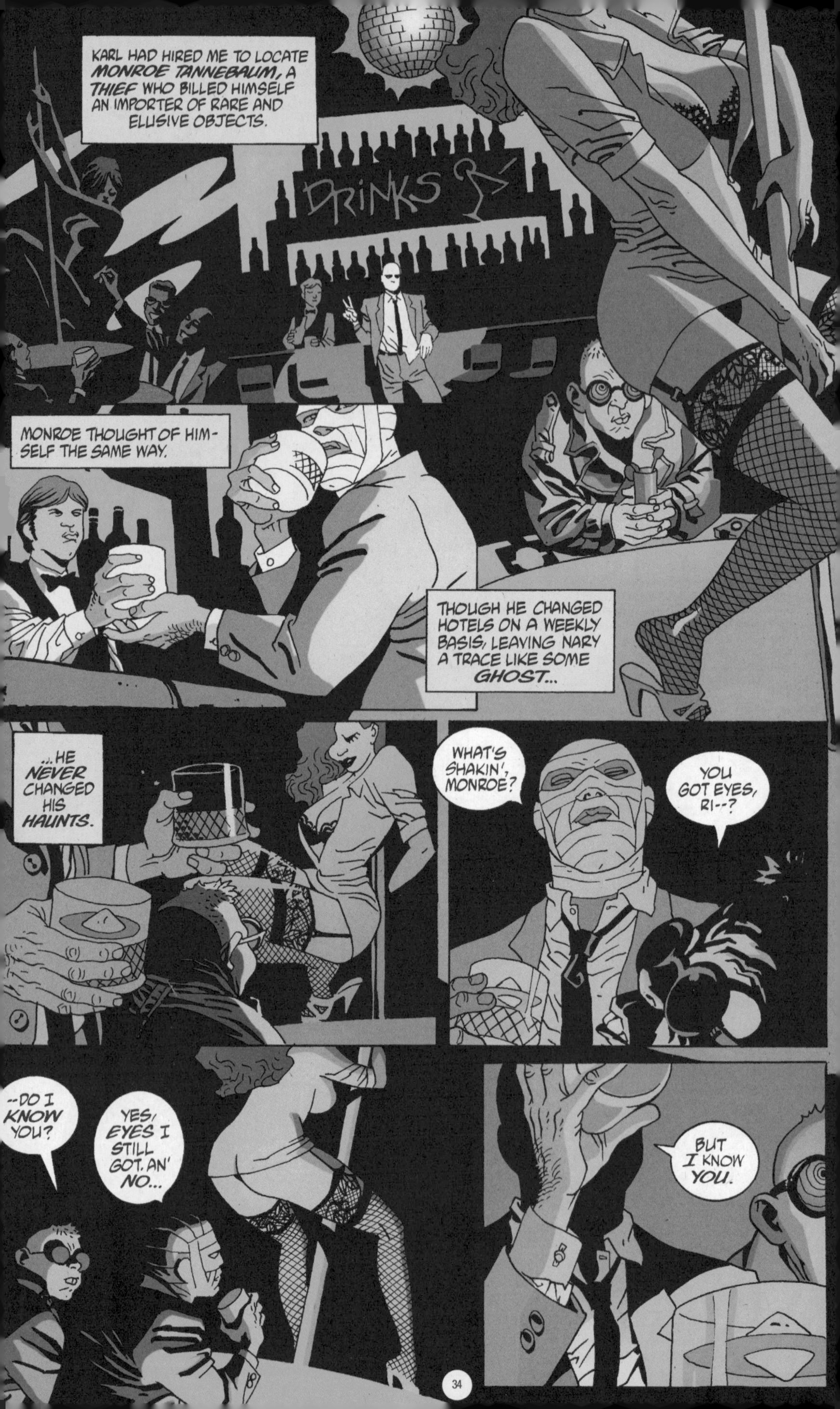
KARL HAD HIRED ME TO LOCATE MONROE TANNEBAUM, A THIEF WHO BILLED HIMSELF AN IMPORTER OF RARE AND ELUSIVE OBJECTS.
DRINKS
MONROE THOUGHT OF HIM-SELF THE SAME WAY.
THOUGH HE CHANGED HOTELS ON A WEEKLY BASIS, LEAVING NARY A TRACE LIKE SOME GHOST...
...HE NEVER CHANGED HIS HAUNTS.
WHAT'S SHAKIN', MONROE?
YOU GOT EYES, RI--?
--DO I KNOW YOU?
YES, EYES I STILL GOT. AN' NO...
BUT I KNOW YOU.

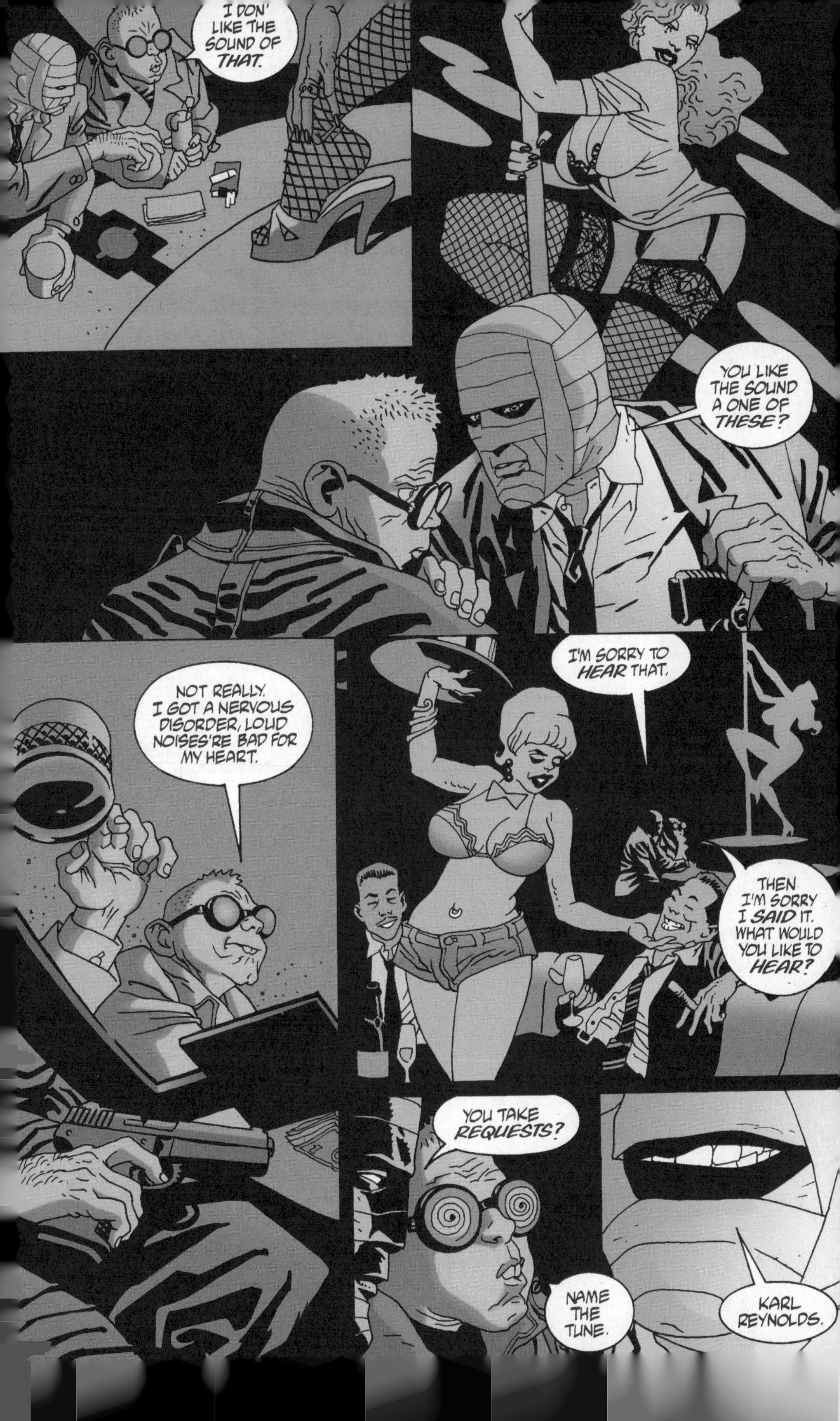
I DON' LIKE THE SOUND OF THAT.
YOU LIKE THE SOUND A ONE OF THESE?
NOT REALLY. I GOT A NERVOUS DISORDER, LOUD NOISES'RE BAD FOR MY HEART.
I'M SORRY TO HEAR THAT.
THEN I'M SORRY I SAID IT. WHAT WOULD YOU LIKE TO HEAR?
YOU TAKE REQUESTS?
NAME THE TUNE.
KARL REYNOLDS.

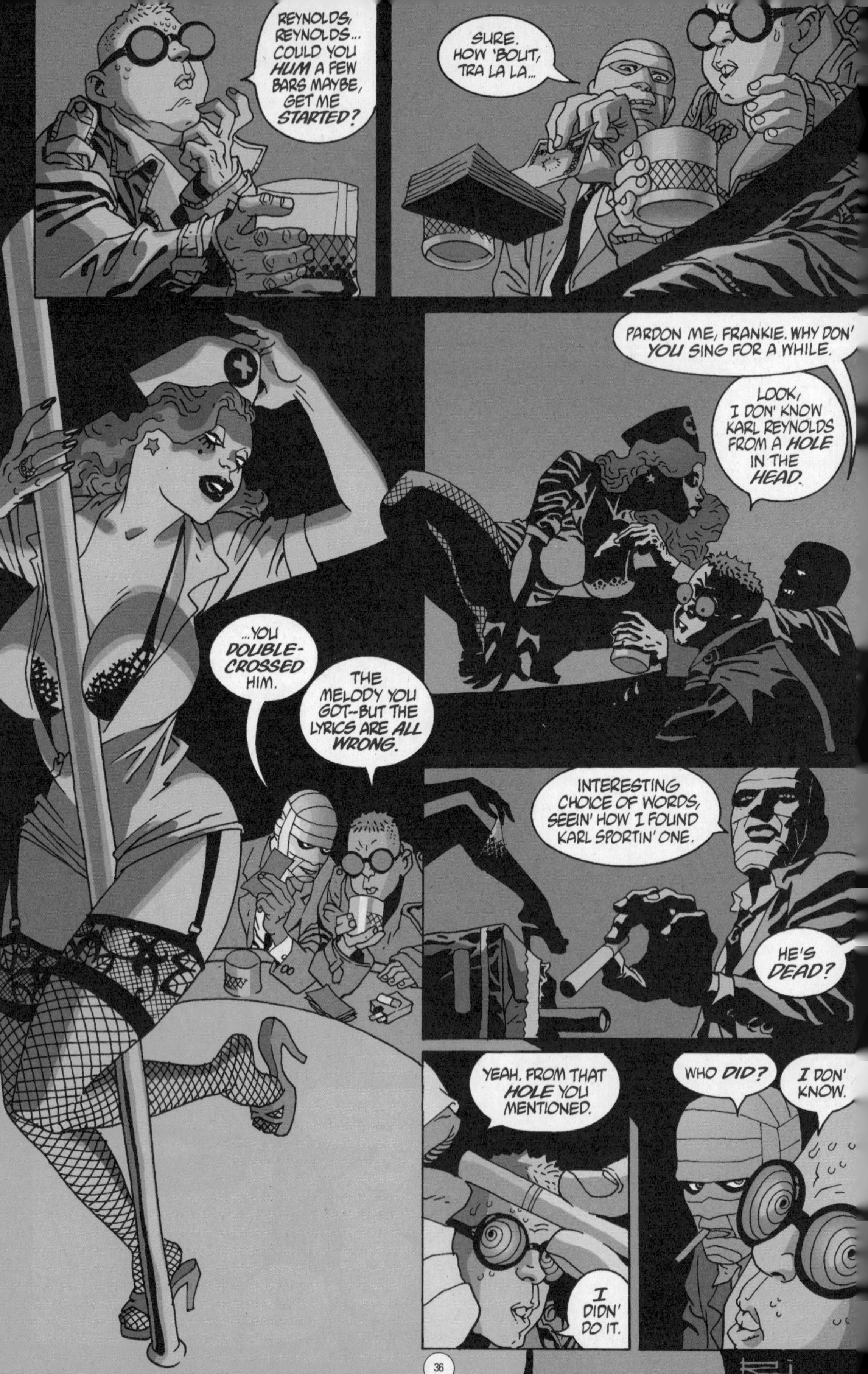
REYNOLDS, REYNOLDS... COULD YOU HUM A FEW BARS MAYBE, GET ME STARTED?
SURE. HOW 'BOUT, TRA LA LA...
PARDON ME, FRANKIE. WHY DON' YOU SING FOR A WHILE.
LOOK, I DON' KNOW KARL REYNOLDS FROM A HOLE IN THE HEAD.
...YOU DOUBLE-CROSSED HIM.
THE MELODY YOU GOT--BUT THE LYRICS ARE ALL WRONG.
INTERESTING CHOICE OF WORDS, SEEIN' HOW I FOUND KARL SPORTIN' ONE.
HE'S DEAD?
YEAH. FROM THAT HOLE YOU MENTIONED.
I DIDN' DO IT.
WHO DID?
I DON' KNOW.

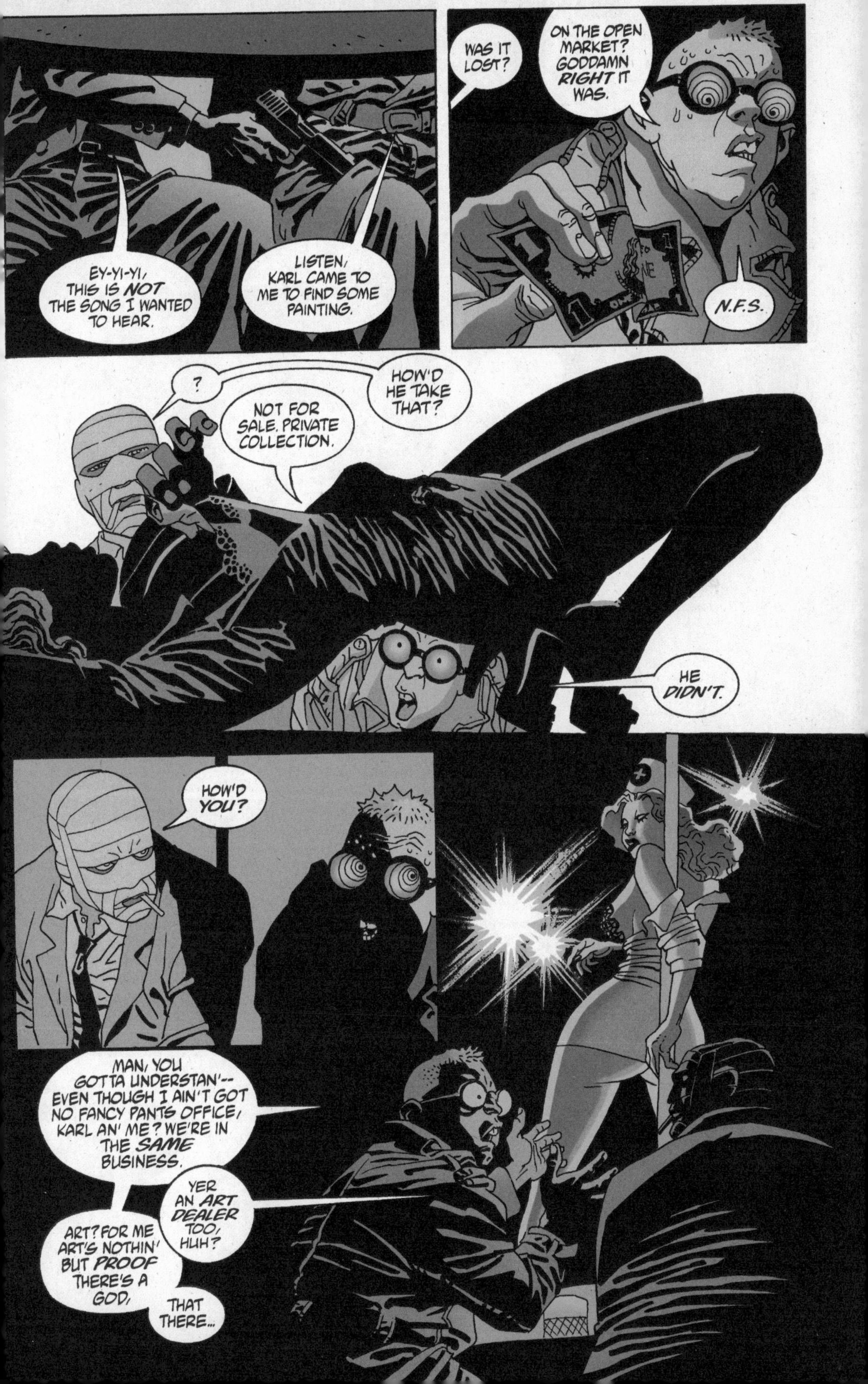
EY-YI-YI, THIS IS *NOT* THE SONG I WANTED TO HEAR.
LISTEN, KARL CAME TO ME TO FIND SOME PAINTING.
WAS IT LOST?
ON THE OPEN MARKET? GODDAMN *RIGHT* IT WAS.
N.F.S.
?
NOT FOR SALE. PRIVATE COLLECTION.
HOW'D HE TAKE THAT?
HE *DIDN'T*.
HOW'D *YOU*?
MAN, YOU GOTTA UNDERSTAN'-- EVEN THOUGH I AIN'T GOT NO FANCY PANTS OFFICE, KARL AN' ME? WE'RE IN THE *SAME* BUSINESS.
YER AN *ART DEALER* TOO, HUH?
ART? FOR ME ART'S NOTHIN' BUT *PROOF* THERE'S A GOD,
THAT THERE...

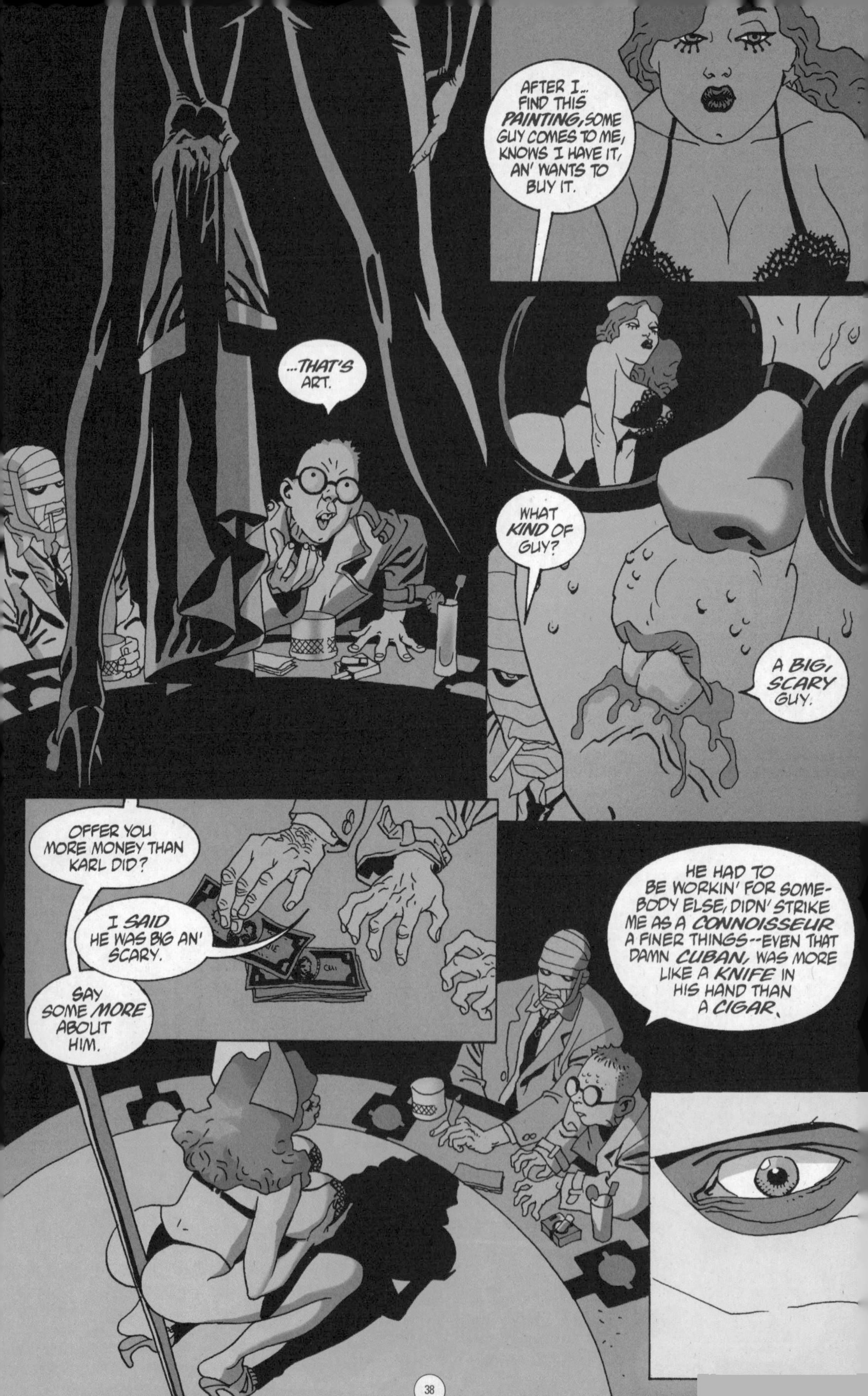

...THAT'S ART.
AFTER I... FIND THIS PAINTING, SOME GUY COMES TO ME, KNOWS I HAVE IT, AN' WANTS TO BUY IT.
WHAT KIND OF GUY?
A BIG, SCARY GUY.
OFFER YOU MORE MONEY THAN KARL DID?
I SAID HE WAS BIG AN' SCARY.
SAY SOME MORE ABOUT HIM.
HE HAD TO BE WORKIN' FOR SOMEBODY ELSE, DIDN' STRIKE ME AS A CONNOISSEUR A FINER THINGS--EVEN THAT DAMN CUBAN, WAS MORE LIKE A KNIFE IN HIS HAND THAN A CIGAR.

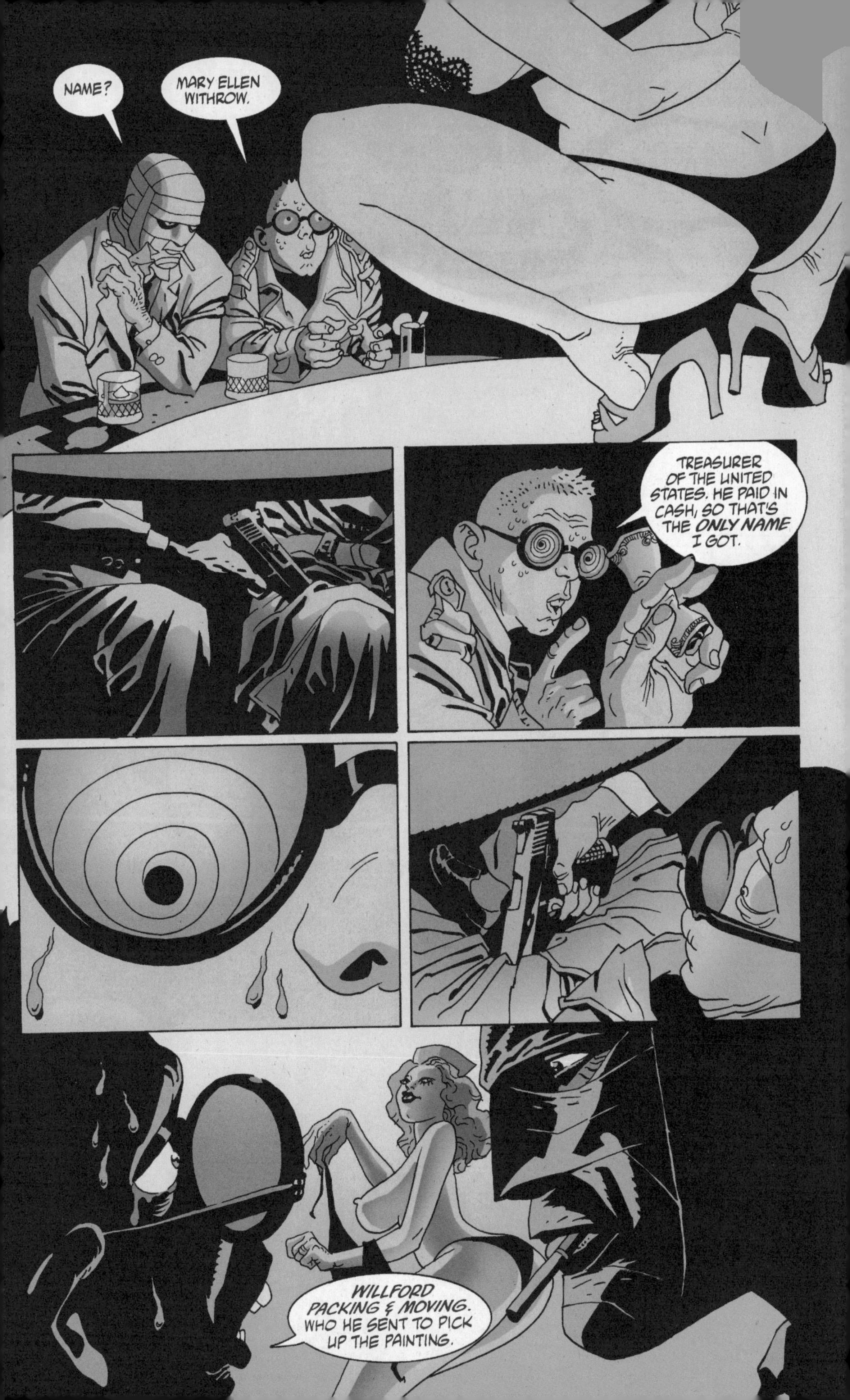
NAME?
MARY ELLEN WITHROW.
TREASURER OF THE UNITED STATES. HE PAID IN CASH, SO THAT'S THE *ONLY NAME* I GOT.
WILLFORD PACKING & MOVING. WHO HE SENT TO PICK UP THE PAINTING.

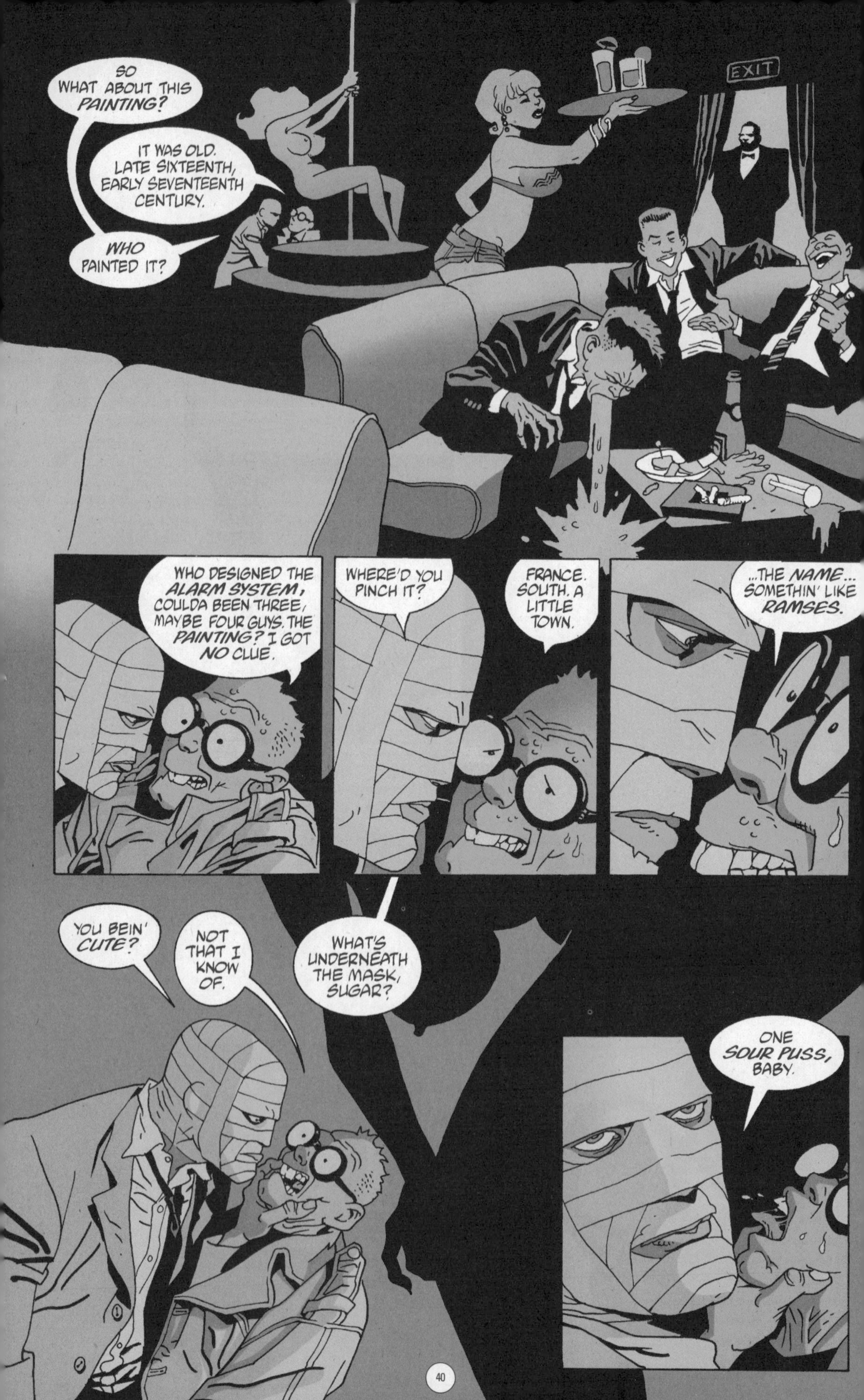
SO WHAT ABOUT THIS PAINTING?
IT WAS OLD. LATE SIXTEENTH, EARLY SEVENTEENTH CENTURY.
WHO PAINTED IT?
EXIT
WHO DESIGNED THE ALARM SYSTEM, COULDA BEEN THREE, MAYBE FOUR GUYS. THE PAINTING? I GOT NO CLUE.
WHERE'D YOU PINCH IT?
FRANCE. SOUTH. A LITTLE TOWN.
...THE NAME... SOMETHIN' LIKE RAMSES.
YOU BEIN' CUTE?
NOT THAT I KNOW OF.
WHAT'S UNDERNEATH THE MASK, SUGAR?
ONE SOUR PUSS, BABY.

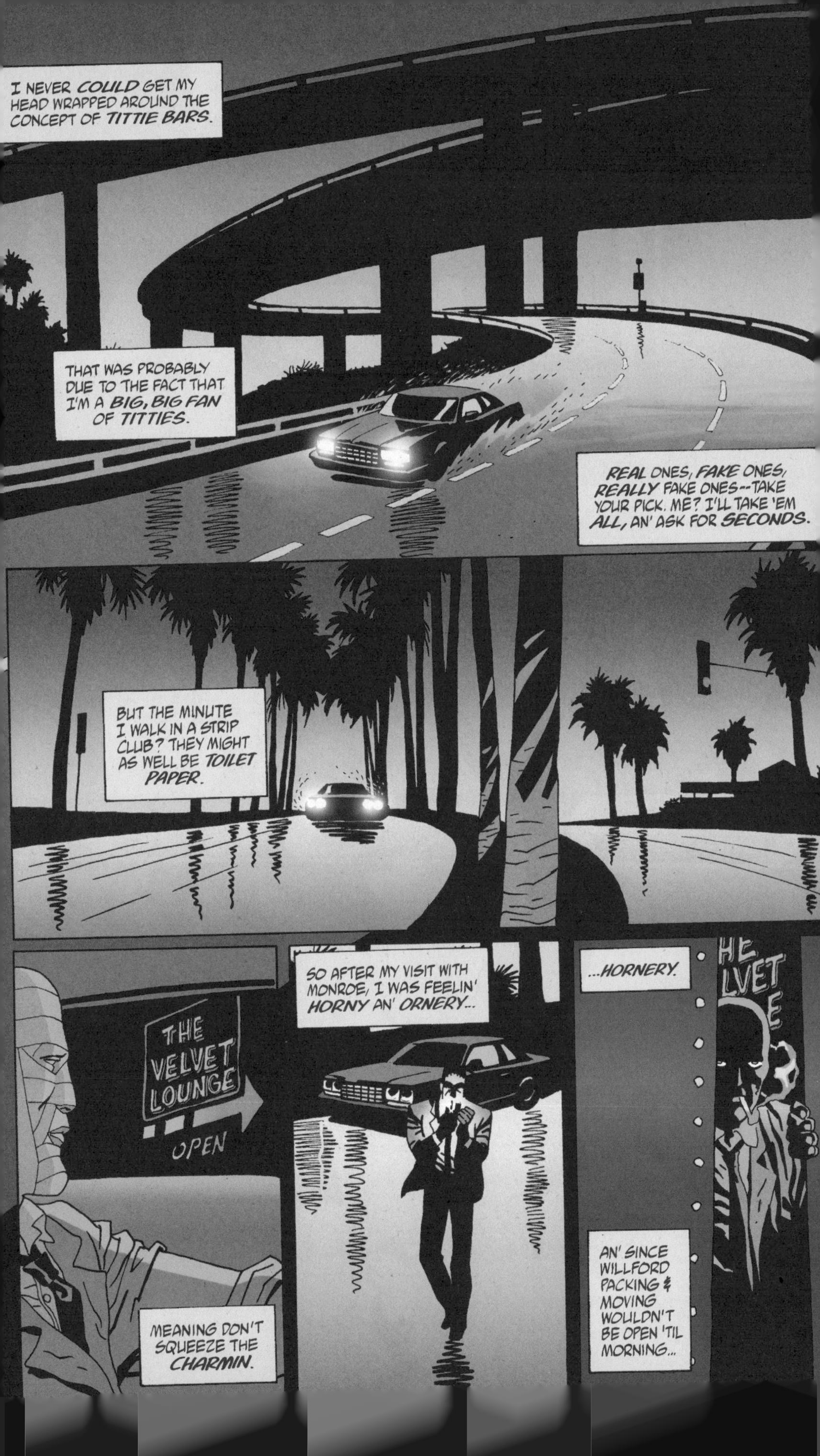
I NEVER COULD GET MY HEAD WRAPPED AROUND THE CONCEPT OF TITTIE BARS.
THAT WAS PROBABLY DUE TO THE FACT THAT I'M A BIG, BIG FAN OF TITTIES.
REAL ONES, FAKE ONES, REALLY FAKE ONES--TAKE YOUR PICK. ME? I'LL TAKE 'EM ALL, AN' ASK FOR SECONDS.
BUT THE MINUTE I WALK IN A STRIP CLUB? THEY MIGHT AS WELL BE TOILET PAPER.
THE VELVET LOUNGE
OPEN
MEANING DON'T SQUEEZE THE CHARMIN.
SO AFTER MY VISIT WITH MONROE, I WAS FEELIN' HORNY AN' ORNERY...
...HORNERY.
AN' SINCE WILLFORD PACKING & MOVING WOULDN'T BE OPEN 'TIL MORNING...

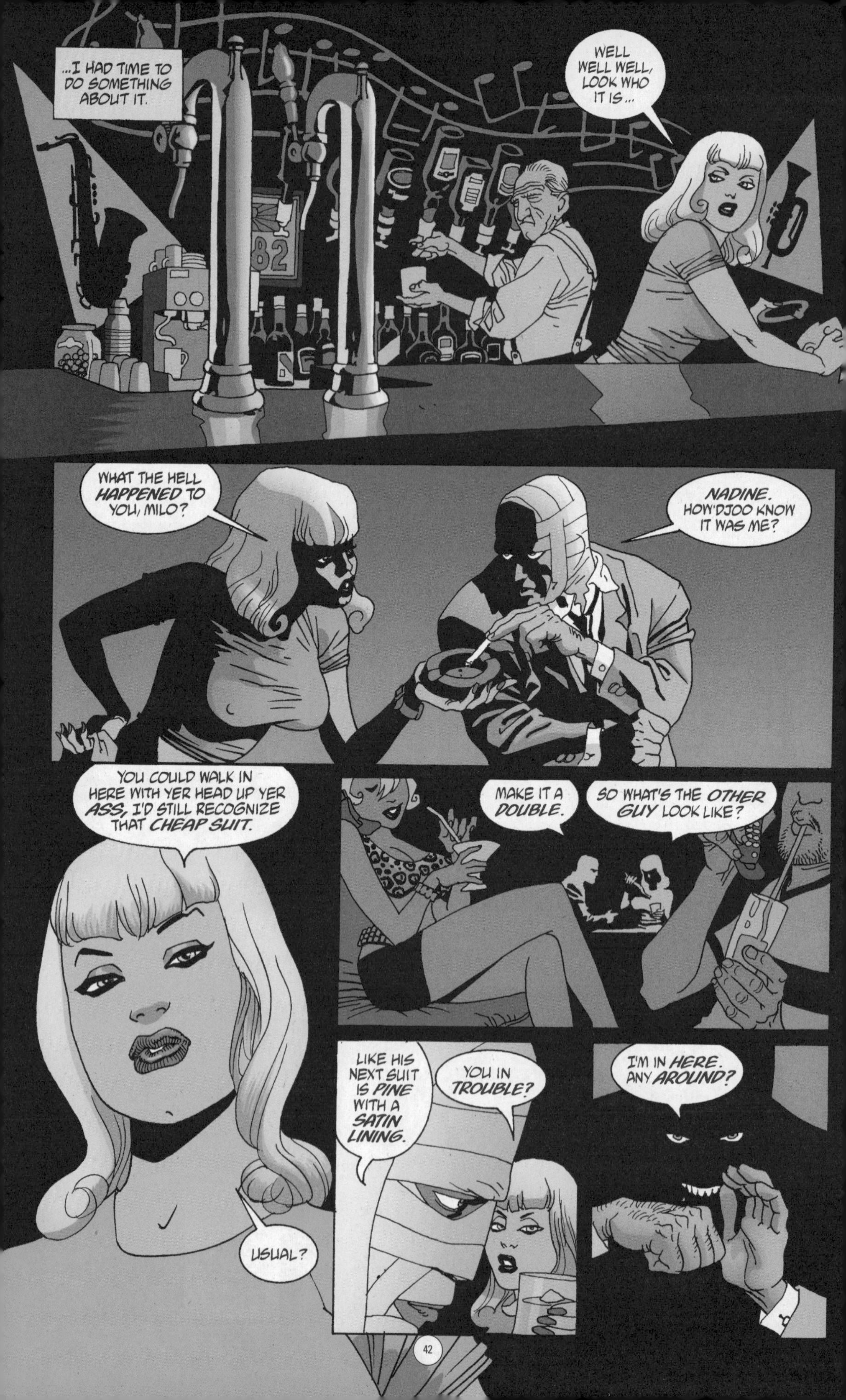
...I HAD TIME TO DO SOMETHING ABOUT IT.
WELL WELL WELL, LOOK WHO IT IS...
WHAT THE HELL HAPPENED TO YOU, MILO?
NADINE. HOW'DJOO KNOW IT WAS ME?
YOU COULD WALK IN HERE WITH YER HEAD UP YER ASS, I'D STILL RECOGNIZE THAT CHEAP SUIT.
USUAL?
MAKE IT A DOUBLE.
SO WHAT'S THE OTHER GUY LOOK LIKE?
LIKE HIS NEXT SUIT IS PINE WITH A SATIN LINING.
YOU IN TROUBLE?
I'M IN HERE. ANY AROUND?

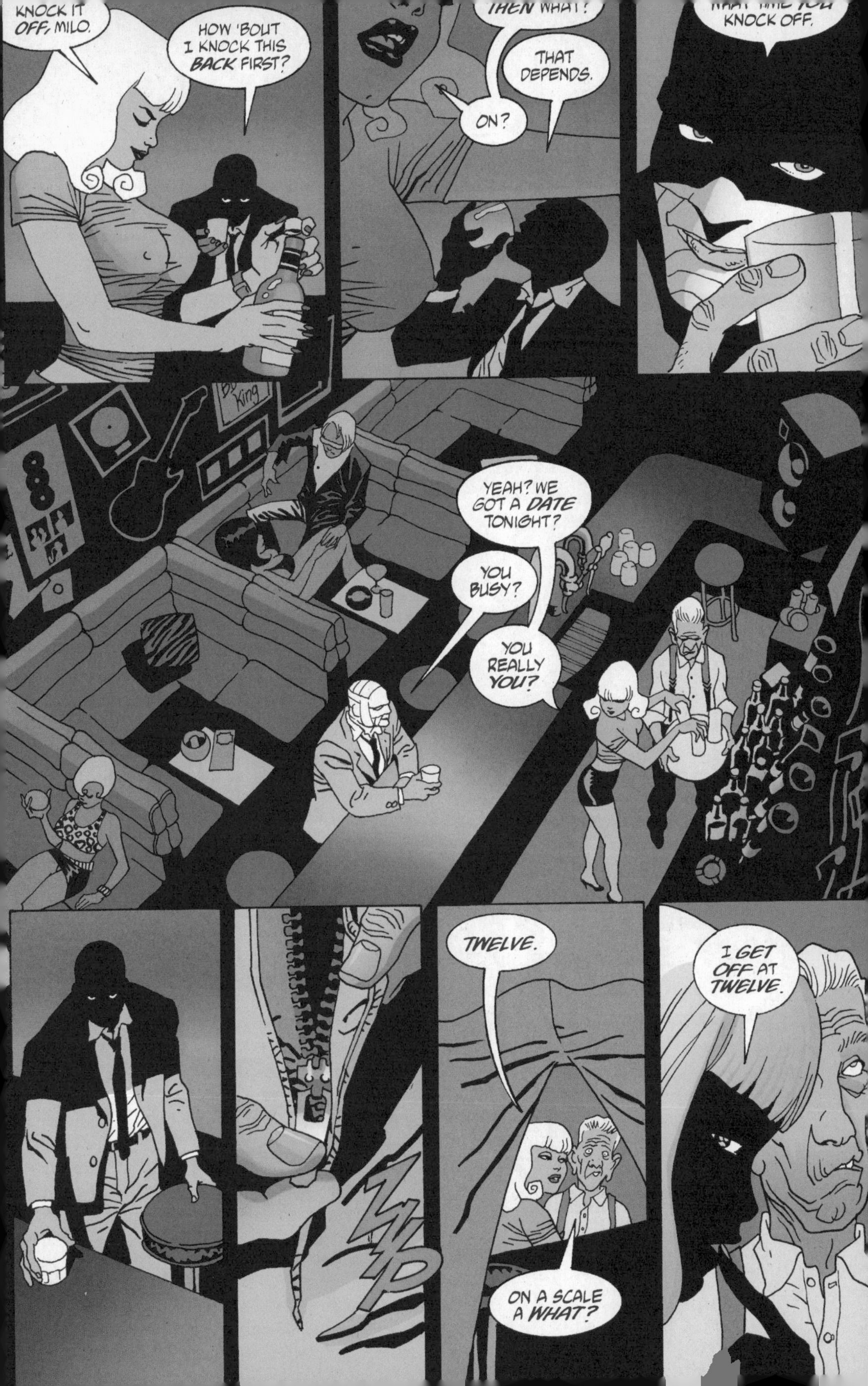

KNOCK IT OFF, MILO.
HOW 'BOUT I KNOCK THIS BACK FIRST?
THEN WHAT?
ON?
THAT DEPENDS.
KNOCK OFF.
YEAH? WE GOT A DATE TONIGHT?
YOU BUSY?
YOU REALLY YOU?
WHIP
TWELVE.
ON A SCALE A WHAT?
I GET OFF AT TWELVE.

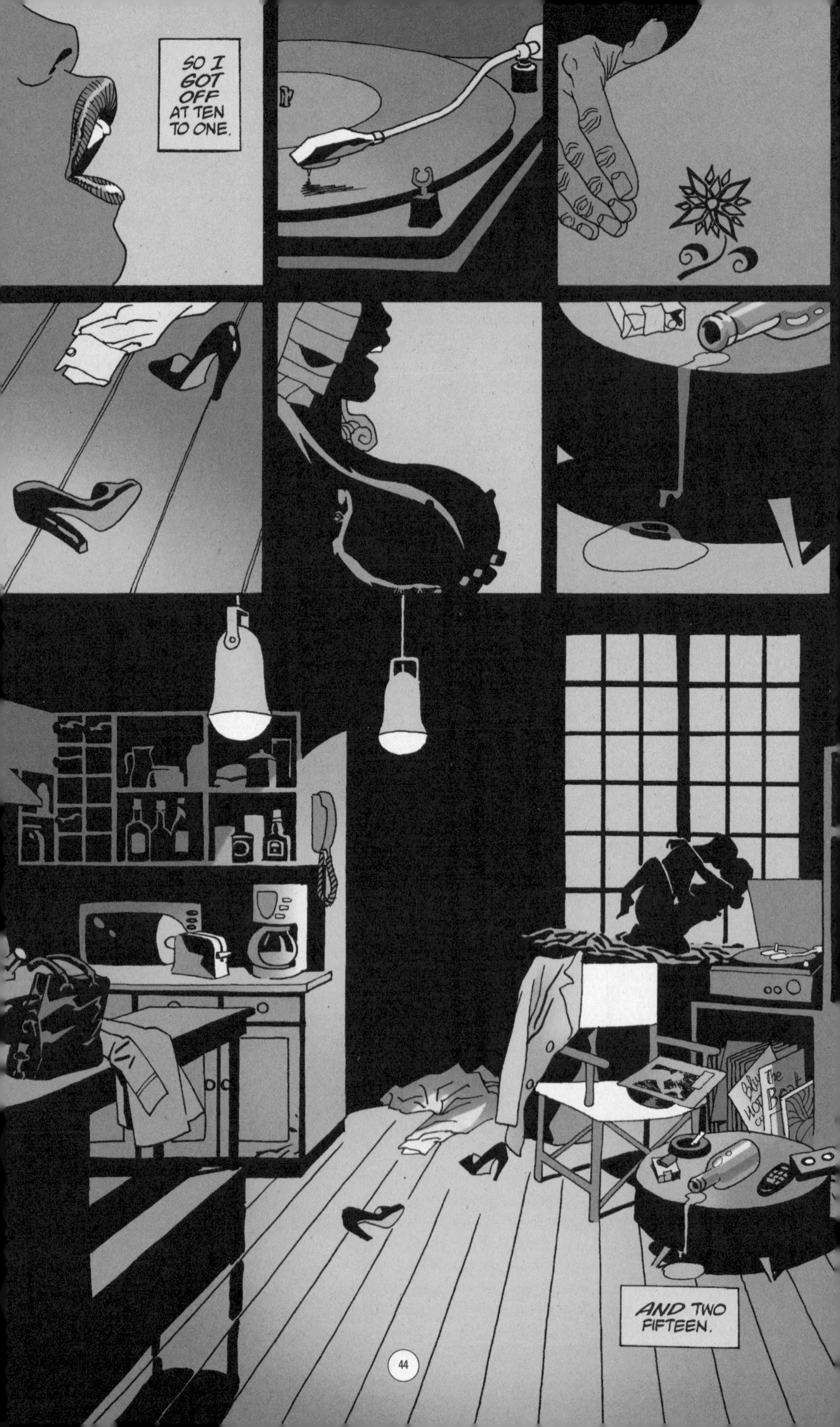
SO I GOT OFF AT TEN TO ONE.
AND TWO FIFTEEN.

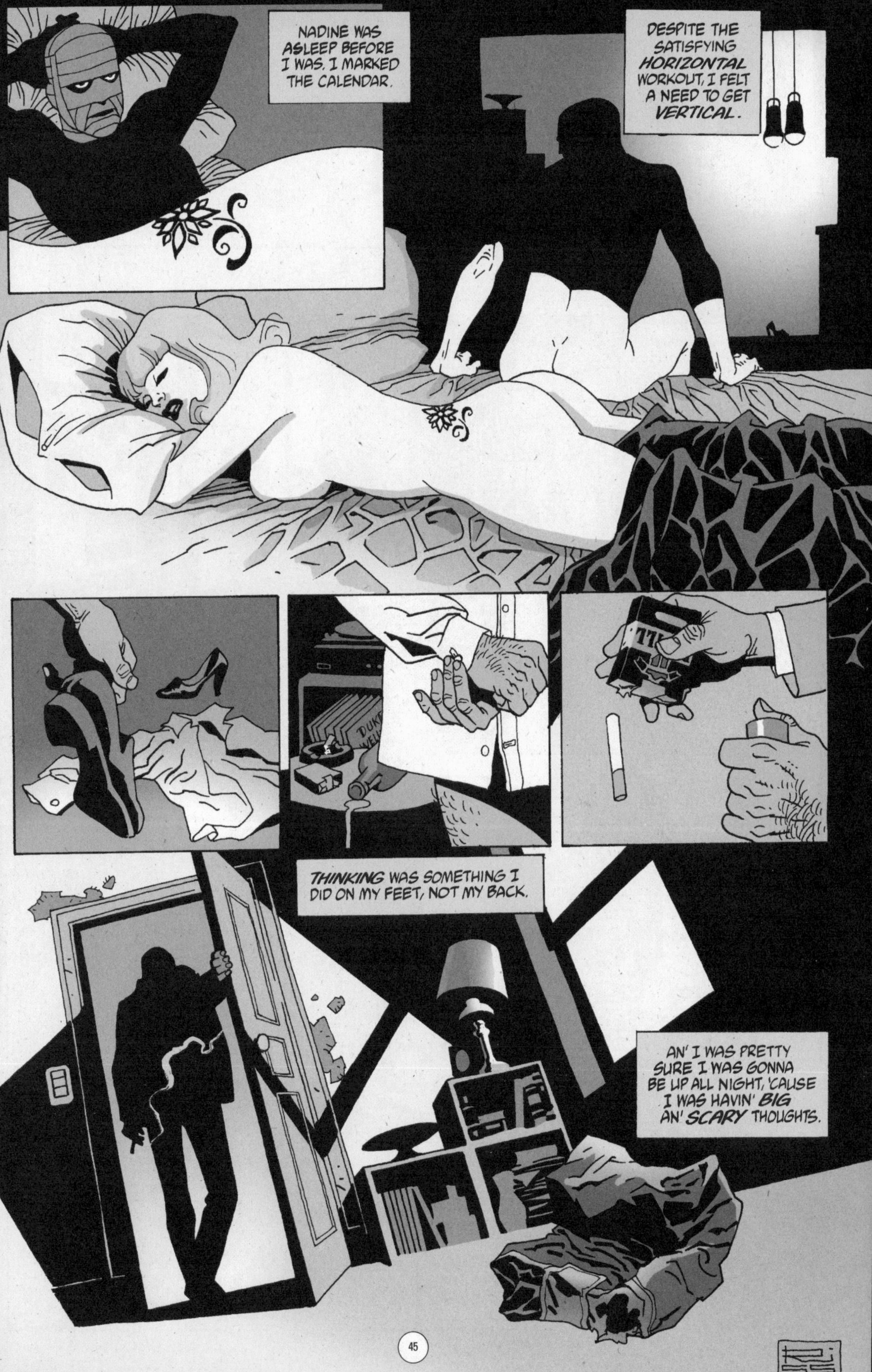
NADINE WAS ASLEEP BEFORE I WAS. I MARKED THE CALENDAR.
DESPITE THE SATISFYING HORIZONTAL WORKOUT, I FELT A NEED TO GET VERTICAL.
THINKING WAS SOMETHING I DID ON MY FEET, NOT MY BACK.
AN' I WAS PRETTY SURE I WAS GONNA BE UP ALL NIGHT, 'CAUSE I WAS HAVIN' BIG AN' SCARY THOUGHTS.

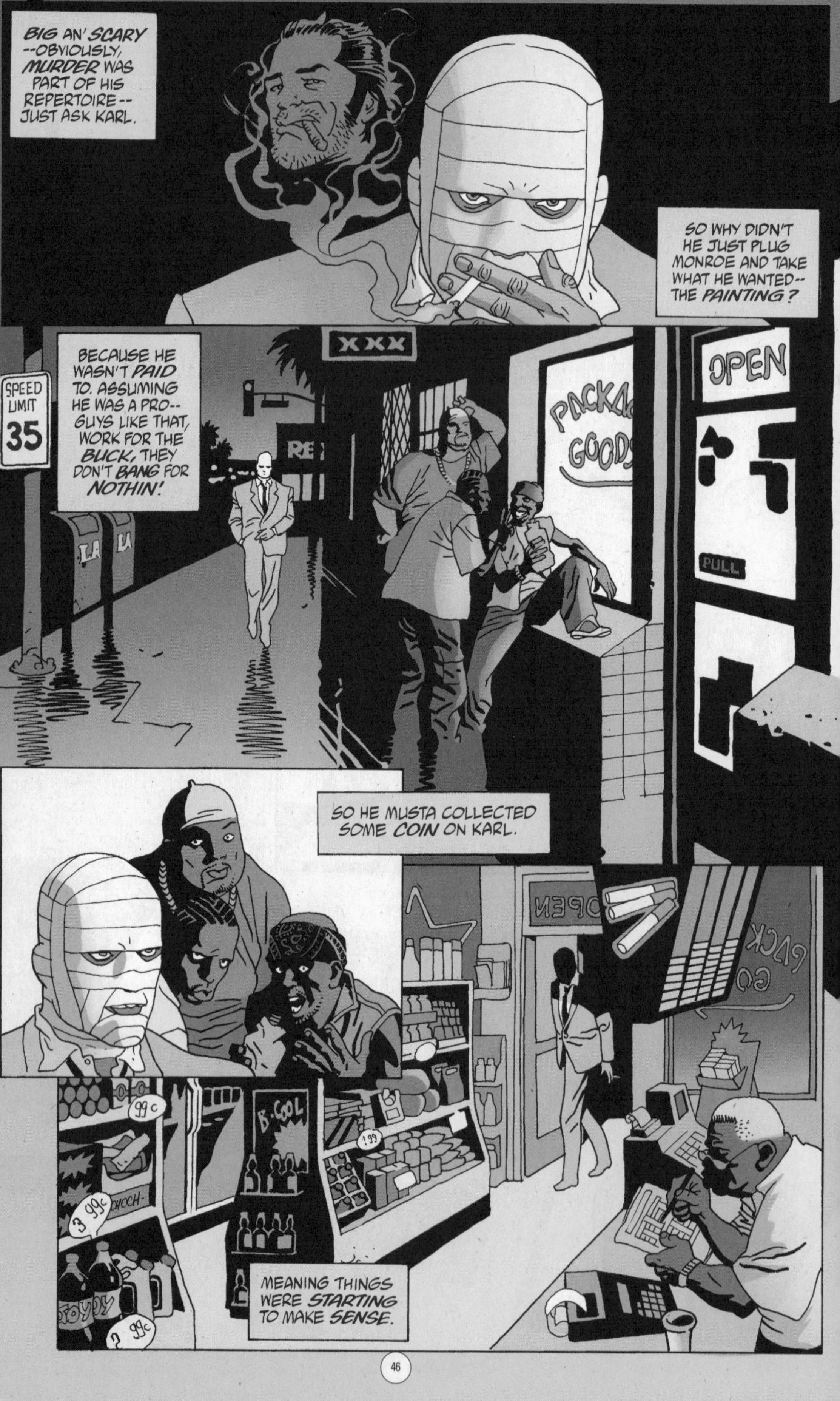
BIG AN' SCARY --OBVIOUSLY, MURDER WAS PART OF HIS REPERTOIRE -- JUST ASK KARL.
SO WHY DIDN'T HE JUST PLUG MONROE AND TAKE WHAT HE WANTED-- THE PAINTING?
XXX
SPEED LIMIT 35
BECAUSE HE WASN'T PAID TO. ASSUMING HE WAS A PRO-- GUYS LIKE THAT, WORK FOR THE BUCK, THEY DON'T BANG FOR NOTHIN'!
OPEN
PULL
SO HE MUSTA COLLECTED SOME COIN ON KARL.
99¢
1.99
MEANING THINGS WERE STARTING TO MAKE SENSE.

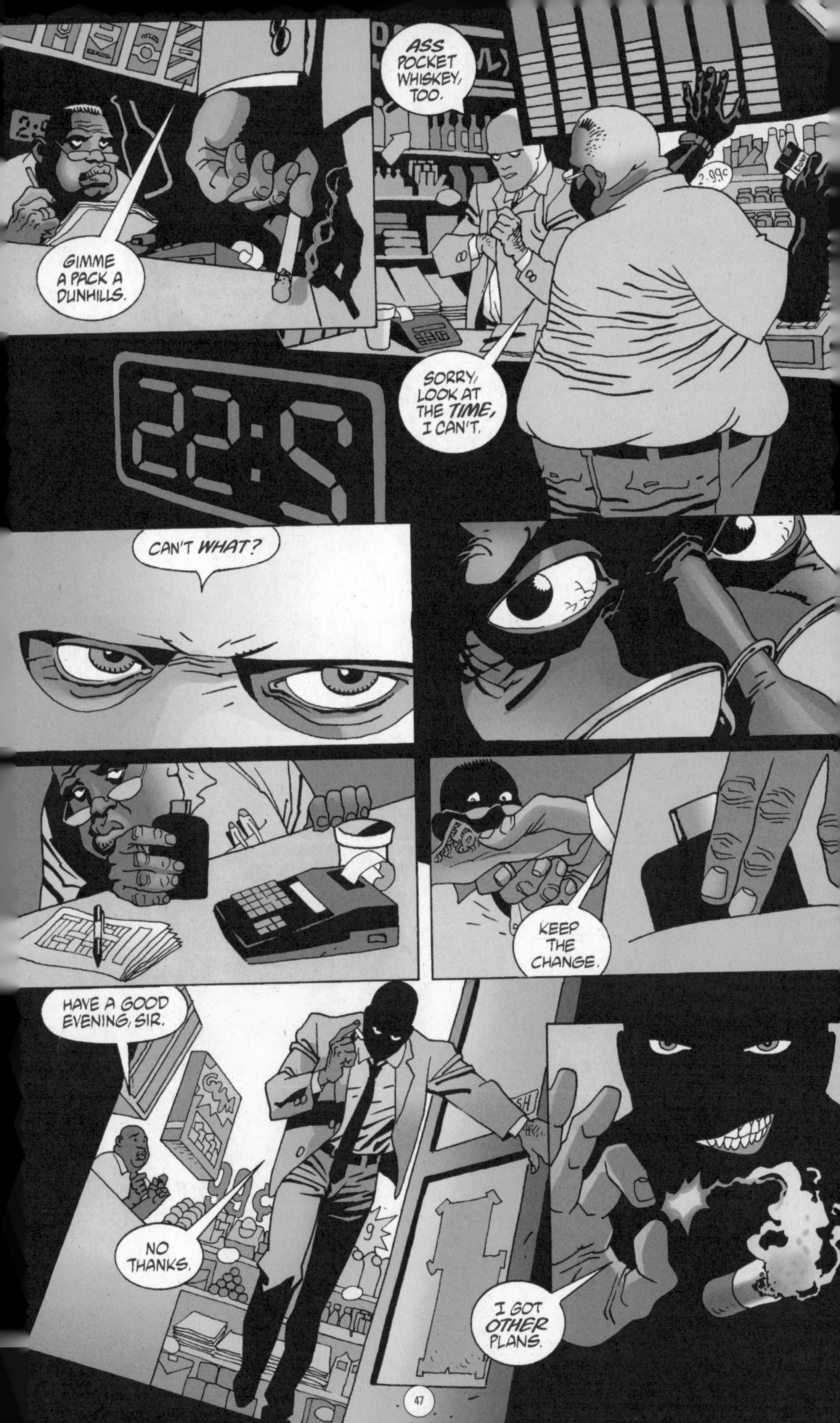
GIMME A PACK A DUNHILLS.
ASS POCKET WHISKEY, TOO.
SORRY, LOOK AT THE TIME, I CAN'T.
CAN'T WHAT?
KEEP THE CHANGE.
HAVE A GOOD EVENING, SIR.
NO THANKS.
I GOT OTHER PLANS.

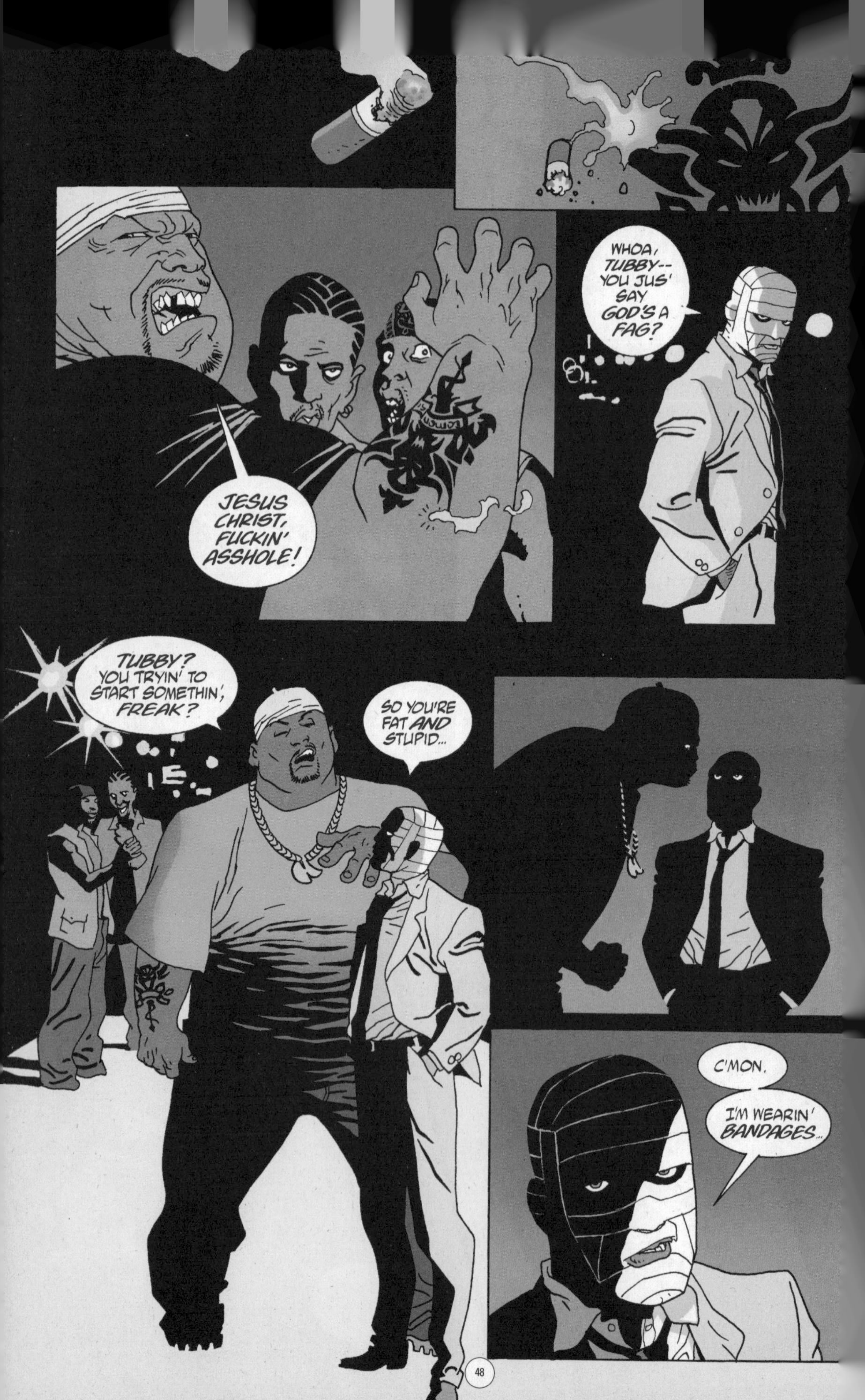
JESUS CHRIST, FUCKIN' ASSHOLE!
WHOA, TUBBY-- YOU JUS' SAY GOD'S A FAG?
TUBBY? YOU TRYIN' TO START SOMETHIN', FREAK?
SO YOU'RE FAT AND STUPID...
C'MON.
I'M WEARIN' BANDAGES...

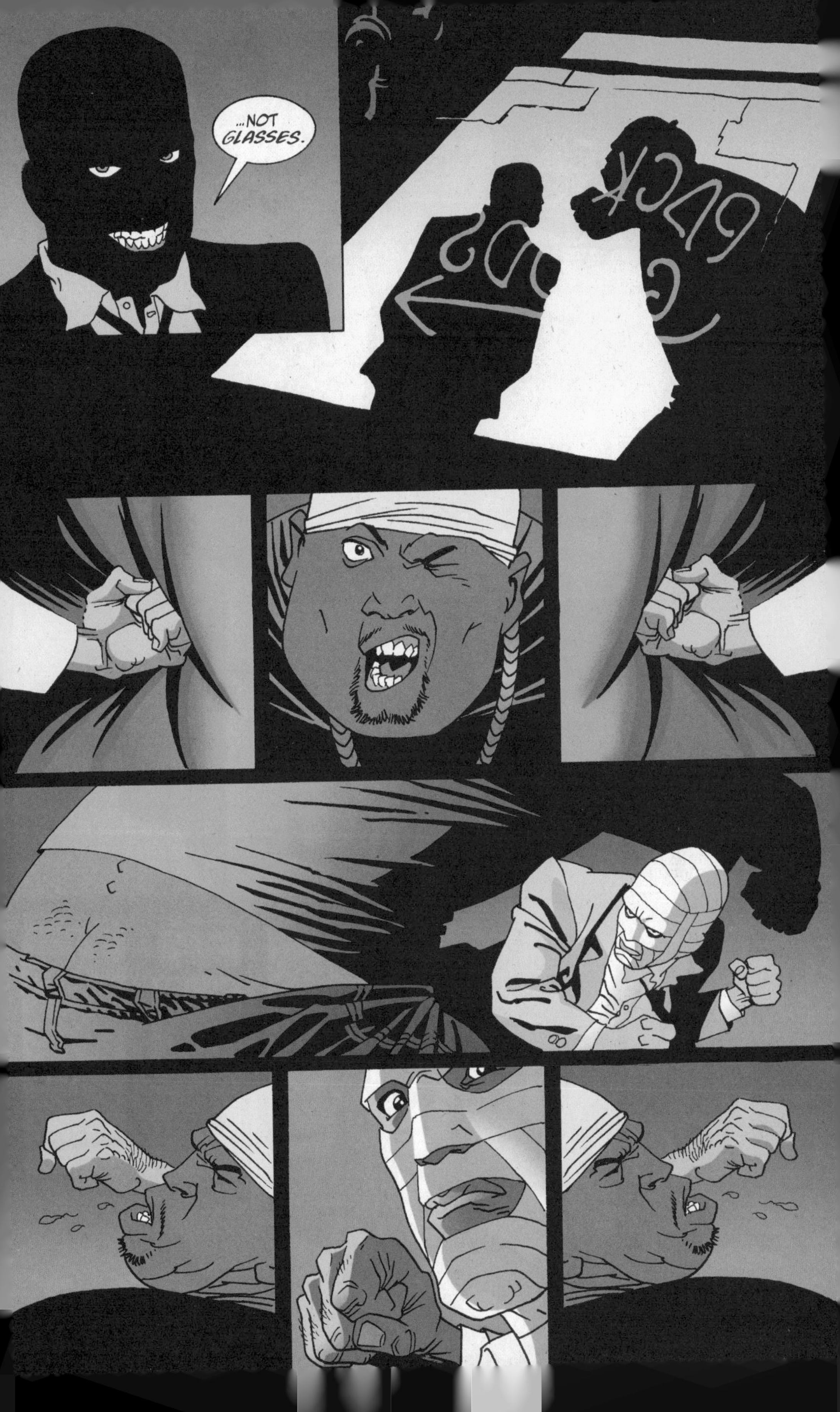
...NOT GLASSES.

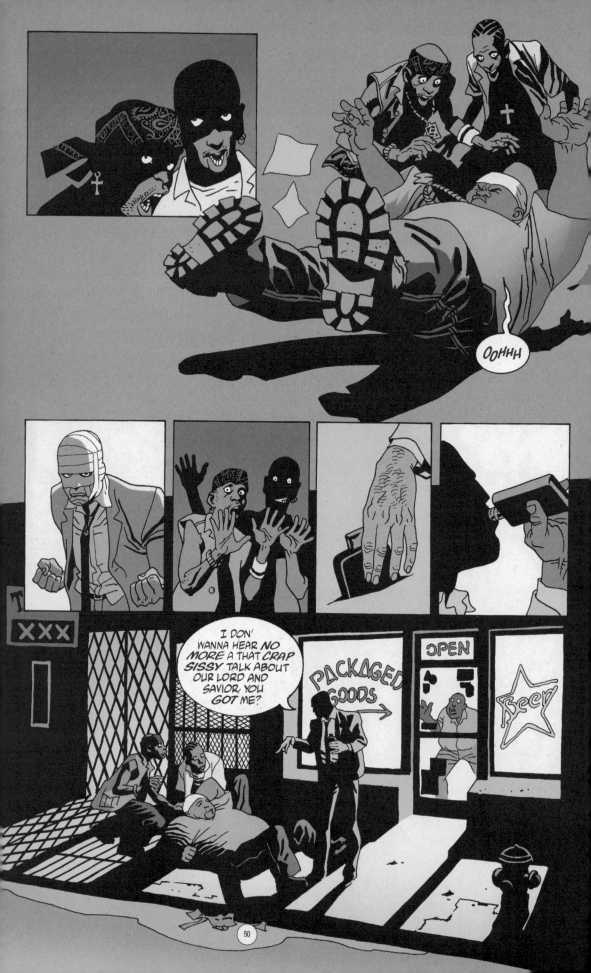

OOHHH

I DON' WANNA HEAR NO MORE A THAT CRAP SISSY TALK ABOUT OUR LORD AND SAVIOR, YOU GOT ME?

T
XXX

PACKAGED GOODS →

OPEN

Beer

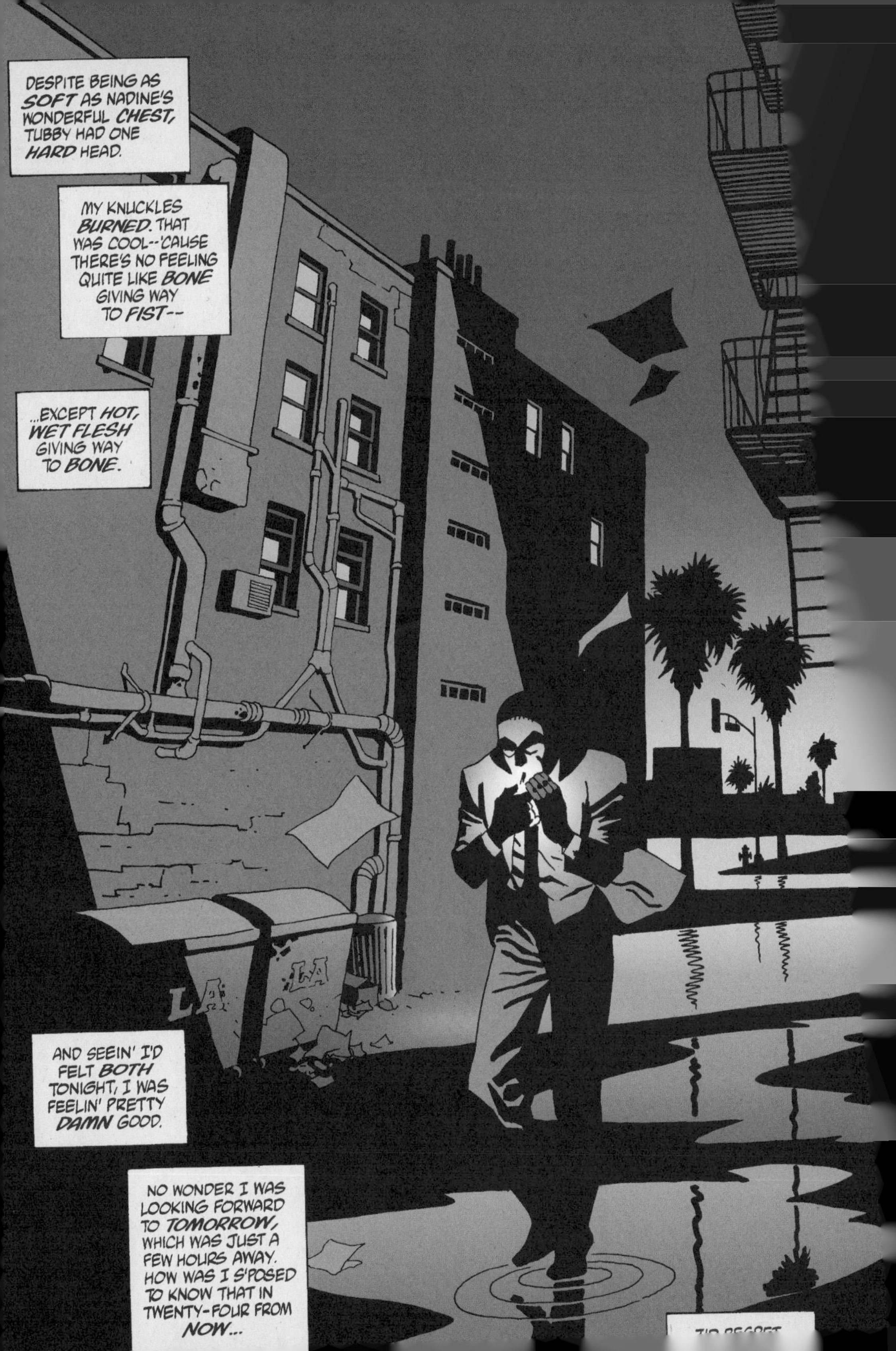
DESPITE BEING AS SOFT AS NADINE'S WONDERFUL CHEST, TUBBY HAD ONE HARD HEAD.
MY KNUCKLES BURNED. THAT WAS COOL--'CAUSE THERE'S NO FEELING QUITE LIKE BONE GIVING WAY TO FIST--
...EXCEPT HOT, WET FLESH GIVING WAY TO BONE.
AND SEEIN' I'D FELT BOTH TONIGHT, I WAS FEELIN' PRETTY DAMN GOOD.
NO WONDER I WAS LOOKING FORWARD TO TOMORROW, WHICH WAS JUST A FEW HOURS AWAY. HOW WAS I S'POSED TO KNOW THAT IN TWENTY-FOUR FROM NOW...

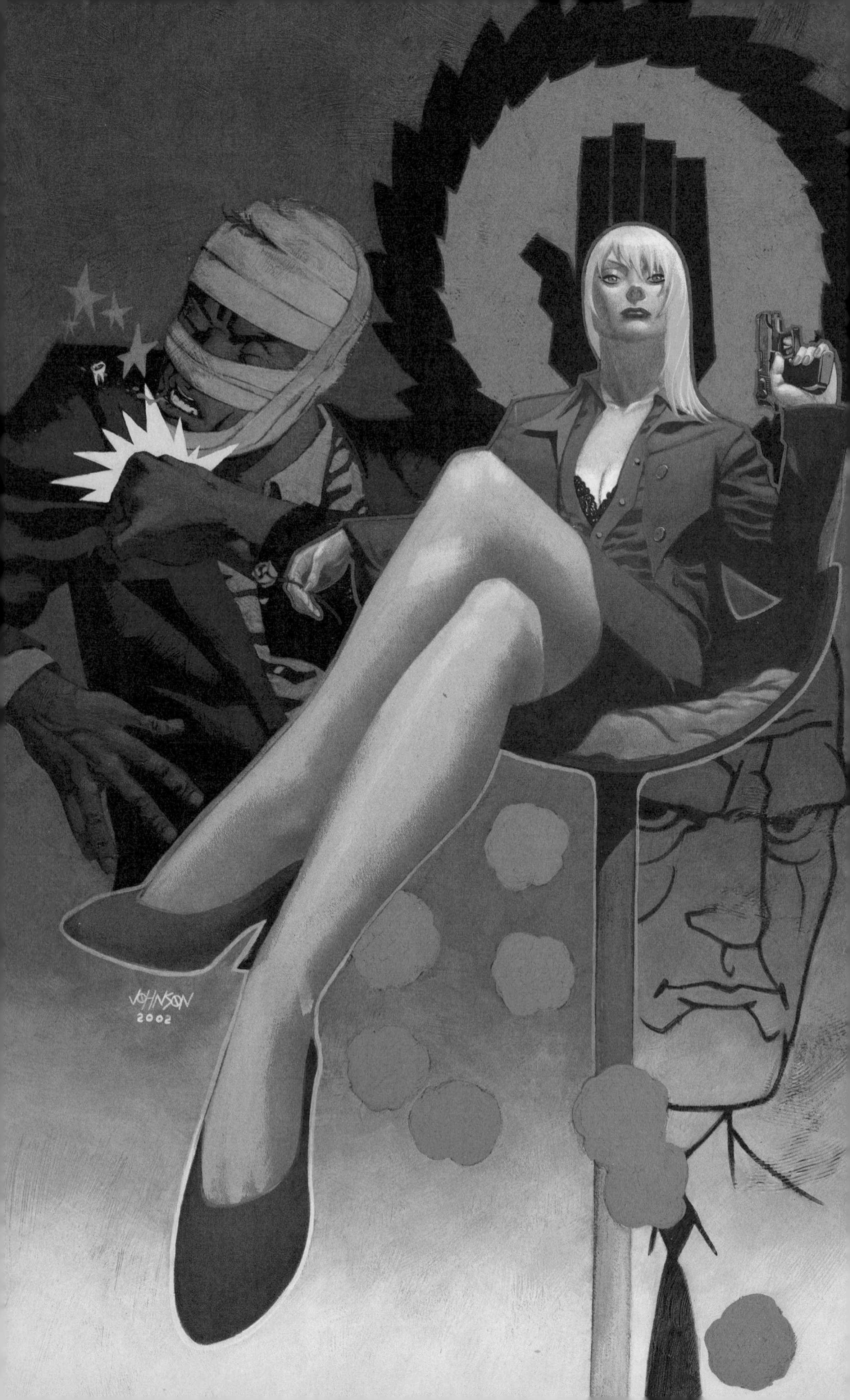
JOHNSON
2002

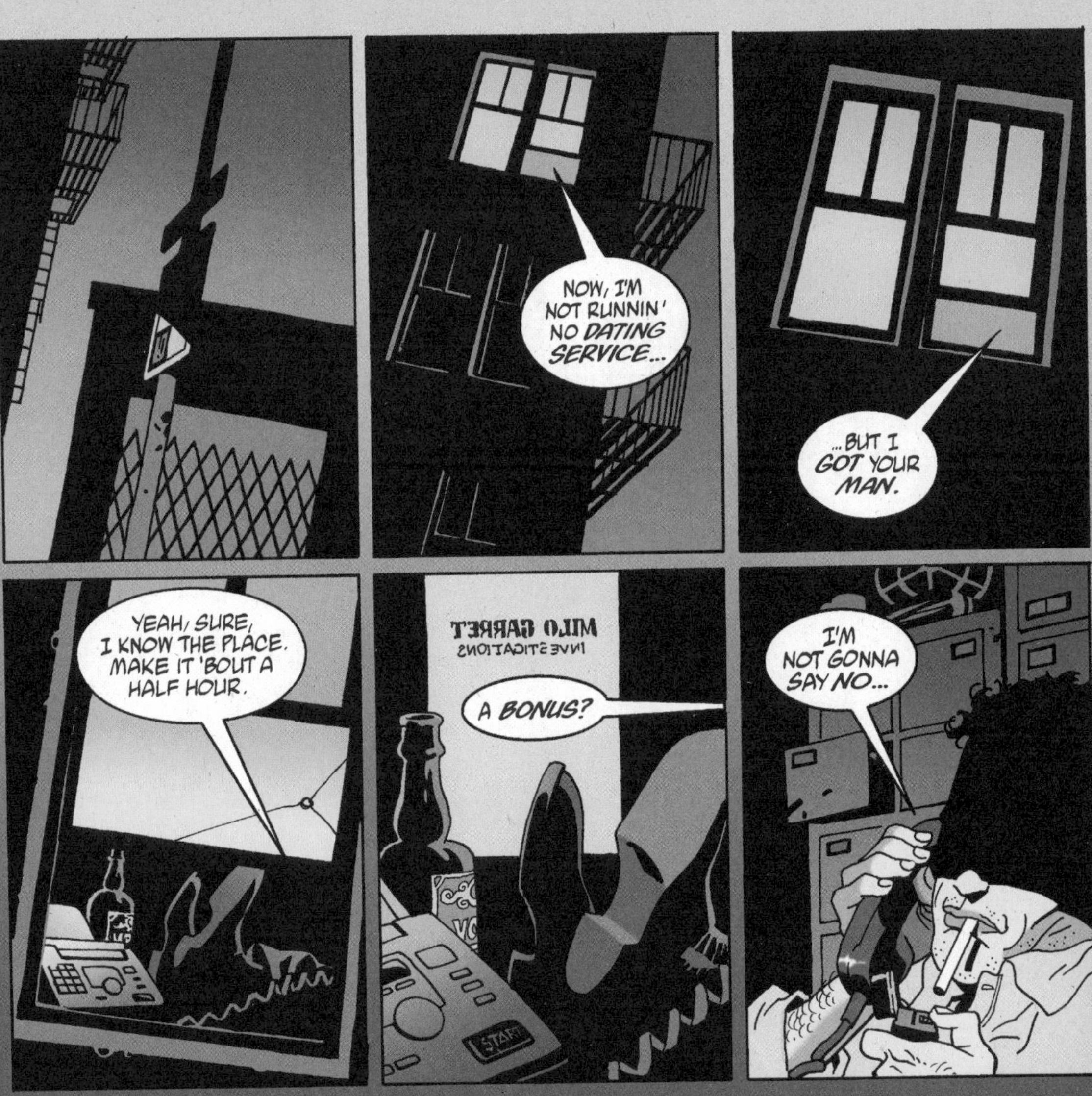
NOW, I'M NOT RUNNIN' NO DATING SERVICE...
...BUT I GOT YOUR MAN.
YEAH, SURE, I KNOW THE PLACE. MAKE IT 'BOUT A HALF HOUR.
MILO GARRET INVESTIGATIONS
A BONUS?
START
I'M NOT GONNA SAY NO...

THE COUNTERFIFTH DETECTIVE PART 3

BRIAN AZZARELLO writer · EDUARDO RISSO artist · PATRICIA MULVIHILL colorist · CLEM ROBINS letterer · DIGITAL CHAMELEON separations · DAVE JOHNSON cover artist · ZACHARY RAU ass't ed. · WILL DENNIS editor

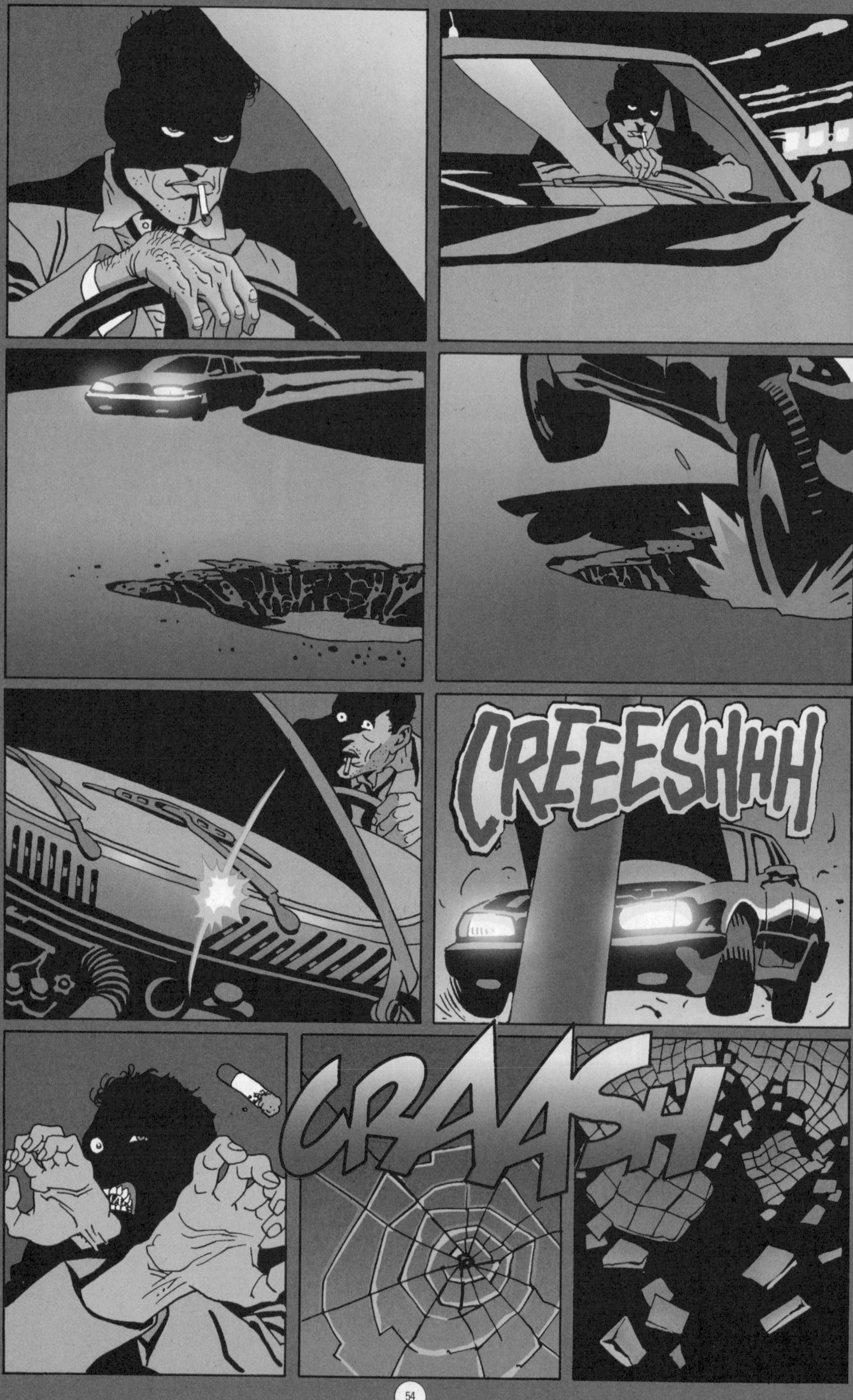
CREEESHHH
CRAASH

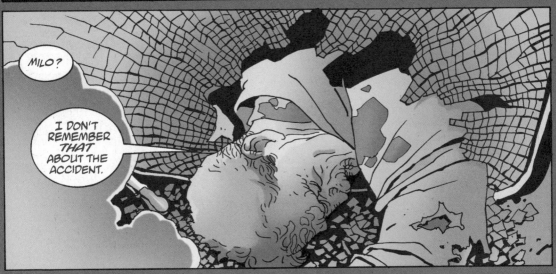

MILO?

I DON'T REMEMBER *THAT* ABOUT THE ACCIDENT.

MILO?

SOMEONE *THERE*, WHO KNEW MY *NAME*...

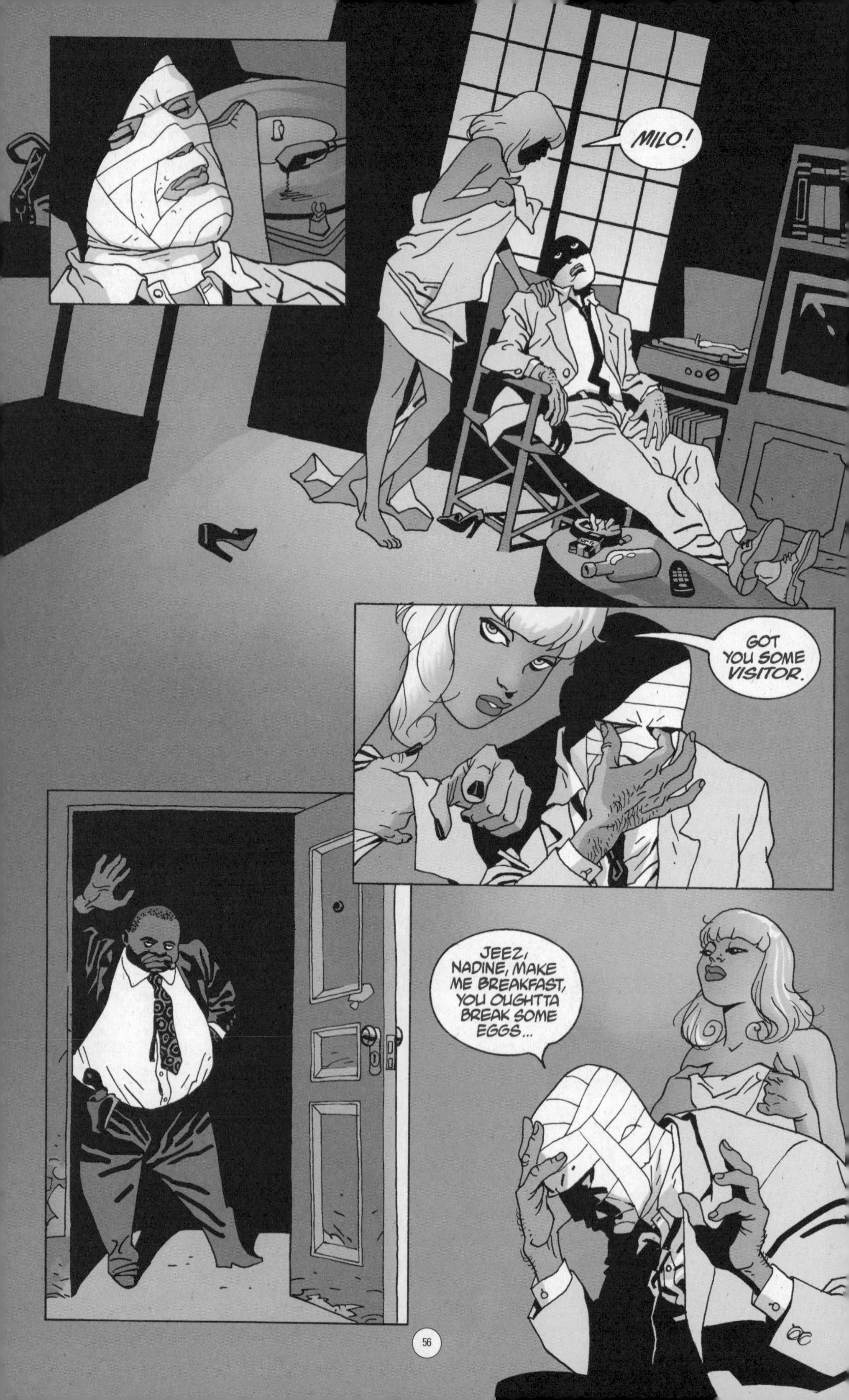
MILO!
GOT YOU SOME VISITOR.
JEEZ, NADINE, MAKE ME BREAKFAST, YOU OUGHTTA BREAK SOME EGGS...

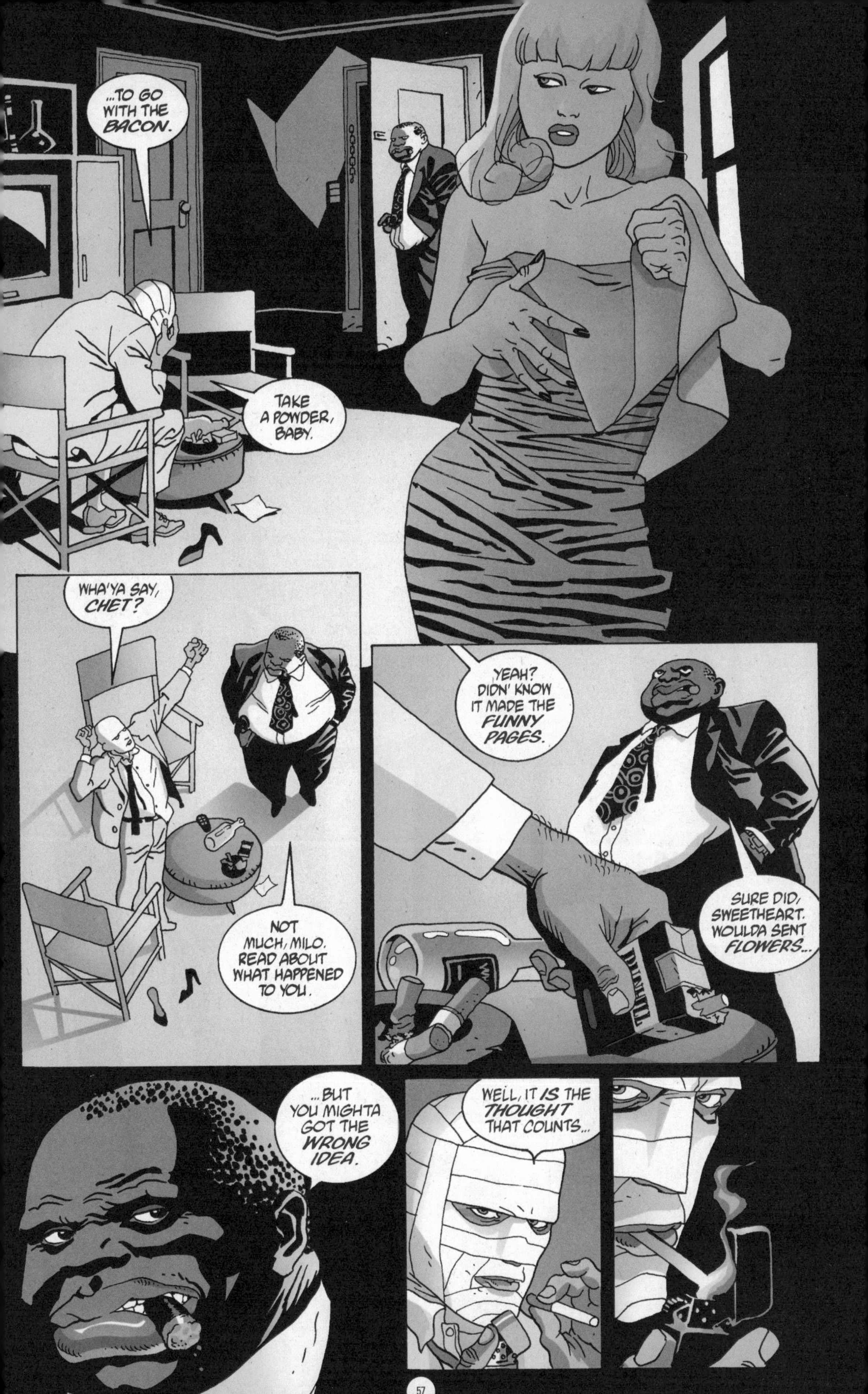
...TO GO WITH THE BACON.
TAKE A POWDER, BABY.
WHA'YA SAY, CHET?
NOT MUCH, MILO. READ ABOUT WHAT HAPPENED TO YOU.
YEAH? DIDN' KNOW IT MADE THE FUNNY PAGES.
SURE DID, SWEETHEART. WOULDA SENT FLOWERS...
...BUT YOU MIGHTA GOT THE WRONG IDEA.
WELL, IT IS THE THOUGHT THAT COUNTS...

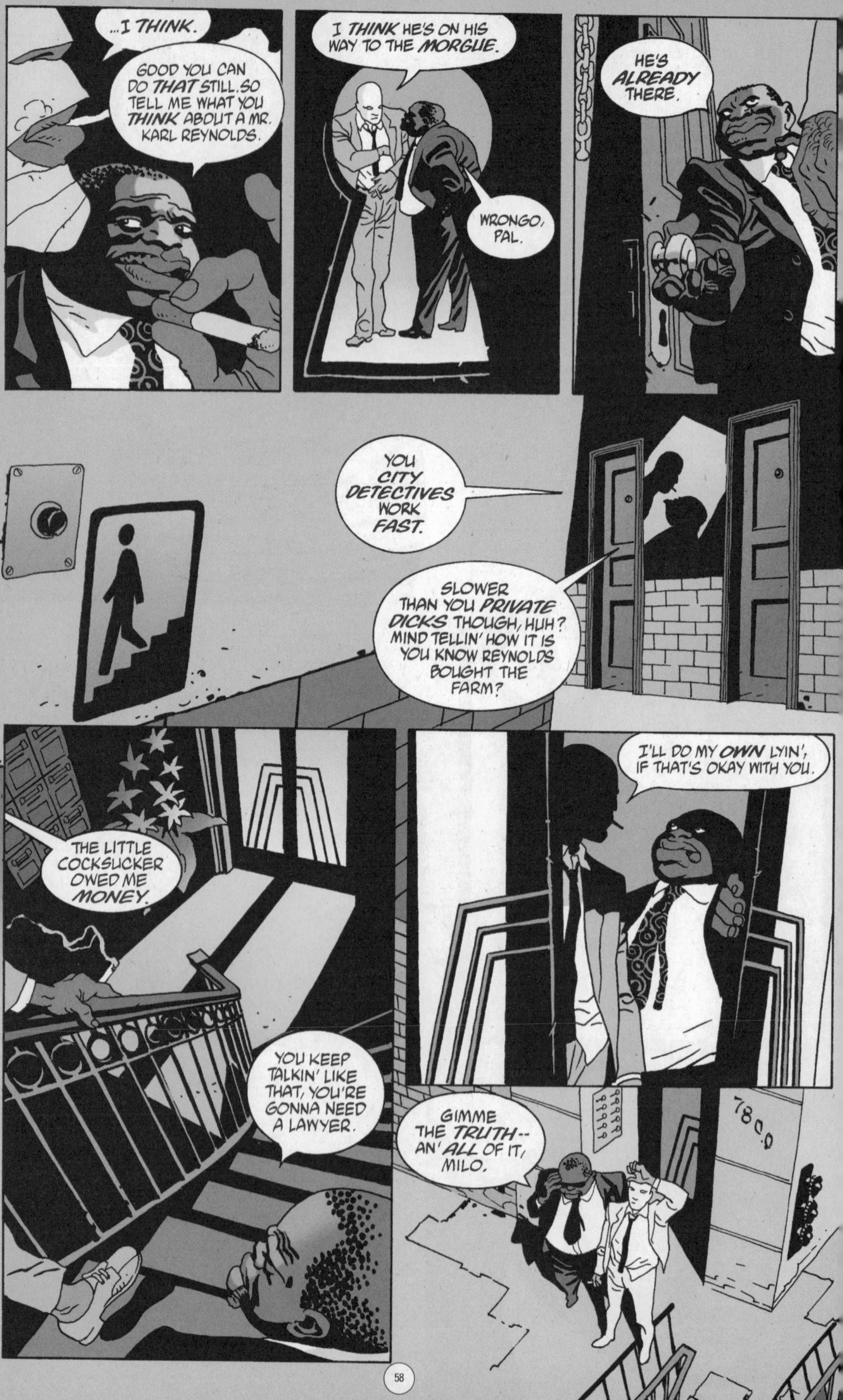
...I THINK.
GOOD YOU CAN DO THAT STILL. SO TELL ME WHAT YOU THINK ABOUT A MR. KARL REYNOLDS.
I THINK HE'S ON HIS WAY TO THE MORGUE.
WRONGO, PAL.
HE'S ALREADY THERE.
YOU CITY DETECTIVES WORK FAST.
SLOWER THAN YOU PRIVATE DICKS THOUGH, HUH? MIND TELLIN' HOW IT IS YOU KNOW REYNOLDS BOUGHT THE FARM?
THE LITTLE COCKSUCKER OWED ME MONEY.
YOU KEEP TALKIN' LIKE THAT, YOU'RE GONNA NEED A LAWYER.
I'LL DO MY OWN LYIN', IF THAT'S OKAY WITH YOU.
GIMME THE TRUTH-- AN' ALL OF IT, MILO.
780

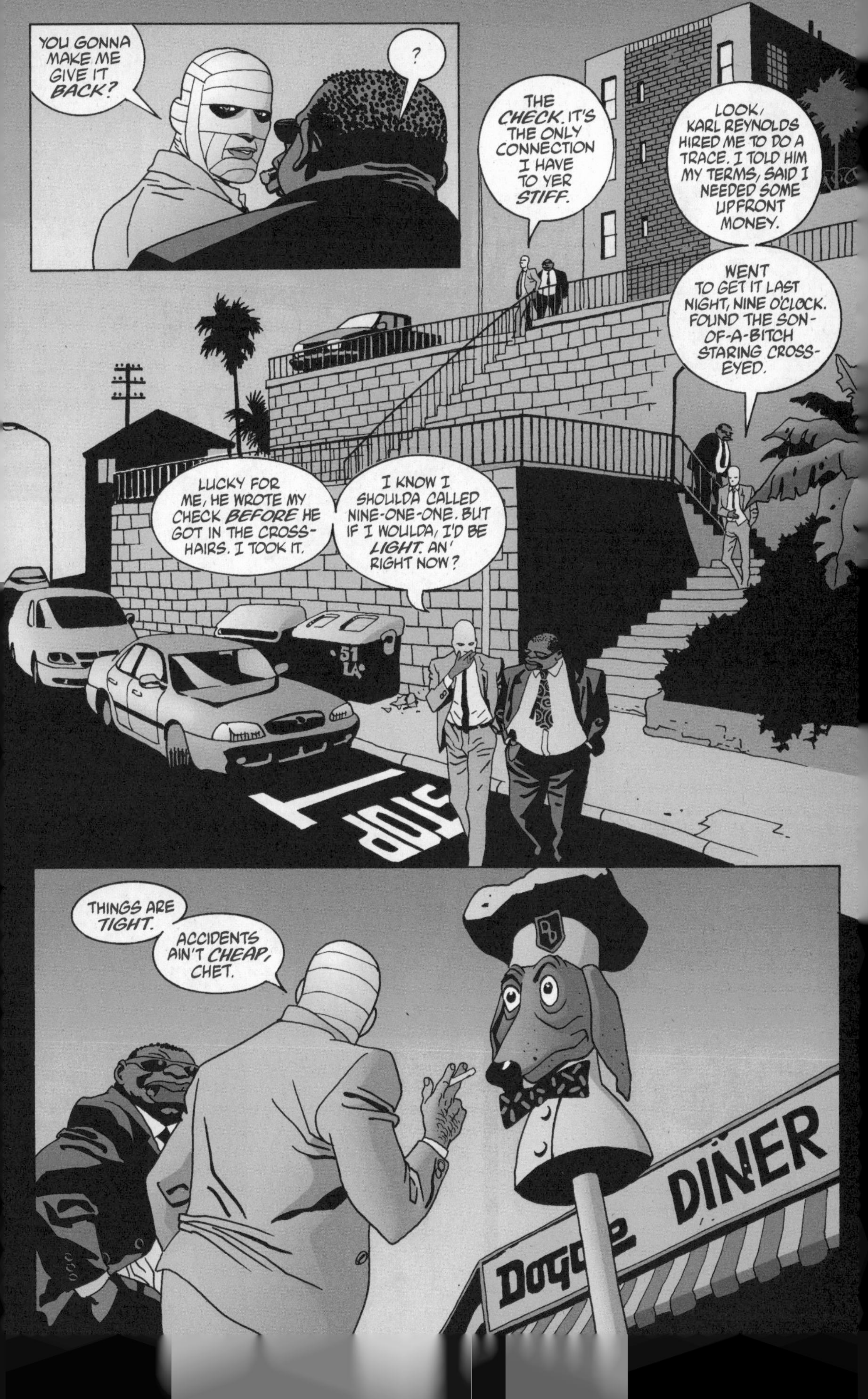
YOU GONNA MAKE ME GIVE IT BACK?
?
THE CHECK. IT'S THE ONLY CONNECTION I HAVE TO YER STIFF.
LOOK, KARL REYNOLDS HIRED ME TO DO A TRACE. I TOLD HIM MY TERMS, SAID I NEEDED SOME UPFRONT MONEY.
WENT TO GET IT LAST NIGHT, NINE O'CLOCK. FOUND THE SON-OF-A-BITCH STARING CROSS-EYED.
LUCKY FOR ME, HE WROTE MY CHECK BEFORE HE GOT IN THE CROSS-HAIRS. I TOOK IT.
I KNOW I SHOULDA CALLED NINE-ONE-ONE. BUT IF I WOULDA, I'D BE LIGHT. AN' RIGHT NOW?
51 LA
STOP
THINGS ARE TIGHT.
ACCIDENTS AIN'T CHEAP, CHET.
DD
Doggie DINER

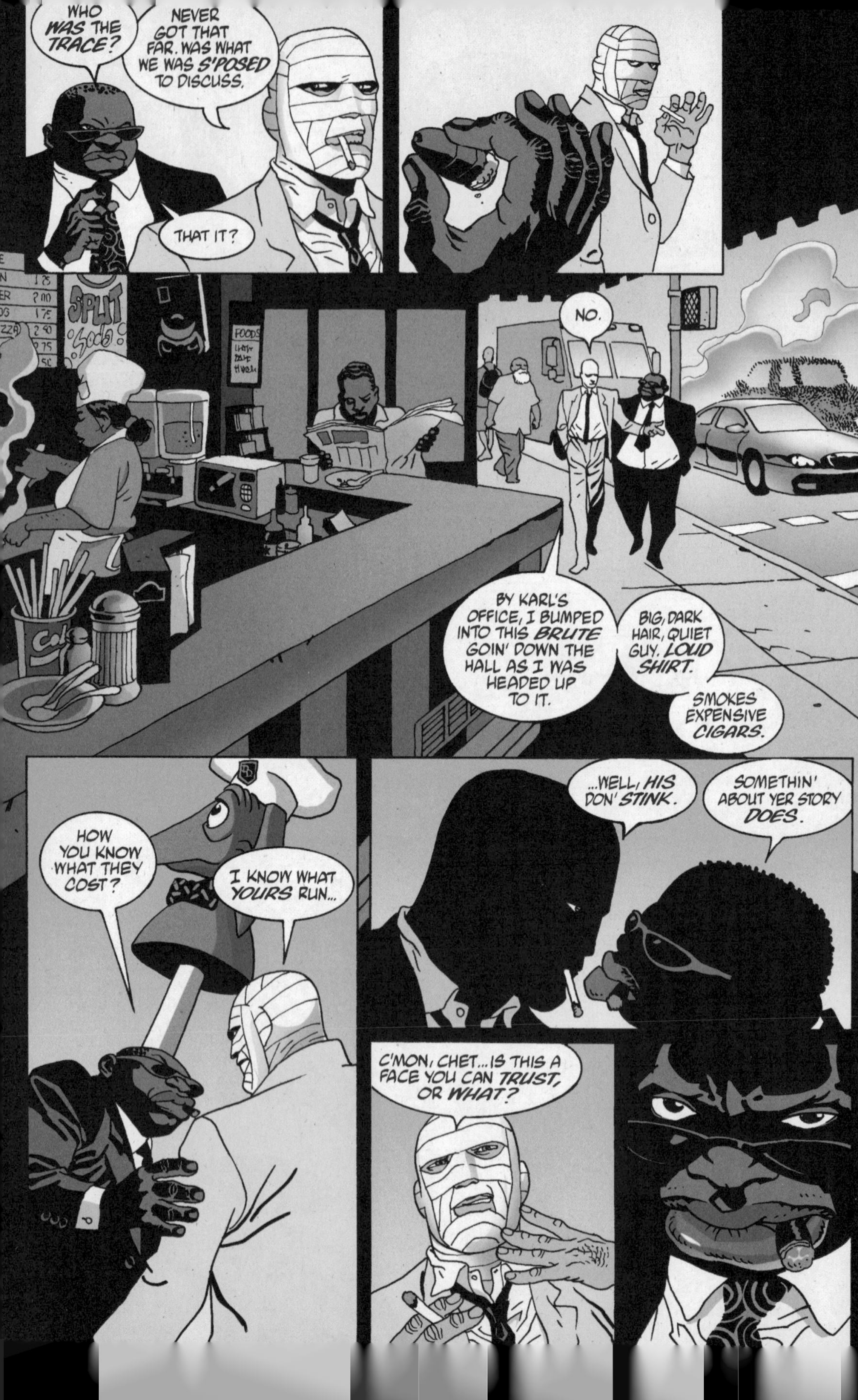
WHO WAS THE TRACE?
NEVER GOT THAT FAR. WAS WHAT WE WAS S'POSED TO DISCUSS.
THAT IT?
NO.
BY KARL'S OFFICE, I BUMPED INTO THIS BRUTE GOIN' DOWN THE HALL AS I WAS HEADED UP TO IT.
BIG, DARK HAIR, QUIET GUY. LOUD SHIRT.
SMOKES EXPENSIVE CIGARS.
HOW YOU KNOW WHAT THEY COST?
I KNOW WHAT YOURS RUN...
...WELL, HIS DON' STINK.
SOMETHIN' ABOUT YER STORY DOES.
C'MON, CHET...IS THIS A FACE YOU CAN TRUST, OR WHAT?

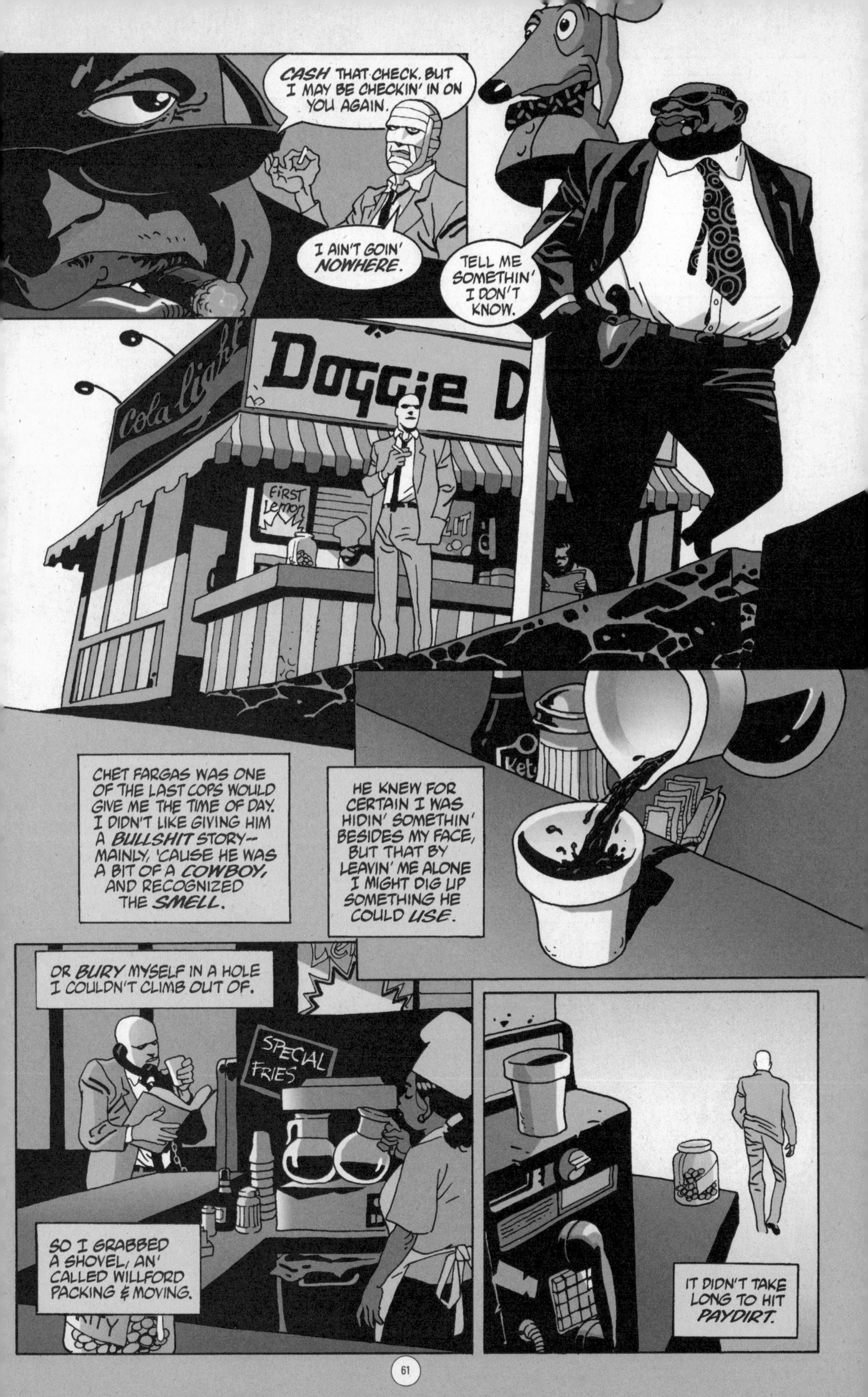
CASH THAT CHECK. BUT I MAY BE CHECKIN' IN ON YOU AGAIN.
I AIN'T GOIN' NOWHERE.
TELL ME SOMETHIN' I DON'T KNOW.
Cola light
Doggie D
FIRST Lemon
CHET FARGAS WAS ONE OF THE LAST COPS WOULD GIVE ME THE TIME OF DAY. I DIDN'T LIKE GIVING HIM A BULLSHIT STORY-- MAINLY, 'CAUSE HE WAS A BIT OF A COWBOY, AND RECOGNIZED THE SMELL.
HE KNEW FOR CERTAIN I WAS HIDIN' SOMETHIN' BESIDES MY FACE, BUT THAT BY LEAVIN' ME ALONE I MIGHT DIG UP SOMETHING HE COULD USE.
OR BURY MYSELF IN A HOLE I COULDN'T CLIMB OUT OF.
SPECIAL FRIES
SO I GRABBED A SHOVEL, AN' CALLED WILLFORD PACKING & MOVING.
IT DIDN'T TAKE LONG TO HIT PAYDIRT.

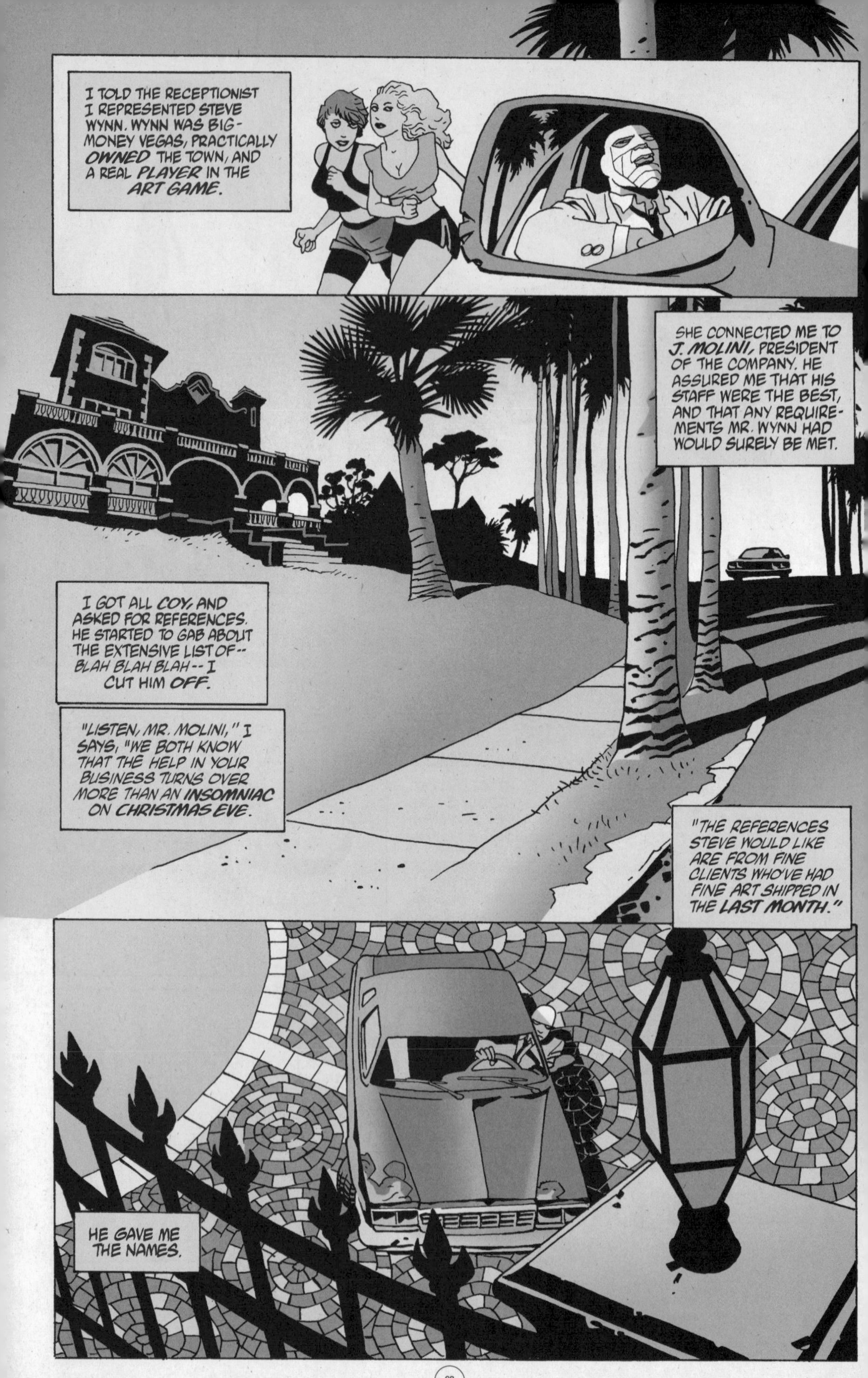
I TOLD THE RECEPTIONIST I REPRESENTED STEVE WYNN. WYNN WAS BIG-MONEY VEGAS, PRACTICALLY OWNED THE TOWN, AND A REAL PLAYER IN THE ART GAME.
SHE CONNECTED ME TO J. MOLINI, PRESIDENT OF THE COMPANY. HE ASSURED ME THAT HIS STAFF WERE THE BEST, AND THAT ANY REQUIREMENTS MR. WYNN HAD WOULD SURELY BE MET.
I GOT ALL COY, AND ASKED FOR REFERENCES. HE STARTED TO GAB ABOUT THE EXTENSIVE LIST OF-- BLAH BLAH BLAH-- I CUT HIM OFF.
"LISTEN, MR. MOLINI," I SAYS, "WE BOTH KNOW THAT THE HELP IN YOUR BUSINESS TURNS OVER MORE THAN AN INSOMNIAC ON CHRISTMAS EVE.
"THE REFERENCES STEVE WOULD LIKE ARE FROM FINE CLIENTS WHO'VE HAD FINE ART SHIPPED IN THE LAST MONTH."
HE GAVE ME THE NAMES.

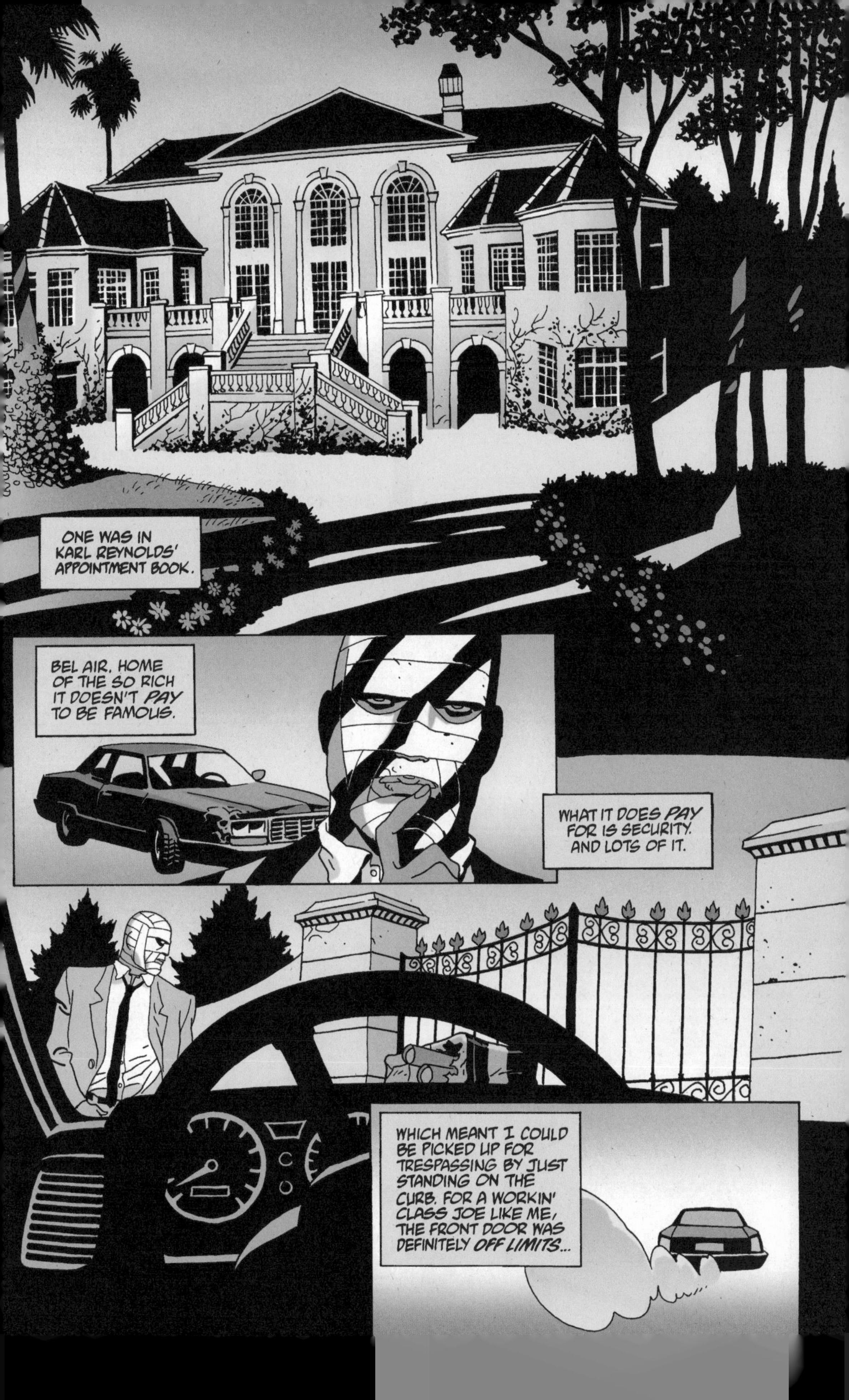
ONE WAS IN KARL REYNOLDS' APPOINTMENT BOOK.
BEL AIR. HOME OF THE SO RICH IT DOESN'T PAY TO BE FAMOUS.
WHAT IT DOES PAY FOR IS SECURITY. AND LOTS OF IT.
WHICH MEANT I COULD BE PICKED UP FOR TRESPASSING BY JUST STANDING ON THE CURB. FOR A WORKIN' CLASS JOE LIKE ME, THE FRONT DOOR WAS DEFINITELY OFF LIMITS...

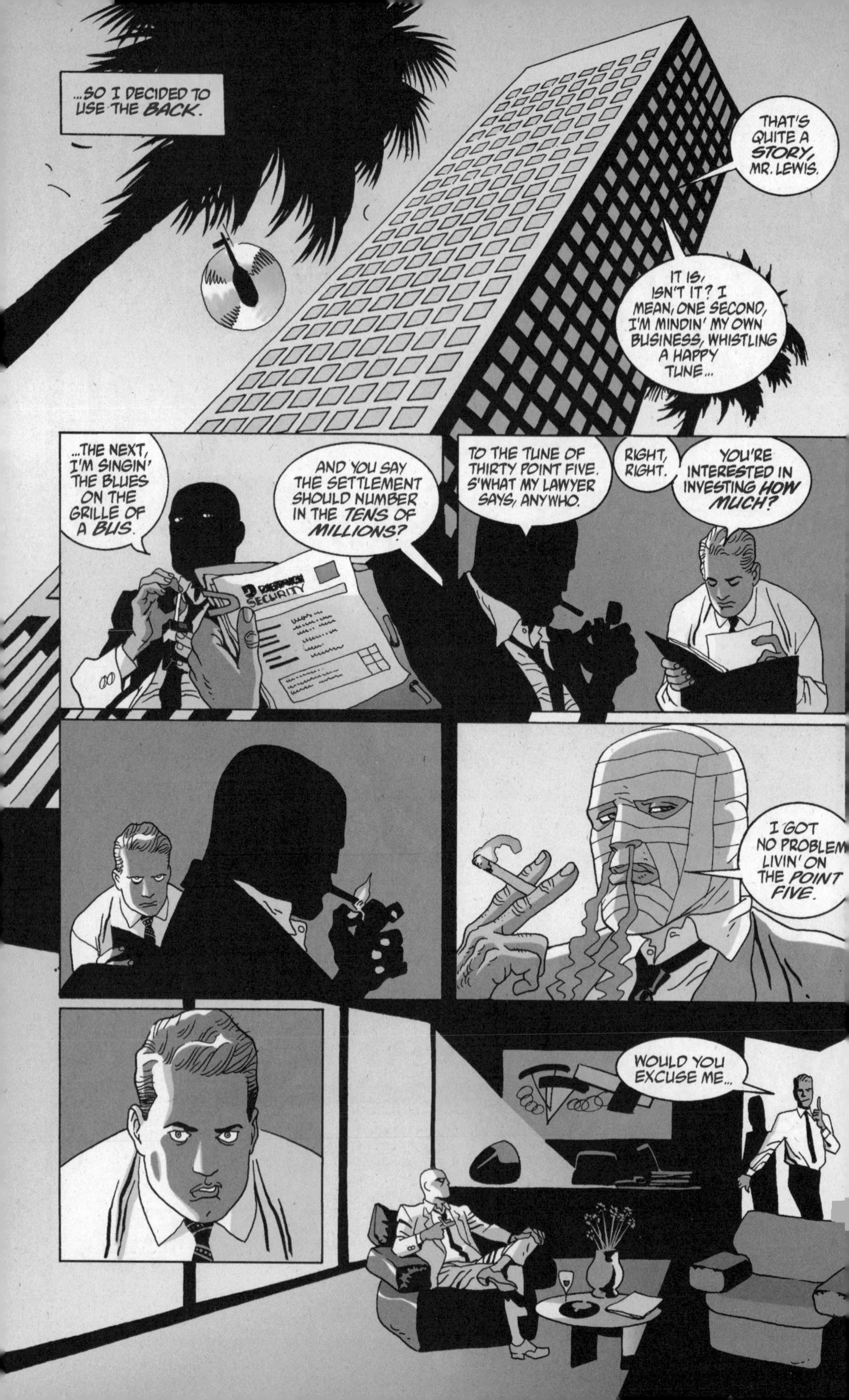
...SO I DECIDED TO USE THE *BACK*.
THAT'S QUITE A *STORY*, MR. LEWIS.
IT IS, ISN'T IT? I MEAN, ONE SECOND, I'M MINDIN' MY OWN BUSINESS, WHISTLING A HAPPY TUNE...
...THE NEXT, I'M SINGIN' THE BLUES ON THE GRILLE OF A *BUS*.
AND YOU SAY THE SETTLEMENT SHOULD NUMBER IN THE *TENS OF MILLIONS?*
SECURITY
TO THE TUNE OF THIRTY POINT FIVE. S'WHAT MY LAWYER SAYS, ANYWHO.
RIGHT, RIGHT.
YOU'RE INTERESTED IN INVESTING *HOW MUCH?*
I GOT NO PROBLEM LIVIN' ON THE *POINT FIVE*.
WOULD YOU EXCUSE ME...

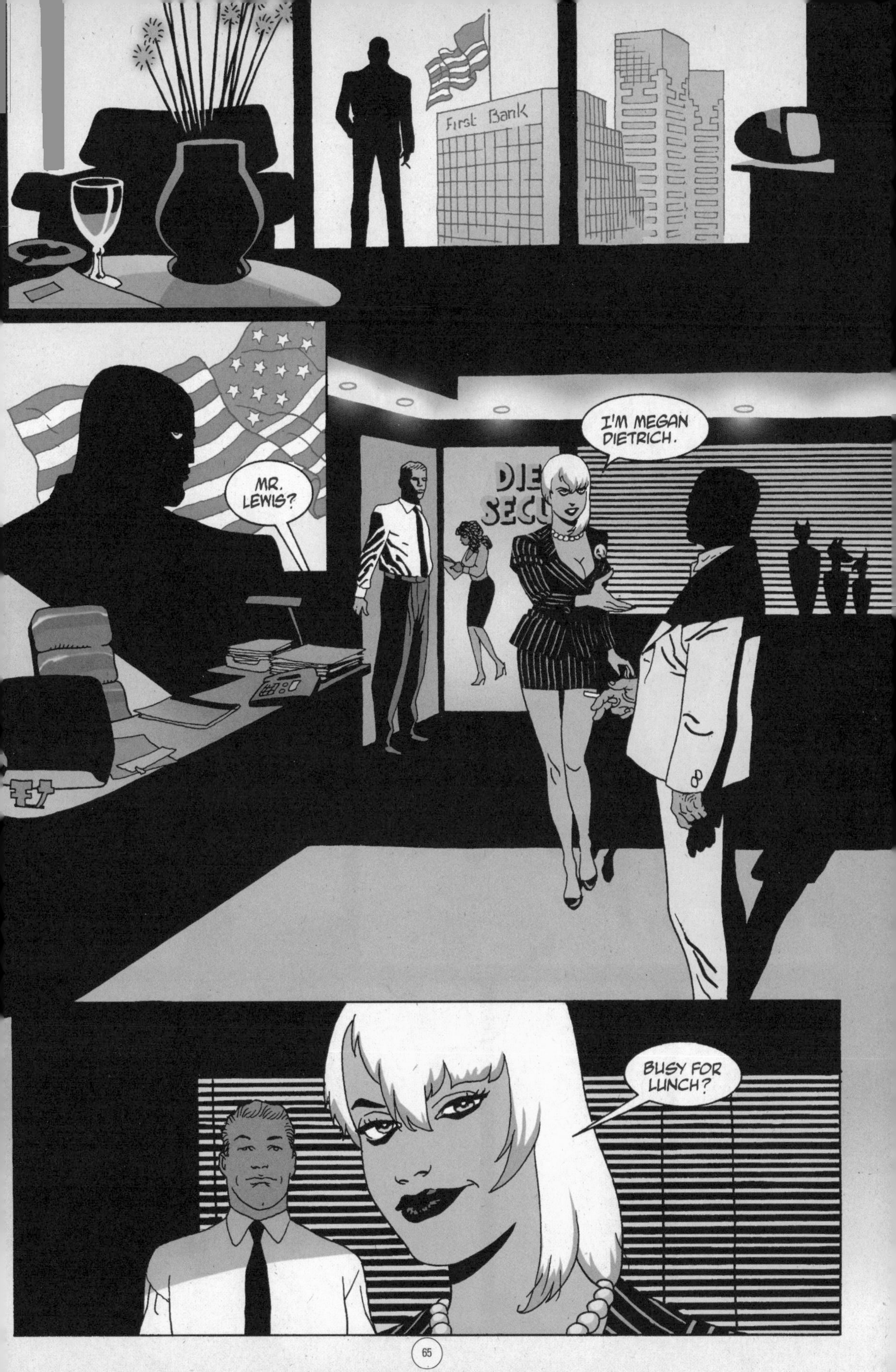
First Bank
MR. LEWIS?
I'M MEGAN DIETRICH.
BUSY FOR LUNCH?

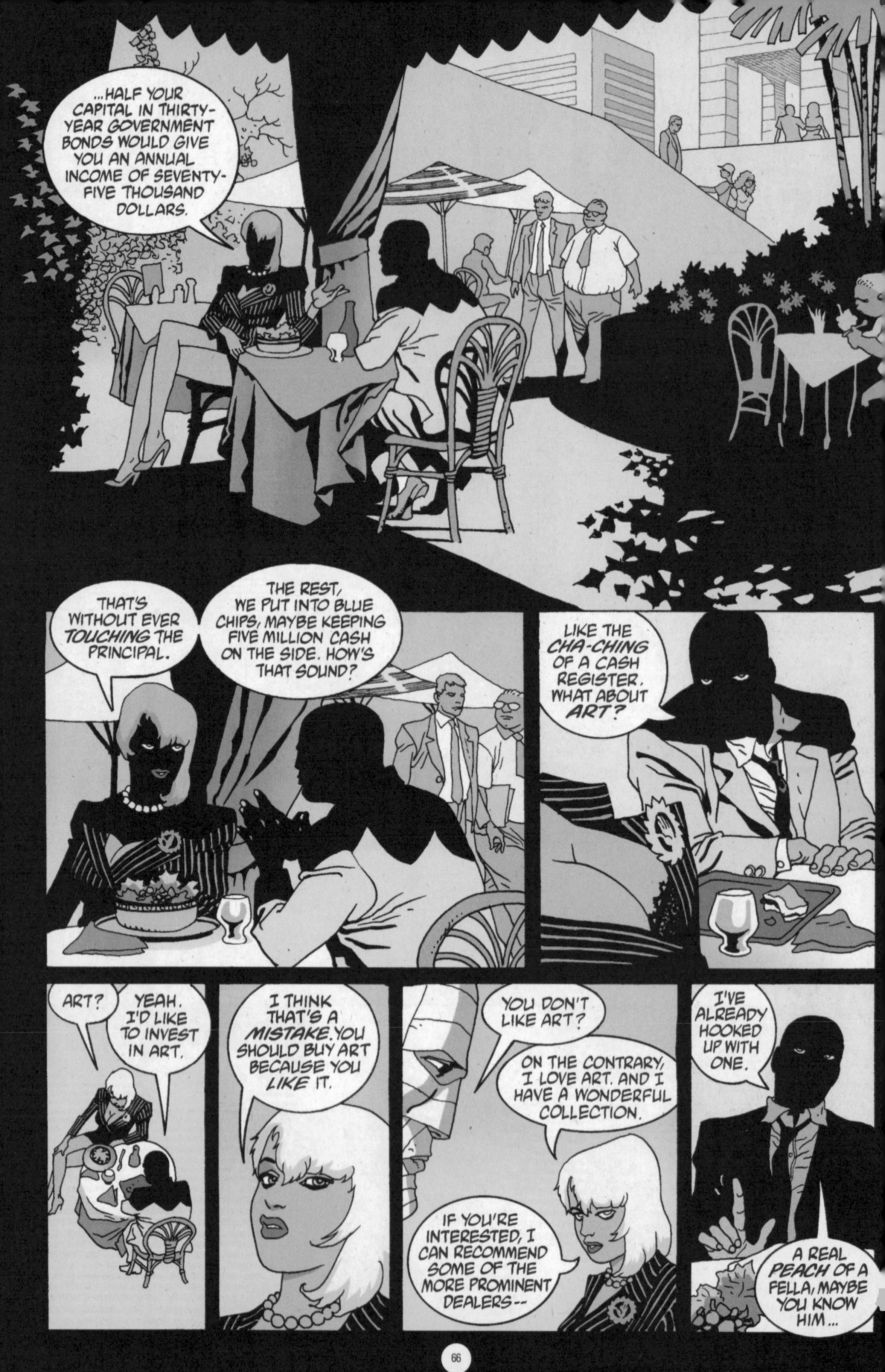
...HALF YOUR CAPITAL IN THIRTY-YEAR GOVERNMENT BONDS WOULD GIVE YOU AN ANNUAL INCOME OF SEVENTY-FIVE THOUSAND DOLLARS.
THAT'S WITHOUT EVER TOUCHING THE PRINCIPAL.
THE REST, WE PUT INTO BLUE CHIPS, MAYBE KEEPING FIVE MILLION CASH ON THE SIDE. HOW'S THAT SOUND?
LIKE THE CHA-CHING OF A CASH REGISTER. WHAT ABOUT ART?
ART?
YEAH. I'D LIKE TO INVEST IN ART.
I THINK THAT'S A MISTAKE. YOU SHOULD BUY ART BECAUSE YOU LIKE IT.
YOU DON'T LIKE ART?
ON THE CONTRARY, I LOVE ART. AND I HAVE A WONDERFUL COLLECTION.
IF YOU'RE INTERESTED, I CAN RECOMMEND SOME OF THE MORE PROMINENT DEALERS--
I'VE ALREADY HOOKED UP WITH ONE.
A REAL PEACH OF A FELLA, MAYBE YOU KNOW HIM...

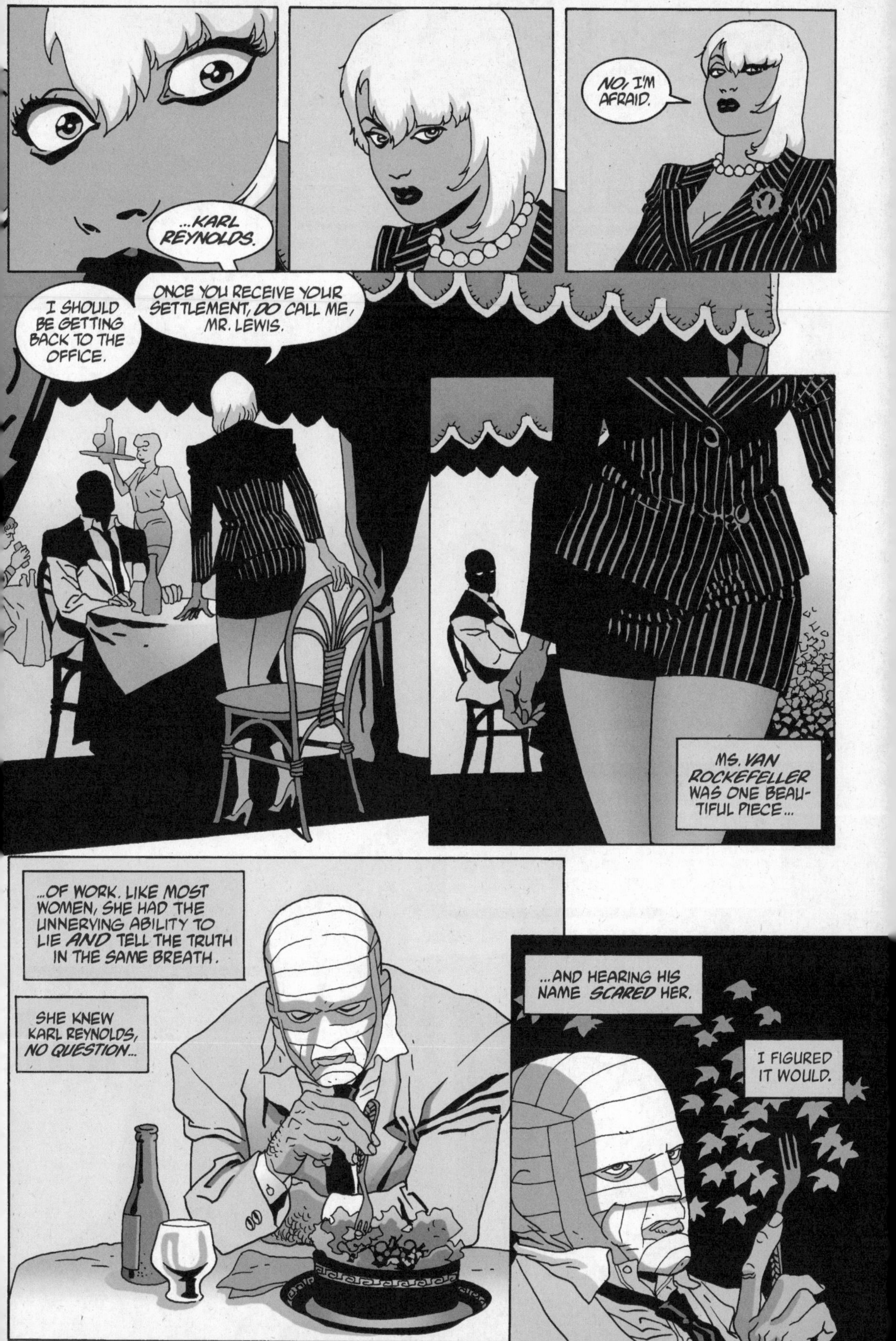
...KARL REYNOLDS.
NO, I'M AFRAID.
I SHOULD BE GETTING BACK TO THE OFFICE.
ONCE YOU RECEIVE YOUR SETTLEMENT, DO CALL ME, MR. LEWIS.
MS. VAN ROCKEFELLER WAS ONE BEAUTIFUL PIECE...
...OF WORK. LIKE MOST WOMEN, SHE HAD THE UNNERVING ABILITY TO LIE AND TELL THE TRUTH IN THE SAME BREATH.
SHE KNEW KARL REYNOLDS, NO QUESTION...
...AND HEARING HIS NAME SCARED HER.
I FIGURED IT WOULD.

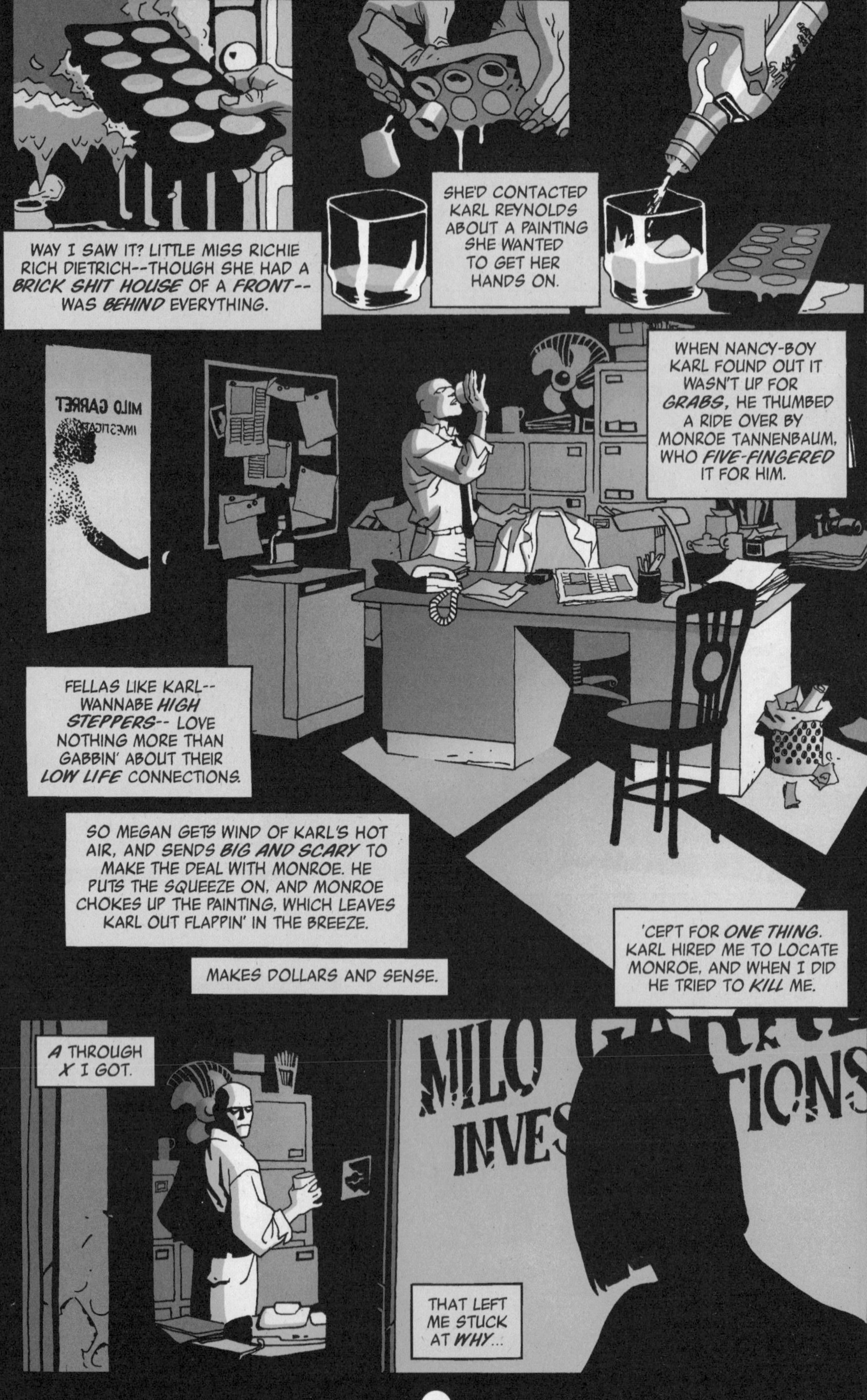

WAY I SAW IT? LITTLE MISS RICHIE RICH DIETRICH--THOUGH SHE HAD A BRICK SHIT HOUSE OF A FRONT--WAS BEHIND EVERYTHING.
SHE'D CONTACTED KARL REYNOLDS ABOUT A PAINTING SHE WANTED TO GET HER HANDS ON.
MILO GARRET INVESTIGATIONS
WHEN NANCY-BOY KARL FOUND OUT IT WASN'T UP FOR GRABS, HE THUMBED A RIDE OVER BY MONROE TANNENBAUM, WHO FIVE-FINGERED IT FOR HIM.
FELLAS LIKE KARL--WANNABE HIGH STEPPERS-- LOVE NOTHING MORE THAN GABBIN' ABOUT THEIR LOW LIFE CONNECTIONS.
SO MEGAN GETS WIND OF KARL'S HOT AIR, AND SENDS BIG AND SCARY TO MAKE THE DEAL WITH MONROE. HE PUTS THE SQUEEZE ON, AND MONROE CHOKES UP THE PAINTING, WHICH LEAVES KARL OUT FLAPPIN' IN THE BREEZE.
MAKES DOLLARS AND SENSE.
'CEPT FOR ONE THING. KARL HIRED ME TO LOCATE MONROE, AND WHEN I DID HE TRIED TO KILL ME.
A THROUGH X I GOT.
MILO
INVES
TIONS
THAT LEFT ME STUCK AT WHY...

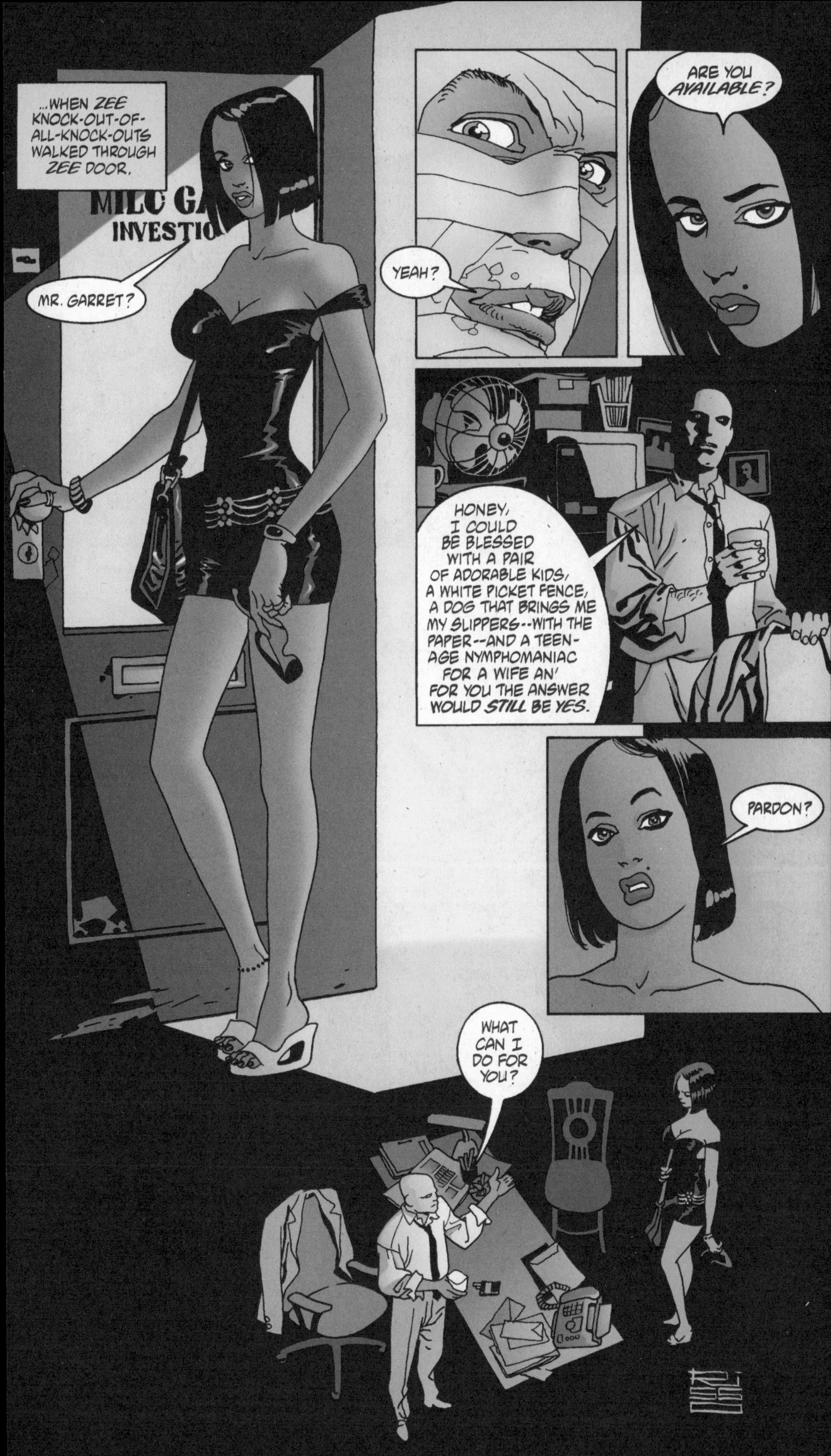

...WHEN ZEE KNOCK-OUT-OF-ALL-KNOCK-OUTS WALKED THROUGH ZEE DOOR.
MILO GA
INVESTIO
MR. GARRET?
YEAH?
ARE YOU AVAILABLE?
HONEY, I COULD BE BLESSED WITH A PAIR OF ADORABLE KIDS, A WHITE PICKET FENCE, A DOG THAT BRINGS ME MY SLIPPERS--WITH THE PAPER--AND A TEEN-AGE NYMPHOMANIAC FOR A WIFE AN' FOR YOU THE ANSWER WOULD STILL BE YES.
PARDON?
WHAT CAN I DO FOR YOU?

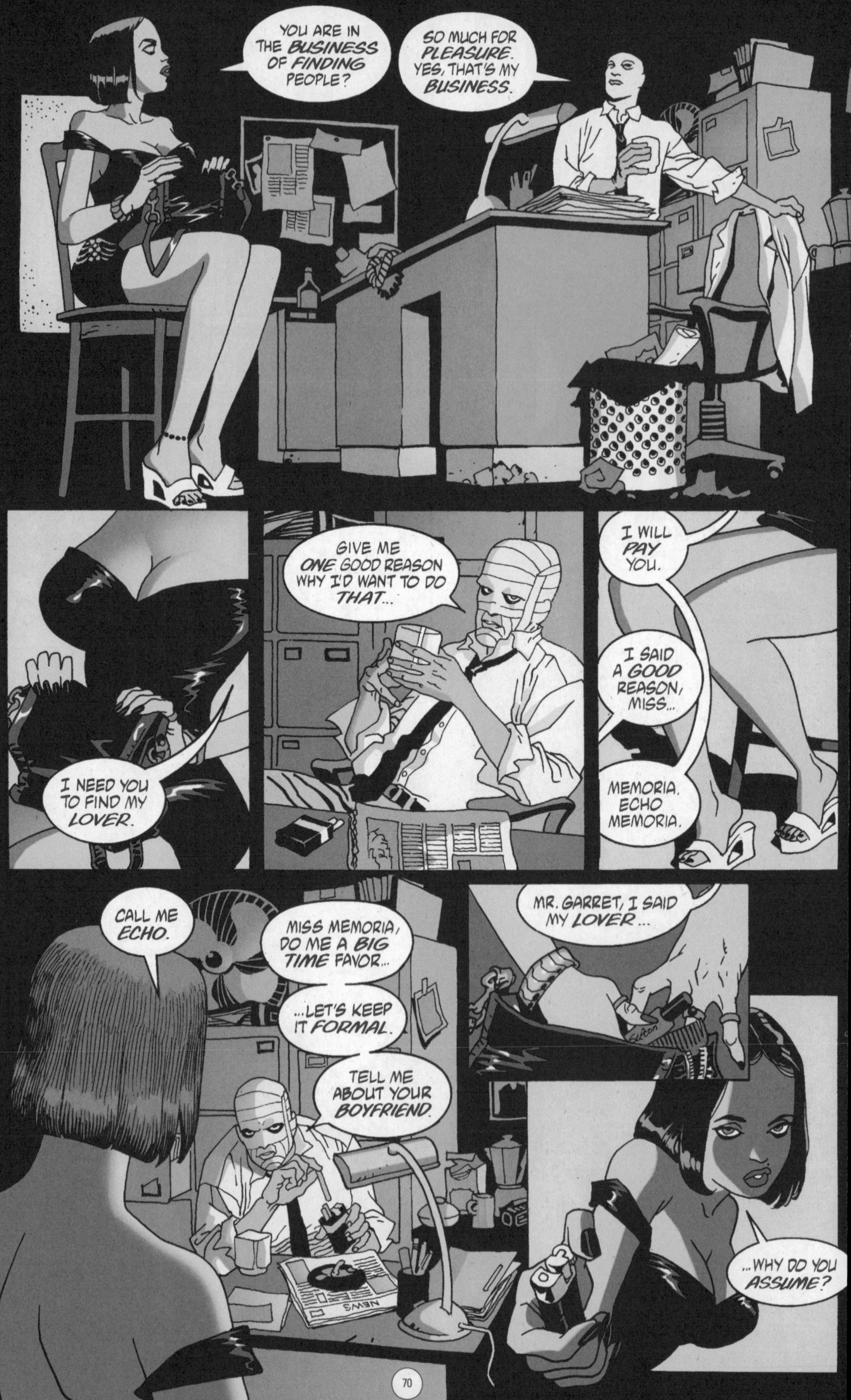
YOU ARE IN THE BUSINESS OF FINDING PEOPLE?
SO MUCH FOR PLEASURE. YES, THAT'S MY BUSINESS.
I NEED YOU TO FIND MY LOVER.
GIVE ME ONE GOOD REASON WHY I'D WANT TO DO THAT...
I WILL PAY YOU.
I SAID A GOOD REASON, MISS...
MEMORIA. ECHO MEMORIA.
CALL ME ECHO.
MISS MEMORIA, DO ME A BIG TIME FAVOR...
...LET'S KEEP IT FORMAL.
TELL ME ABOUT YOUR BOYFRIEND.
MR. GARRET, I SAID MY LOVER...
...WHY DO YOU ASSUME?
NEWS

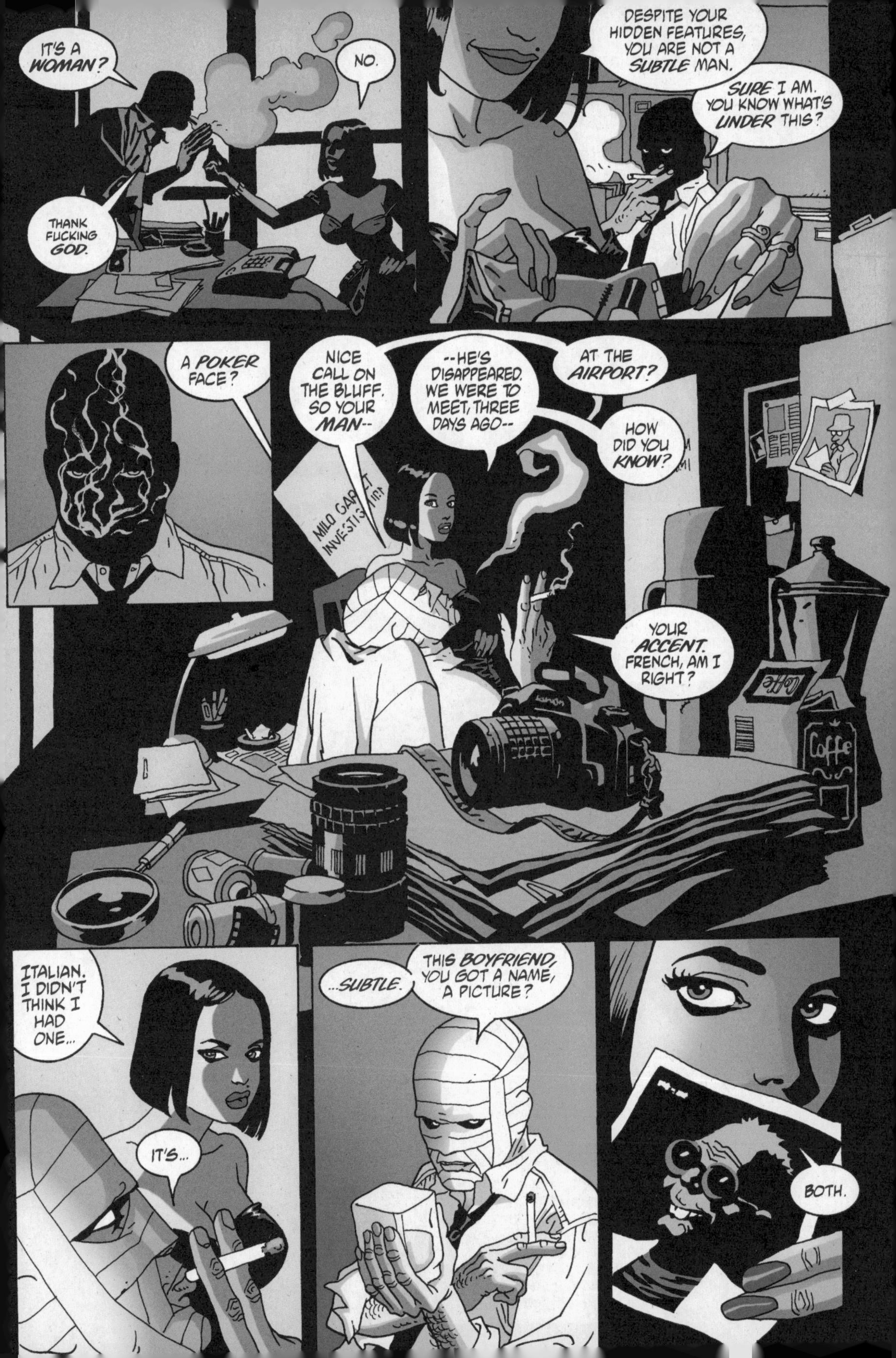
IT'S A WOMAN?
NO.
THANK FUCKING GOD.
DESPITE YOUR HIDDEN FEATURES, YOU ARE NOT A SUBTLE MAN.
SURE I AM. YOU KNOW WHAT'S UNDER THIS?
A POKER FACE?
NICE CALL ON THE BLUFF. SO YOUR MAN--
--HE'S DISAPPEARED. WE WERE TO MEET, THREE DAYS AGO--
AT THE AIRPORT?
HOW DID YOU KNOW?
YOUR ACCENT. FRENCH, AM I RIGHT?
ITALIAN. I DIDN'T THINK I HAD ONE...
IT'S...
...SUBTLE.
THIS BOYFRIEND, YOU GOT A NAME, A PICTURE?
BOTH.

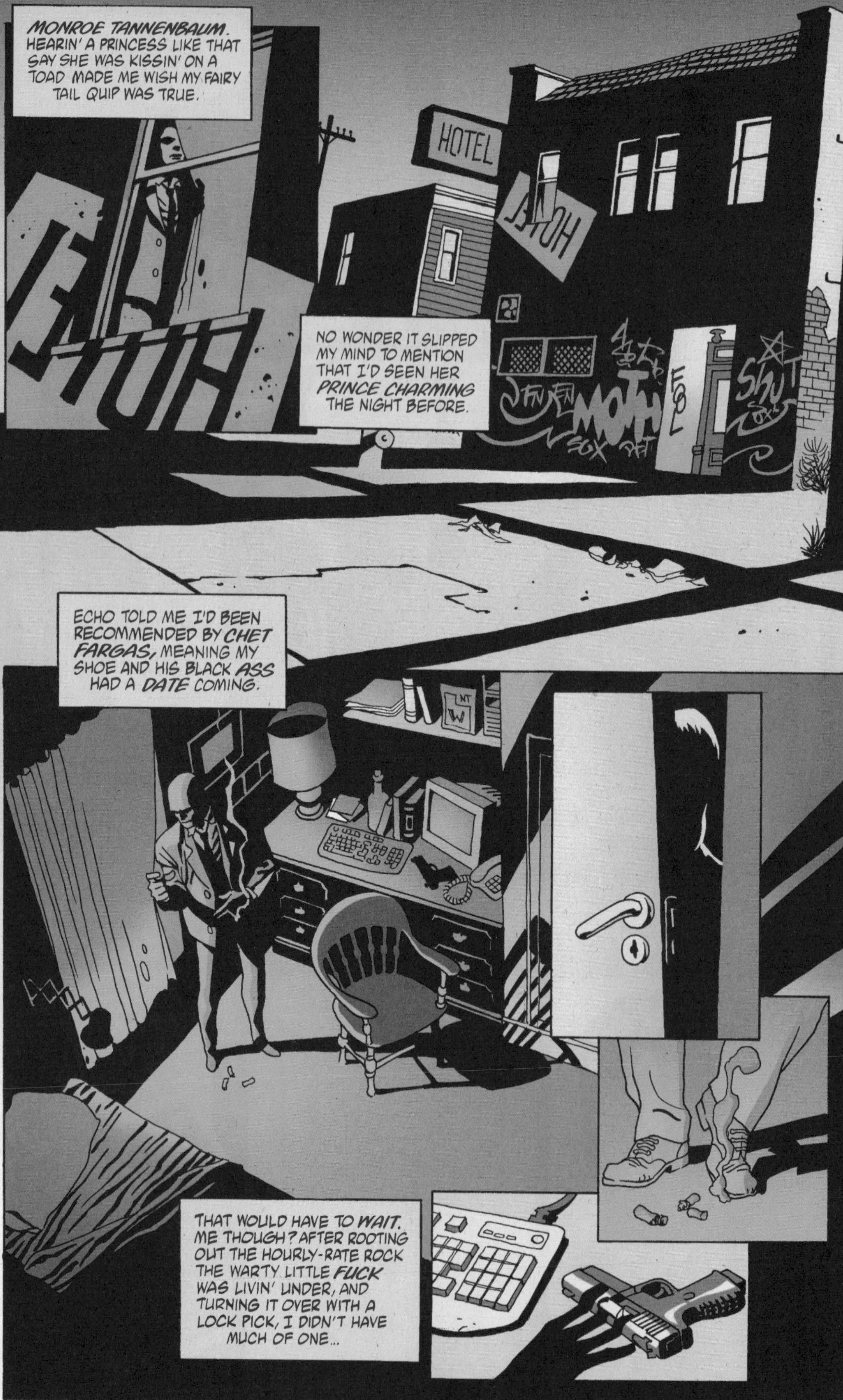
MONROE TANNENBAUM. HEARIN' A PRINCESS LIKE THAT SAY SHE WAS KISSIN' ON A TOAD MADE ME WISH MY FAIRY TAIL QUIP WAS TRUE.
HOTEL
NO WONDER IT SLIPPED MY MIND TO MENTION THAT I'D SEEN HER PRINCE CHARMING THE NIGHT BEFORE.
ECHO TOLD ME I'D BEEN RECOMMENDED BY CHET FARGAS, MEANING MY SHOE AND HIS BLACK ASS HAD A DATE COMING.
THAT WOULD HAVE TO WAIT. ME THOUGH? AFTER ROOTING OUT THE HOURLY-RATE ROCK THE WARTY LITTLE FUCK WAS LIVIN' UNDER, AND TURNING IT OVER WITH A LOCK PICK, I DIDN'T HAVE MUCH OF ONE...

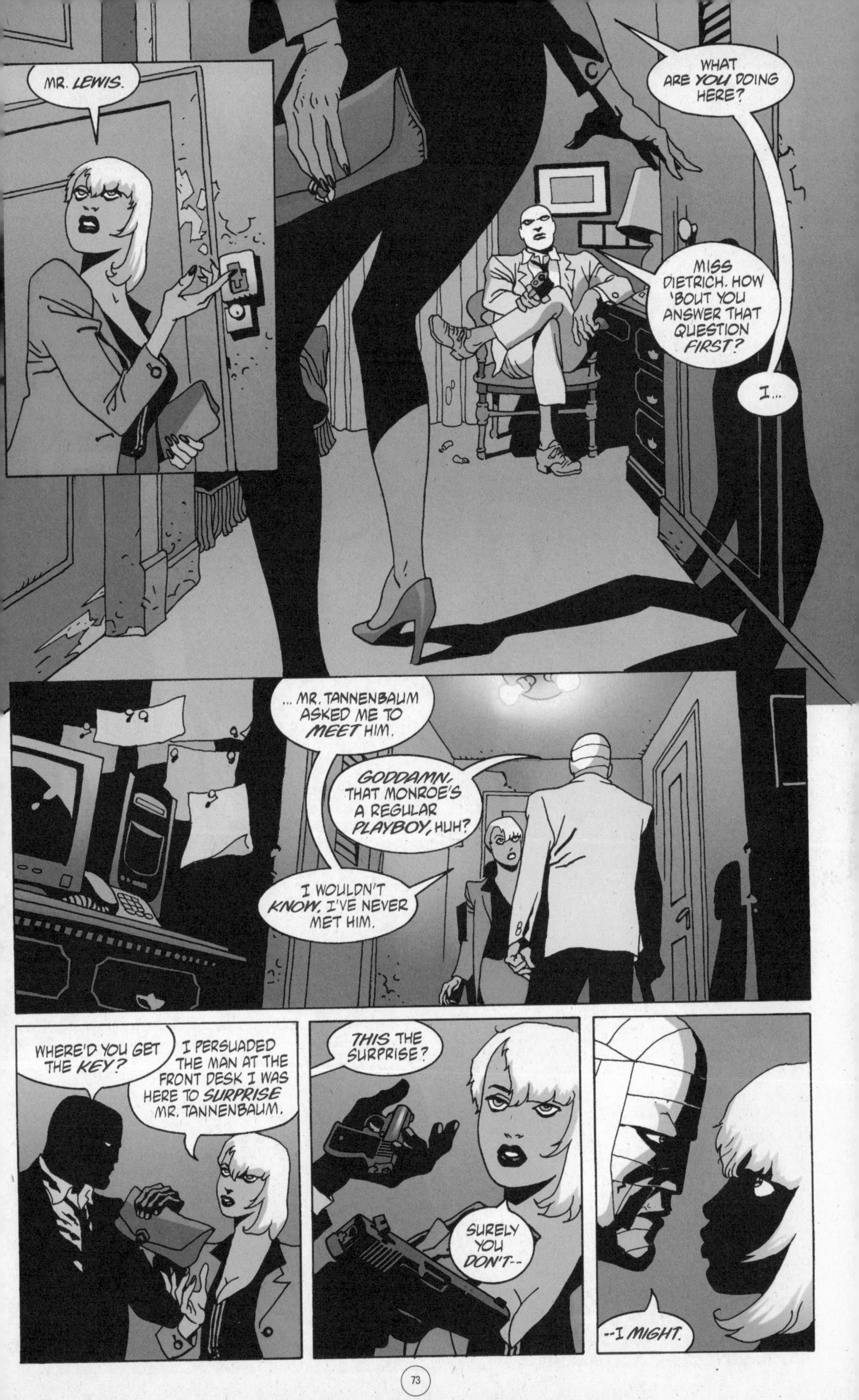
MR. LEWIS.
WHAT ARE YOU DOING HERE?
MISS DIETRICH. HOW 'BOUT YOU ANSWER THAT QUESTION FIRST?
I...
... MR. TANNENBAUM ASKED ME TO MEET HIM.
GODDAMN. THAT MONROE'S A REGULAR PLAYBOY, HUH?
I WOULDN'T KNOW. I'VE NEVER MET HIM.
WHERE'D YOU GET THE KEY?
I PERSUADED THE MAN AT THE FRONT DESK I WAS HERE TO SURPRISE MR. TANNENBAUM.
THIS THE SURPRISE?
SURELY YOU DON'T--
--I MIGHT.

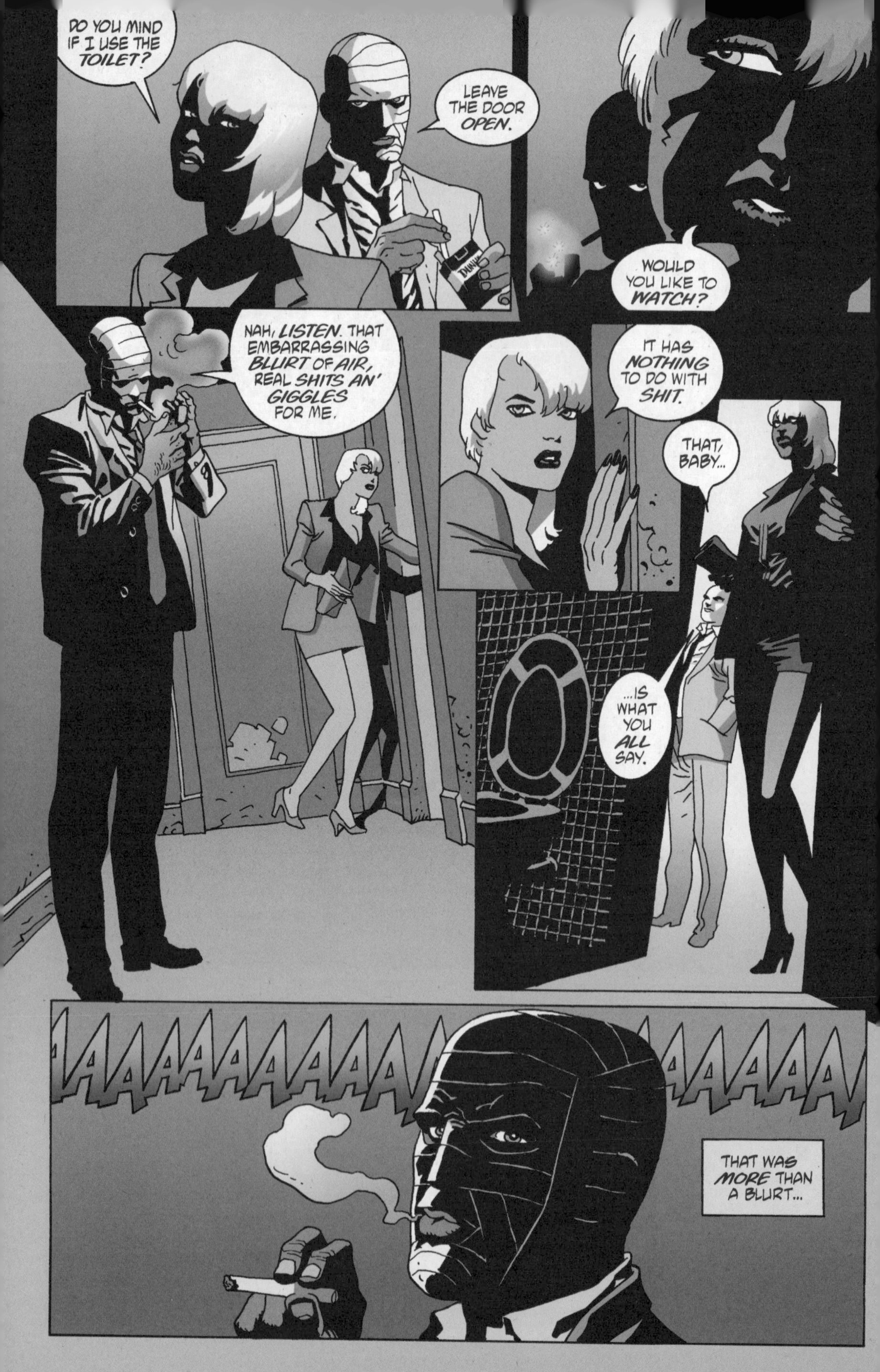
DO YOU MIND IF I USE THE TOILET?
LEAVE THE DOOR OPEN.
WOULD YOU LIKE TO WATCH?
NAH, LISTEN. THAT EMBARRASSING BLURT OF AIR, REAL SHITS AN' GIGGLES FOR ME.
IT HAS NOTHING TO DO WITH SHIT.
THAT, BABY...
...IS WHAT YOU ALL SAY.
AAAAAAAAAAAAAAAAAAAA
THAT WAS MORE THAN A BLURT...

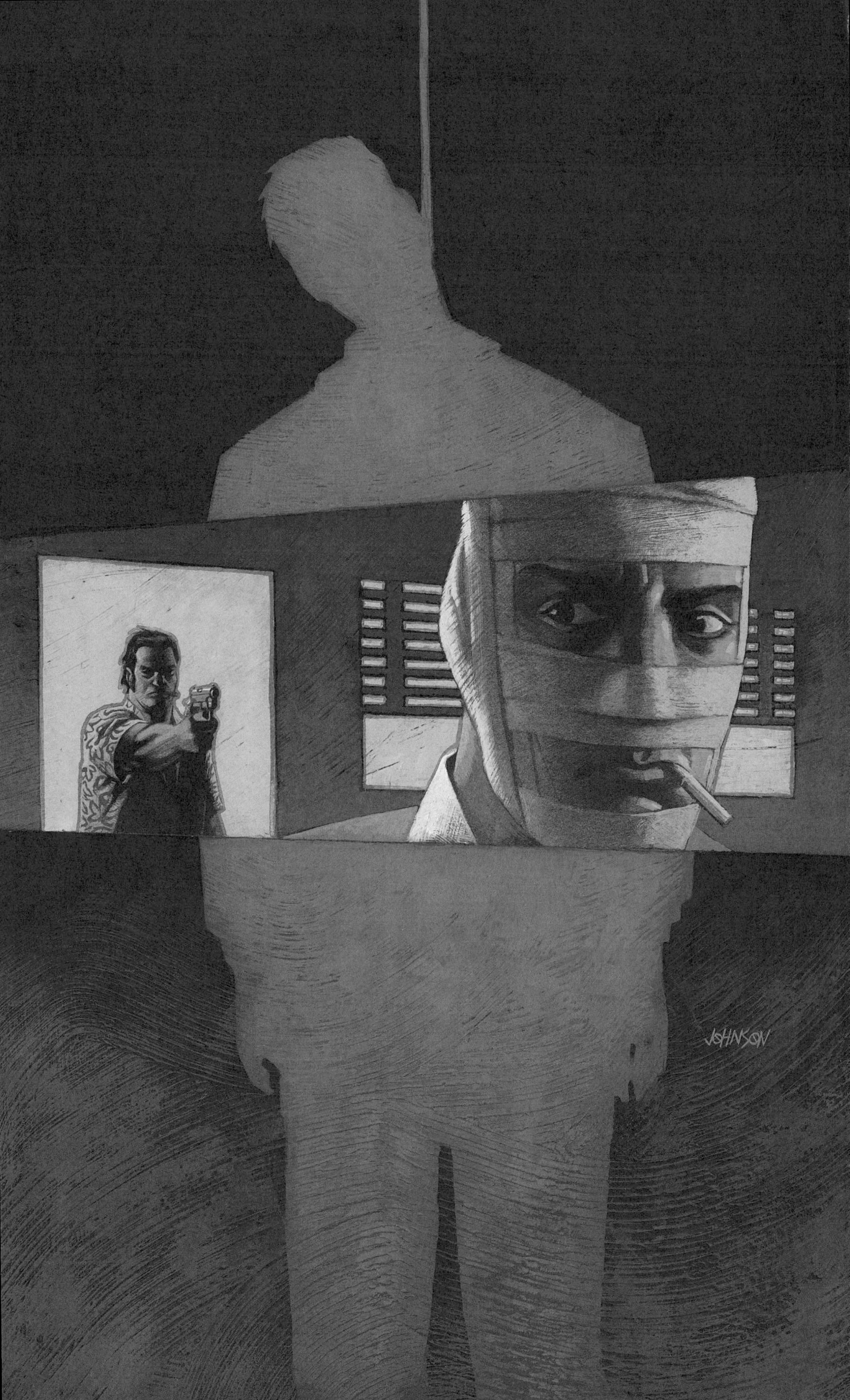
JOHNSON

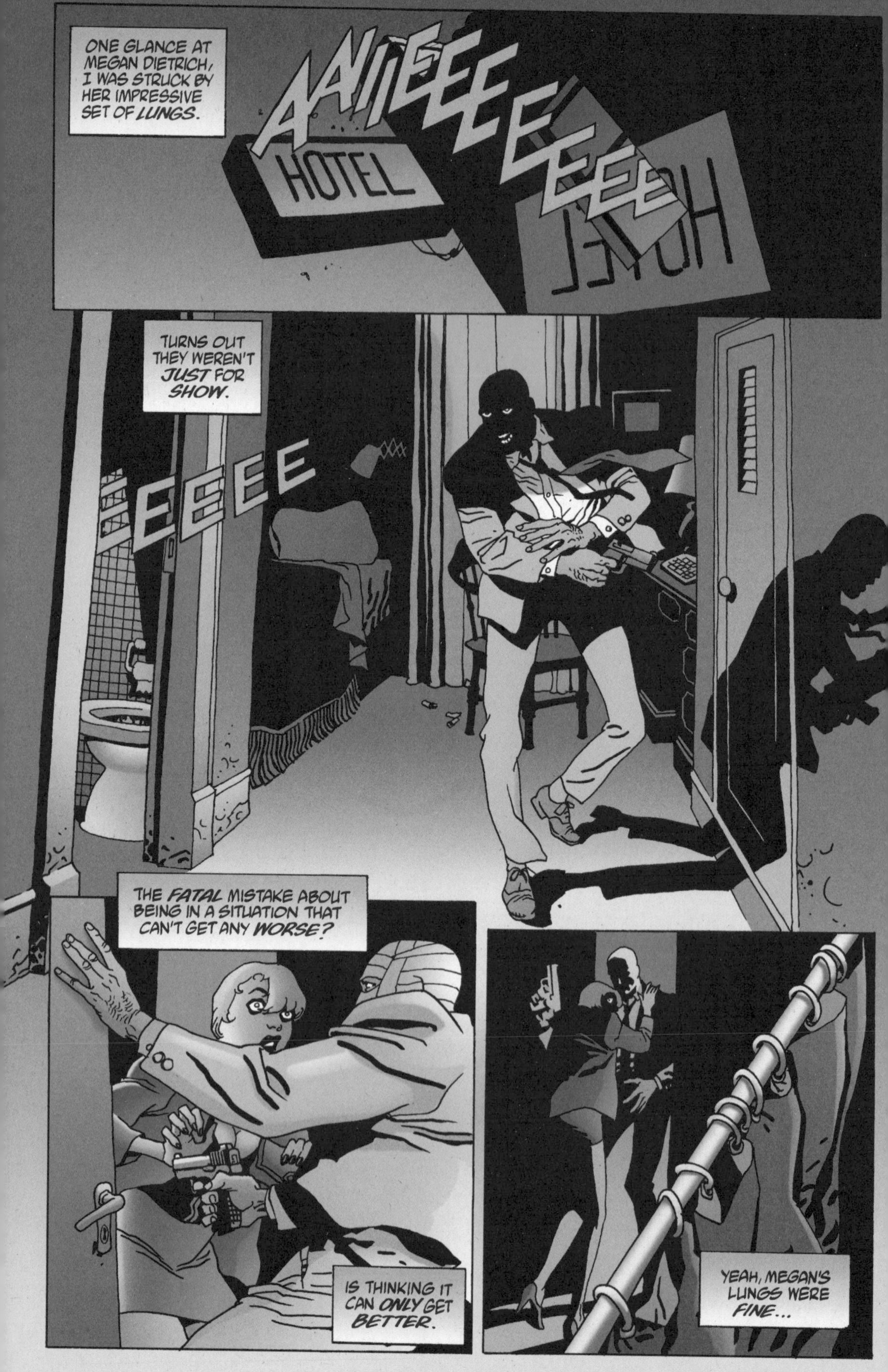
ONE GLANCE AT MEGAN DIETRICH, I WAS STRUCK BY HER IMPRESSIVE SET OF *LUNGS*.
AAIIIEEEEEEEEEEH
HOTEL
HOTEL
TURNS OUT THEY WEREN'T *JUST* FOR *SHOW*.
EEEEE
THE *FATAL* MISTAKE ABOUT BEING IN A SITUATION THAT CAN'T GET ANY *WORSE?*
IS THINKING IT CAN *ONLY* GET *BETTER*.
YEAH, MEGAN'S LUNGS WERE *FINE*...

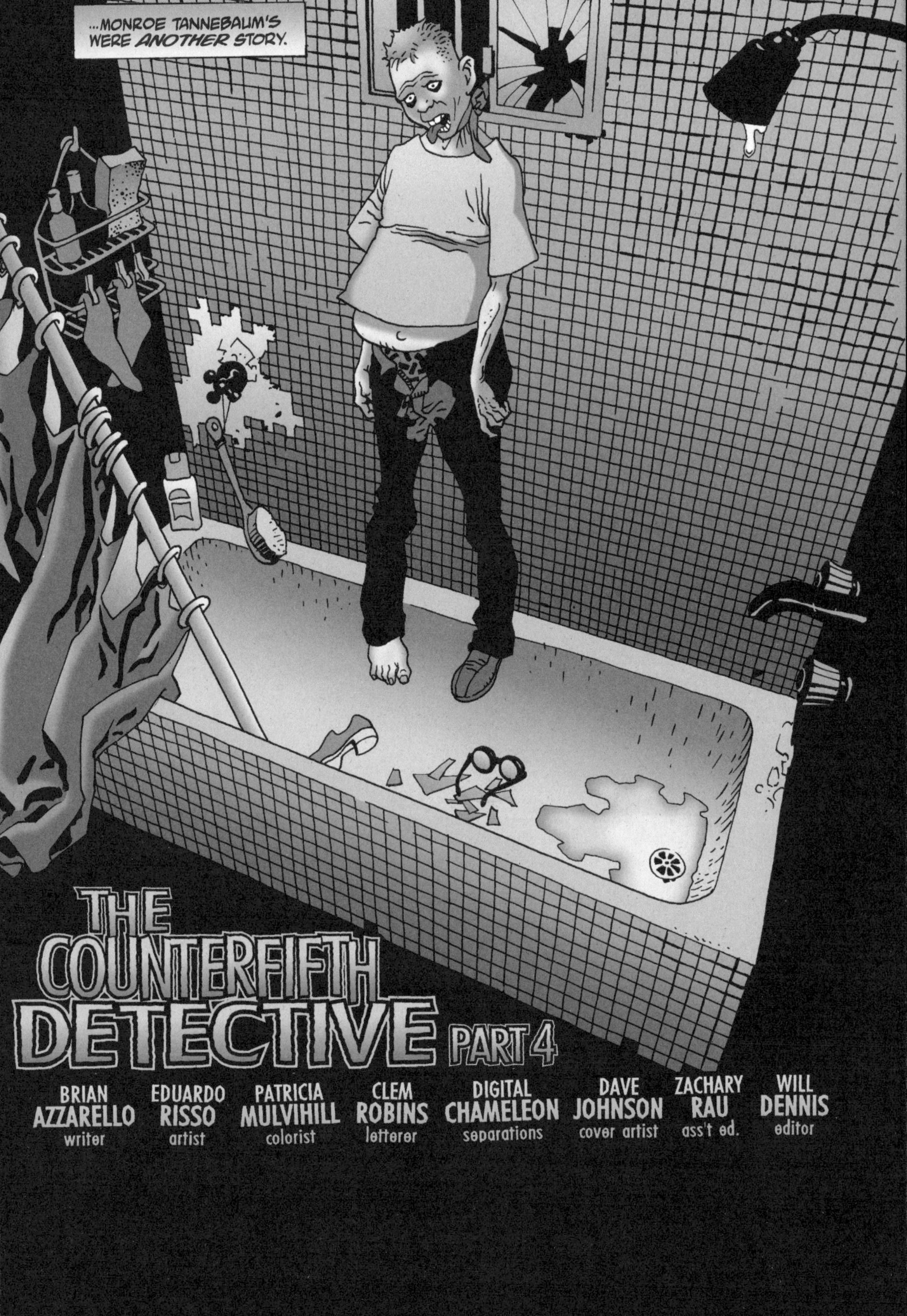
...MONROE TANNEBAUM'S WERE ANOTHER STORY.
THE COUNTERFIFTH DETECTIVE PART 4
BRIAN AZZARELLO writer
EDUARDO RISSO artist
PATRICIA MULVIHILL colorist
CLEM ROBINS letterer
DIGITAL CHAMELEON separations
DAVE JOHNSON cover artist
ZACHARY RAU ass't ed.
WILL DENNIS editor

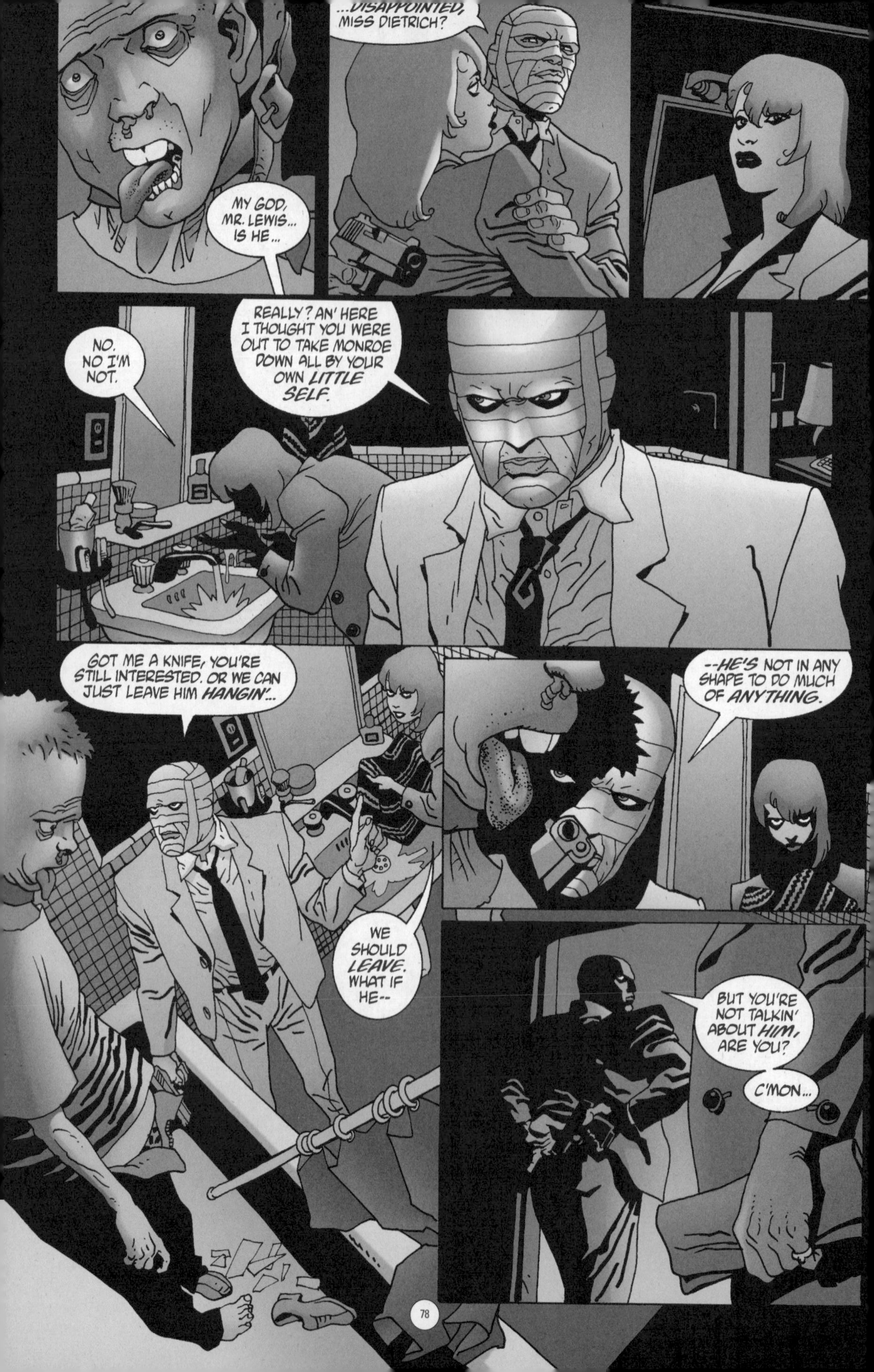

...DISAPPOINTED, MISS DIETRICH?
MY GOD, MR. LEWIS... IS HE...
NO. NO I'M NOT.
REALLY? AN' HERE I THOUGHT YOU WERE OUT TO TAKE MONROE DOWN ALL BY YOUR OWN LITTLE SELF.
GOT ME A KNIFE, YOU'RE STILL INTERESTED. OR WE CAN JUST LEAVE HIM HANGIN'...
WE SHOULD LEAVE. WHAT IF HE--
--HE'S NOT IN ANY SHAPE TO DO MUCH OF ANYTHING.
BUT YOU'RE NOT TALKIN' ABOUT HIM, ARE YOU?
C'MON...

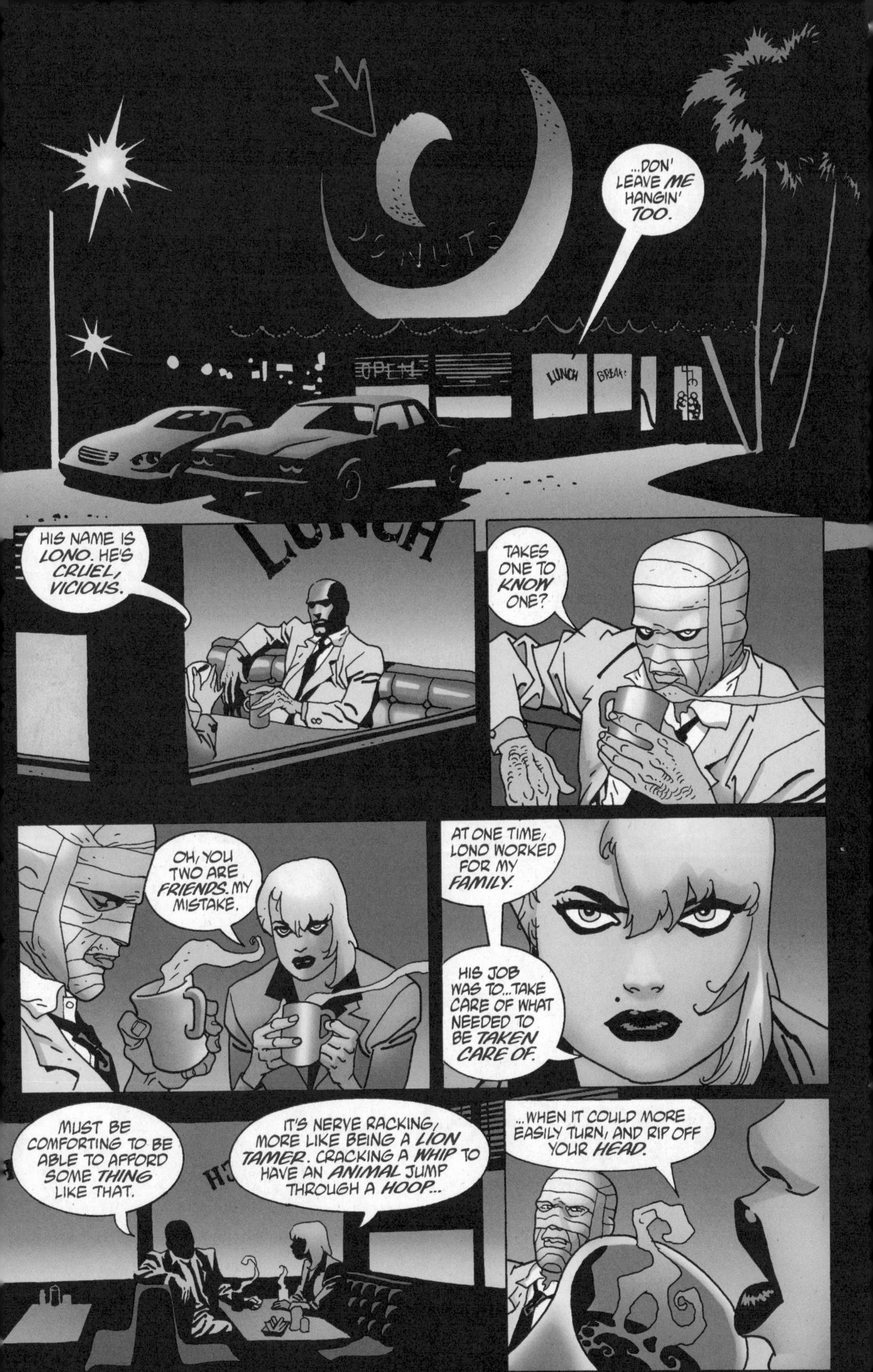

DONUTS
OPEN
LUNCH
BREAK
...DON' LEAVE ME HANGIN' TOO.
LUNCH
HIS NAME IS LONO. HE'S CRUEL, VICIOUS.
TAKES ONE TO KNOW ONE?
OH, YOU TWO ARE FRIENDS. MY MISTAKE.
AT ONE TIME, LONO WORKED FOR MY FAMILY.
HIS JOB WAS TO...TAKE CARE OF WHAT NEEDED TO BE TAKEN CARE OF.
MUST BE COMFORTING TO BE ABLE TO AFFORD SOME THING LIKE THAT.
IT'S NERVE RACKING, MORE LIKE BEING A LION TAMER. CRACKING A WHIP TO HAVE AN ANIMAL JUMP THROUGH A HOOP...
...WHEN IT COULD MORE EASILY TURN, AND RIP OFF YOUR HEAD.

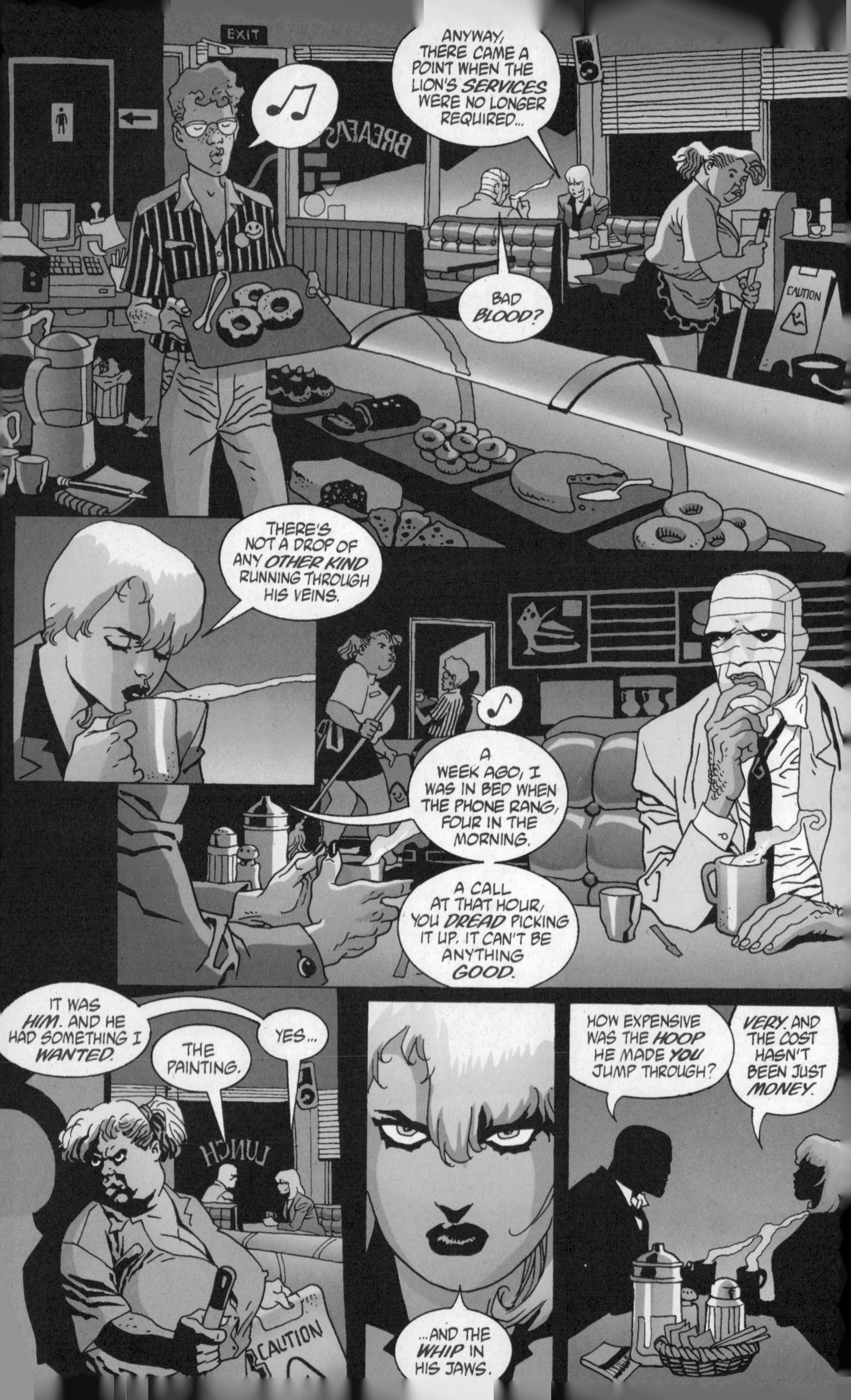
EXIT
ANYWAY, THERE CAME A POINT WHEN THE LION'S SERVICES WERE NO LONGER REQUIRED...
BAD BLOOD?
CAUTION
THERE'S NOT A DROP OF ANY OTHER KIND RUNNING THROUGH HIS VEINS.
A WEEK AGO, I WAS IN BED WHEN THE PHONE RANG, FOUR IN THE MORNING.
A CALL AT THAT HOUR, YOU DREAD PICKING IT UP. IT CAN'T BE ANYTHING GOOD.
IT WAS HIM. AND HE HAD SOMETHING I WANTED.
THE PAINTING.
YES...
LUNCH
CAUTION
...AND THE WHIP IN HIS JAWS.
HOW EXPENSIVE WAS THE HOOP HE MADE YOU JUMP THROUGH?
VERY. AND THE COST HASN'T BEEN JUST MONEY.

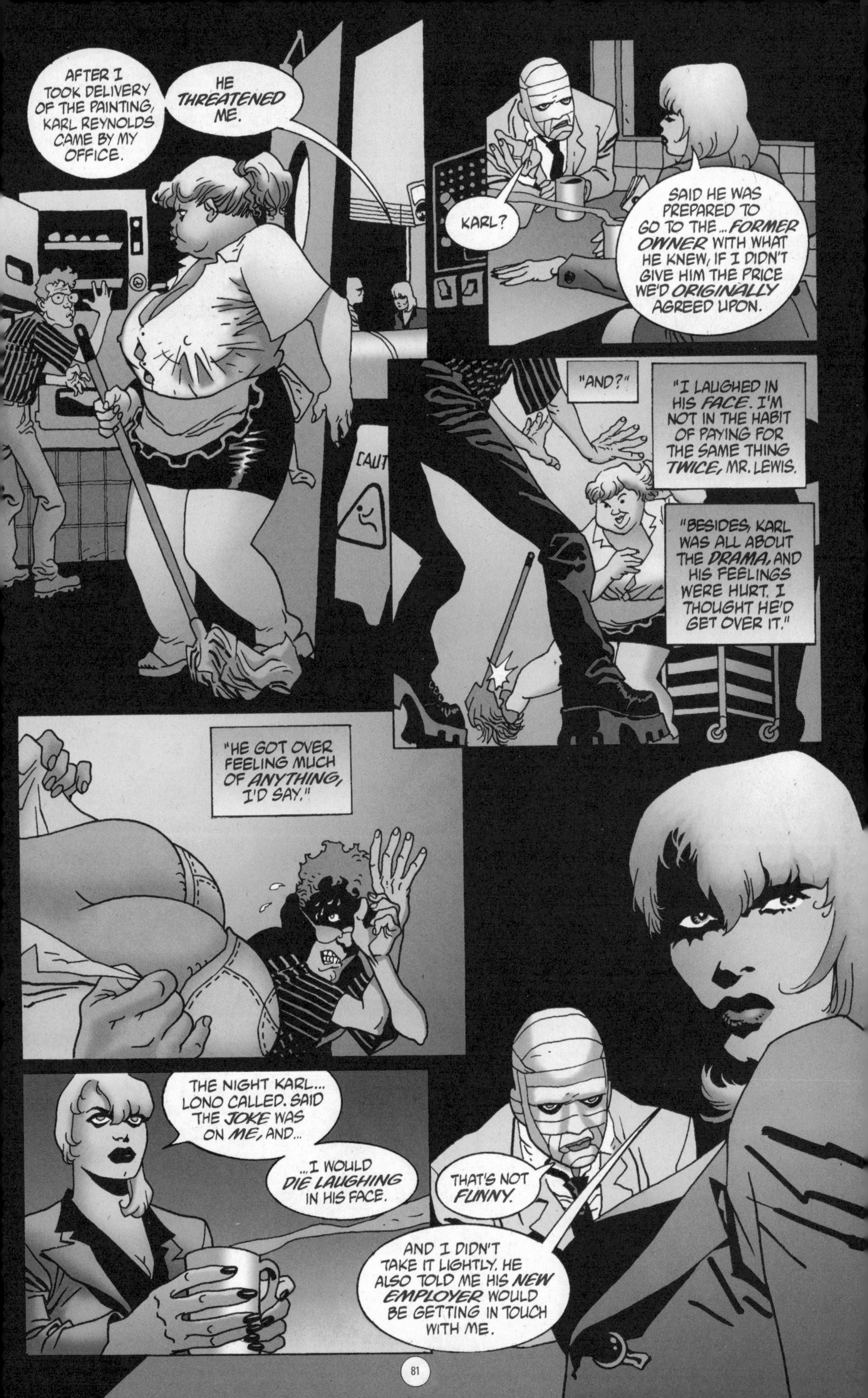
AFTER I TOOK DELIVERY OF THE PAINTING, KARL REYNOLDS CAME BY MY OFFICE.
HE THREATENED ME.
KARL?
SAID HE WAS PREPARED TO GO TO THE... FORMER OWNER WITH WHAT HE KNEW, IF I DIDN'T GIVE HIM THE PRICE WE'D ORIGINALLY AGREED UPON.
"AND?"
"I LAUGHED IN HIS FACE. I'M NOT IN THE HABIT OF PAYING FOR THE SAME THING TWICE, MR. LEWIS.
"BESIDES, KARL WAS ALL ABOUT THE DRAMA, AND HIS FEELINGS WERE HURT. I THOUGHT HE'D GET OVER IT."
"HE GOT OVER FEELING MUCH OF ANYTHING, I'D SAY."
THE NIGHT KARL... LONO CALLED. SAID THE JOKE WAS ON ME, AND...
...I WOULD DIE LAUGHING IN HIS FACE.
THAT'S NOT FUNNY.
AND I DIDN'T TAKE IT LIGHTLY. HE ALSO TOLD ME HIS NEW EMPLOYER WOULD BE GETTING IN TOUCH WITH ME.

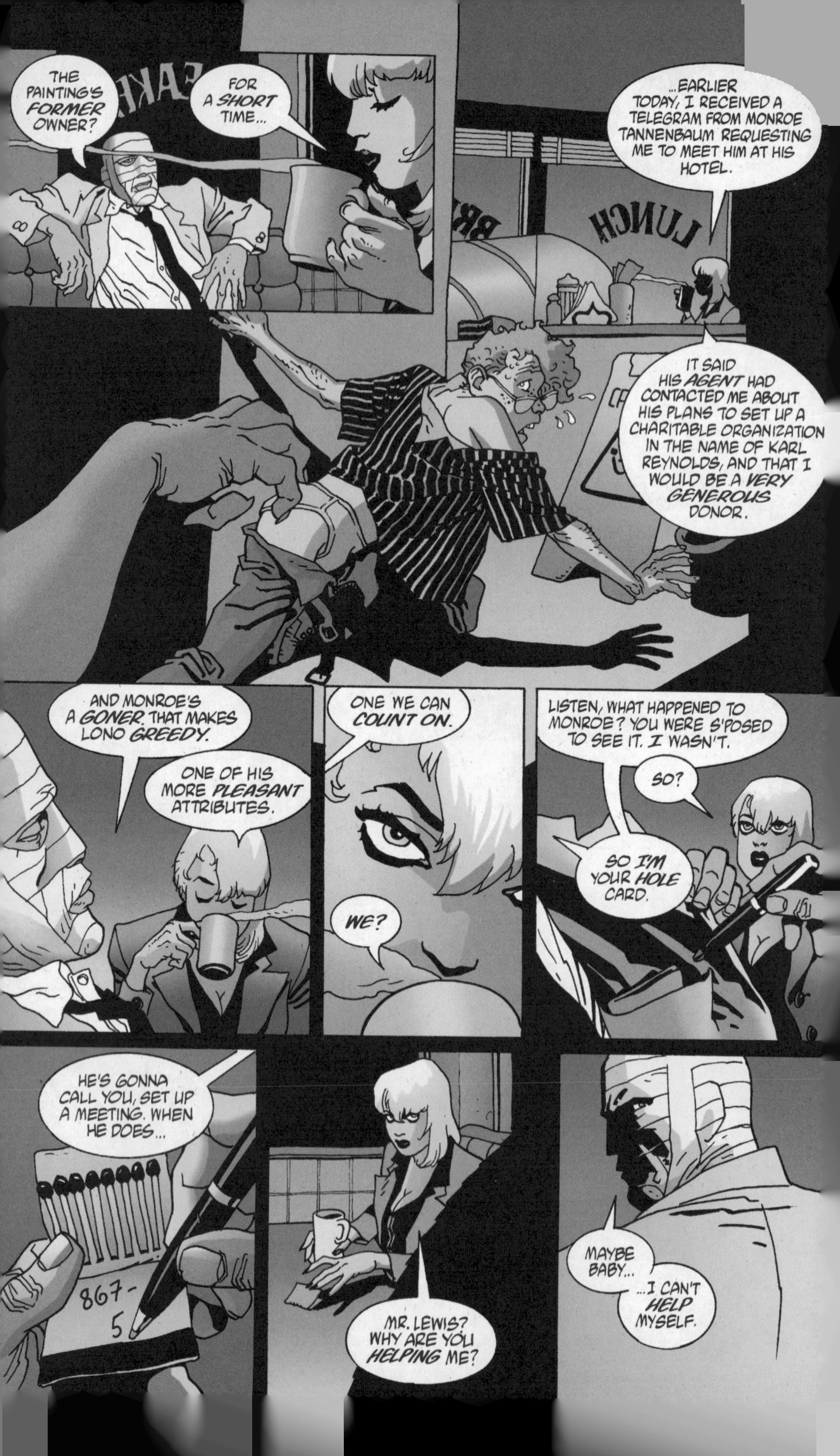
THE PAINTING'S FORMER OWNER?
FOR A SHORT TIME...
...EARLIER TODAY, I RECEIVED A TELEGRAM FROM MONROE TANNENBAUM REQUESTING ME TO MEET HIM AT HIS HOTEL.
LUNCH
IT SAID HIS AGENT HAD CONTACTED ME ABOUT HIS PLANS TO SET UP A CHARITABLE ORGANIZATION IN THE NAME OF KARL REYNOLDS, AND THAT I WOULD BE A VERY GENEROUS DONOR.
AND MONROE'S A GONER. THAT MAKES LONO GREEDY.
ONE OF HIS MORE PLEASANT ATTRIBUTES.
ONE WE CAN COUNT ON.
WE?
LISTEN, WHAT HAPPENED TO MONROE? YOU WERE S'POSED TO SEE IT. I WASN'T.
SO?
SO I'M YOUR HOLE CARD.
HE'S GONNA CALL YOU, SET UP A MEETING. WHEN HE DOES...
867-
5
MR. LEWIS? WHY ARE YOU HELPING ME?
MAYBE BABY...
...I CAN'T HELP MYSELF.

MEGAN HAD TOLD ME THE *TRUTH*, OR AT LEAST *HER PART* IN IT. THAT'S THE THING ABOUT THE *FILTHY RICH* --THEY CAN AFFORD *NOT* TO LIE.

THEY'RE ALSO USED TO *BUYING* THEMSELVES OUT OF A JAM. THIS ONE, THOUGH, WAS A BIT *TOO STICKY* TO BE JUST ABOUT *MONEY*.

MEGAN STOOD TO LOSE HER PRETTY FACE IF WORD GOT OUT THAT SHE FINANCED AN ART HEIST, YET SHE DIDN'T BAT AN EYELASH WHEN I WAS BEATING AROUND THE BUSH ABOUT IT.

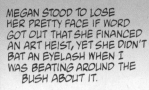

NO SIR, THAT LADY WAS AS *SLICK* AS THE *THIN ICE* SHE'D STUMBLED ONTO.

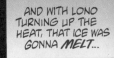

AND WITH LONO TURNING UP THE HEAT, THAT ICE WAS GONNA *MELT*...

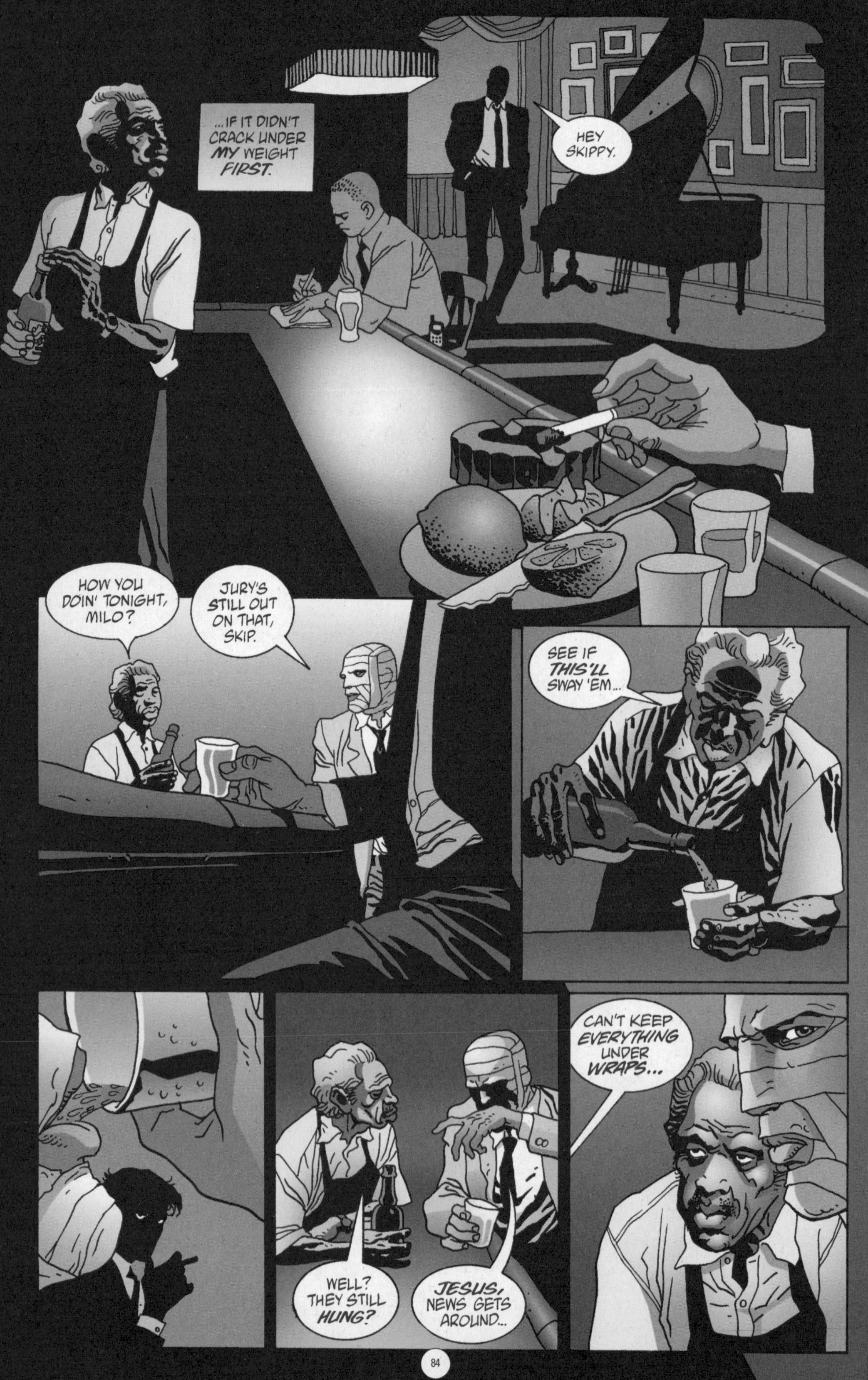
...IF IT DIDN'T CRACK UNDER MY WEIGHT FIRST.
HEY SKIPPY.
HOW YOU DOIN' TONIGHT, MILO?
JURY'S STILL OUT ON THAT, SKIP.
SEE IF THIS'LL SWAY 'EM...
WELL? THEY STILL HUNG?
JESUS, NEWS GETS AROUND...
CAN'T KEEP EVERYTHING UNDER WRAPS...

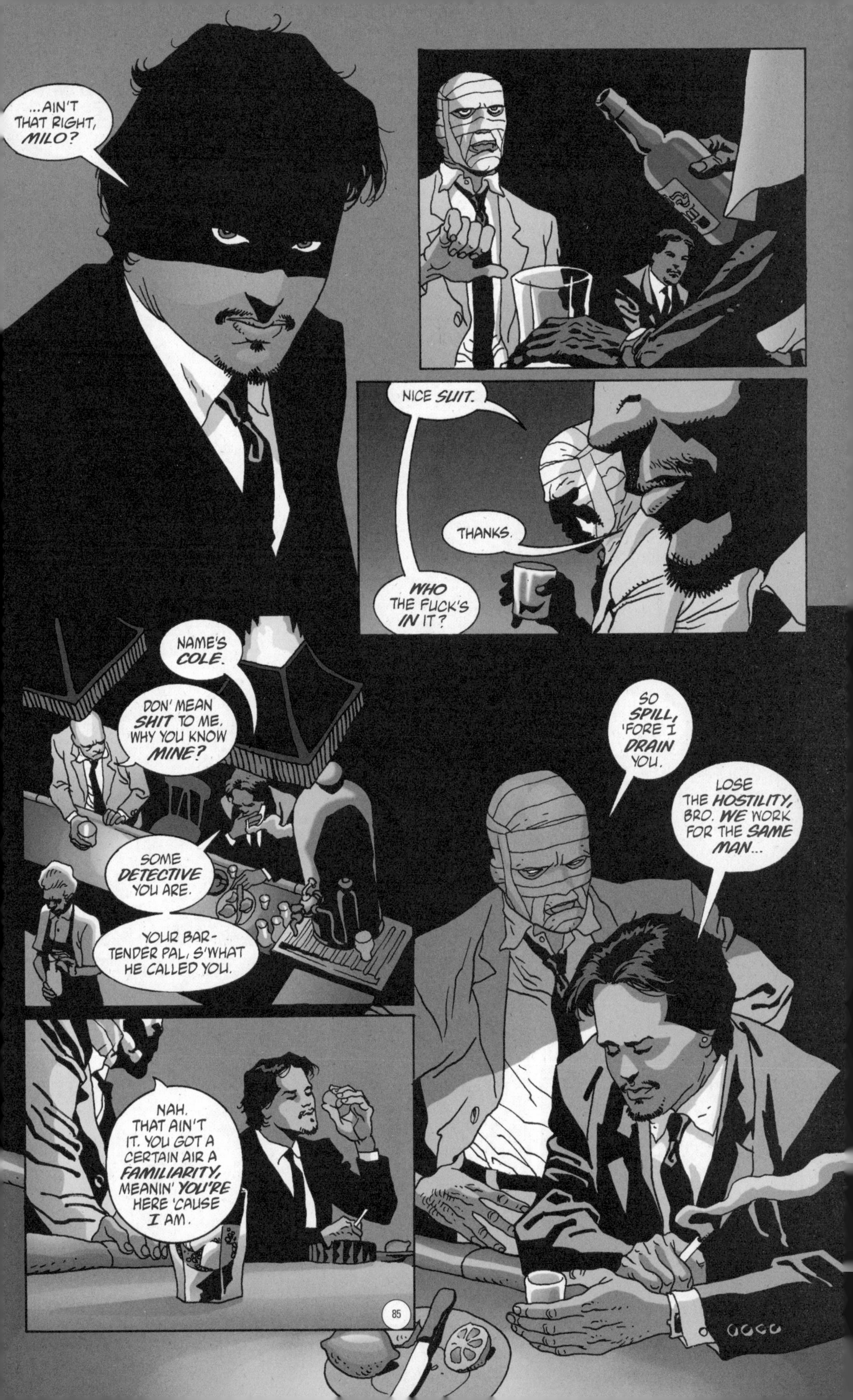
...AIN'T THAT RIGHT, MILO?
NICE SUIT.
THANKS.
WHO THE FUCK'S IN IT?
NAME'S COLE.
DON' MEAN SHIT TO ME. WHY YOU KNOW MINE?
SOME DETECTIVE YOU ARE.
YOUR BAR-TENDER PAL, S'WHAT HE CALLED YOU.
SO SPILL, 'FORE I DRAIN YOU.
LOSE THE HOSTILITY, BRO. WE WORK FOR THE SAME MAN...
NAH. THAT AIN'T IT. YOU GOT A CERTAIN AIR A FAMILIARITY, MEANIN' YOU'RE HERE 'CAUSE I AM.

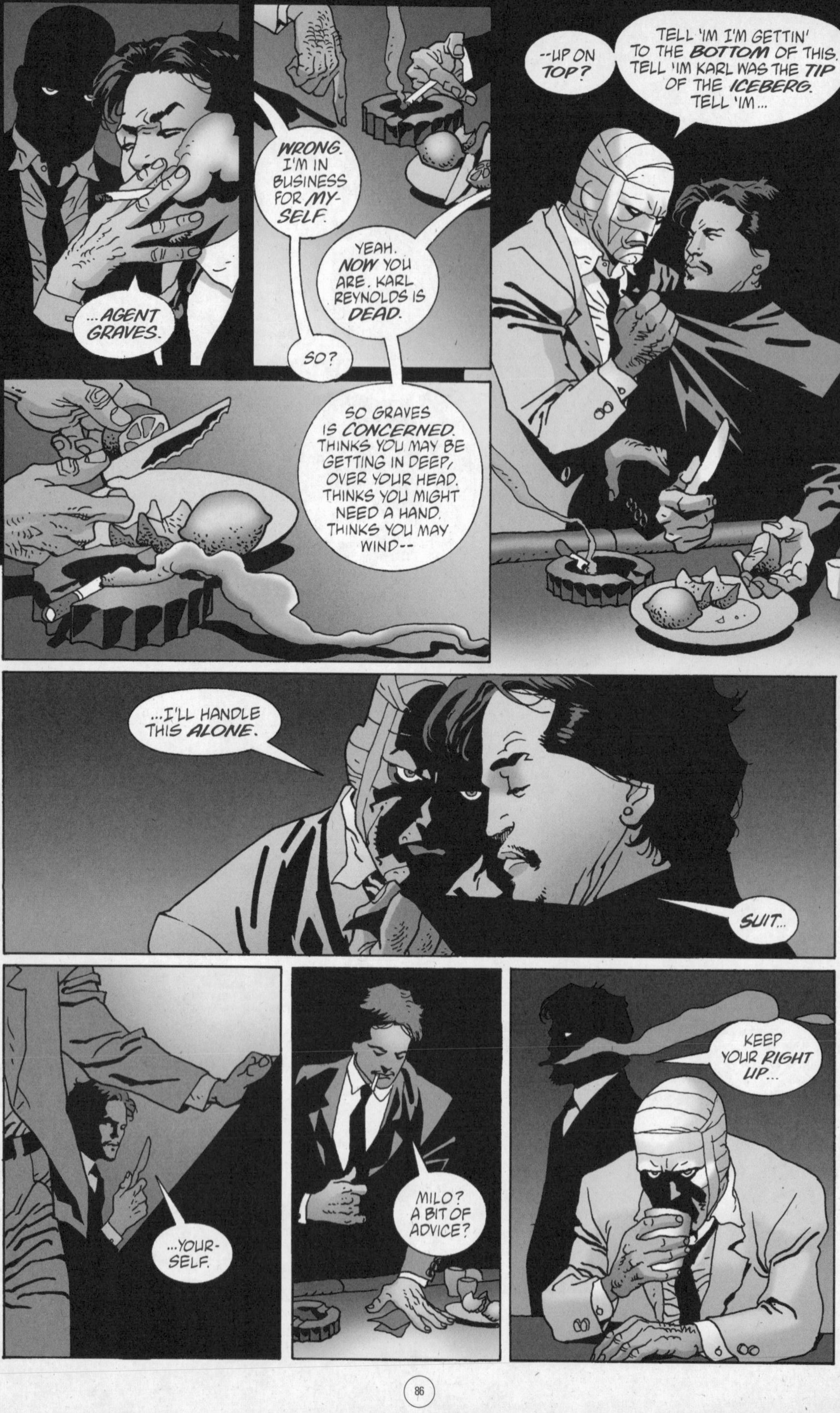

...AGENT GRAVES.
WRONG. I'M IN BUSINESS FOR MYSELF.
SO?
YEAH. NOW YOU ARE. KARL REYNOLDS IS DEAD.
--UP ON TOP?
TELL 'IM I'M GETTIN' TO THE BOTTOM OF THIS. TELL 'IM KARL WAS THE TIP OF THE ICEBERG. TELL 'IM...
SO GRAVES IS CONCERNED. THINKS YOU MAY BE GETTING IN DEEP, OVER YOUR HEAD. THINKS YOU MIGHT NEED A HAND. THINKS YOU MAY WIND--
...I'LL HANDLE THIS ALONE.
SUIT...
...YOURSELF.
MILO? A BIT OF ADVICE?
KEEP YOUR RIGHT UP...

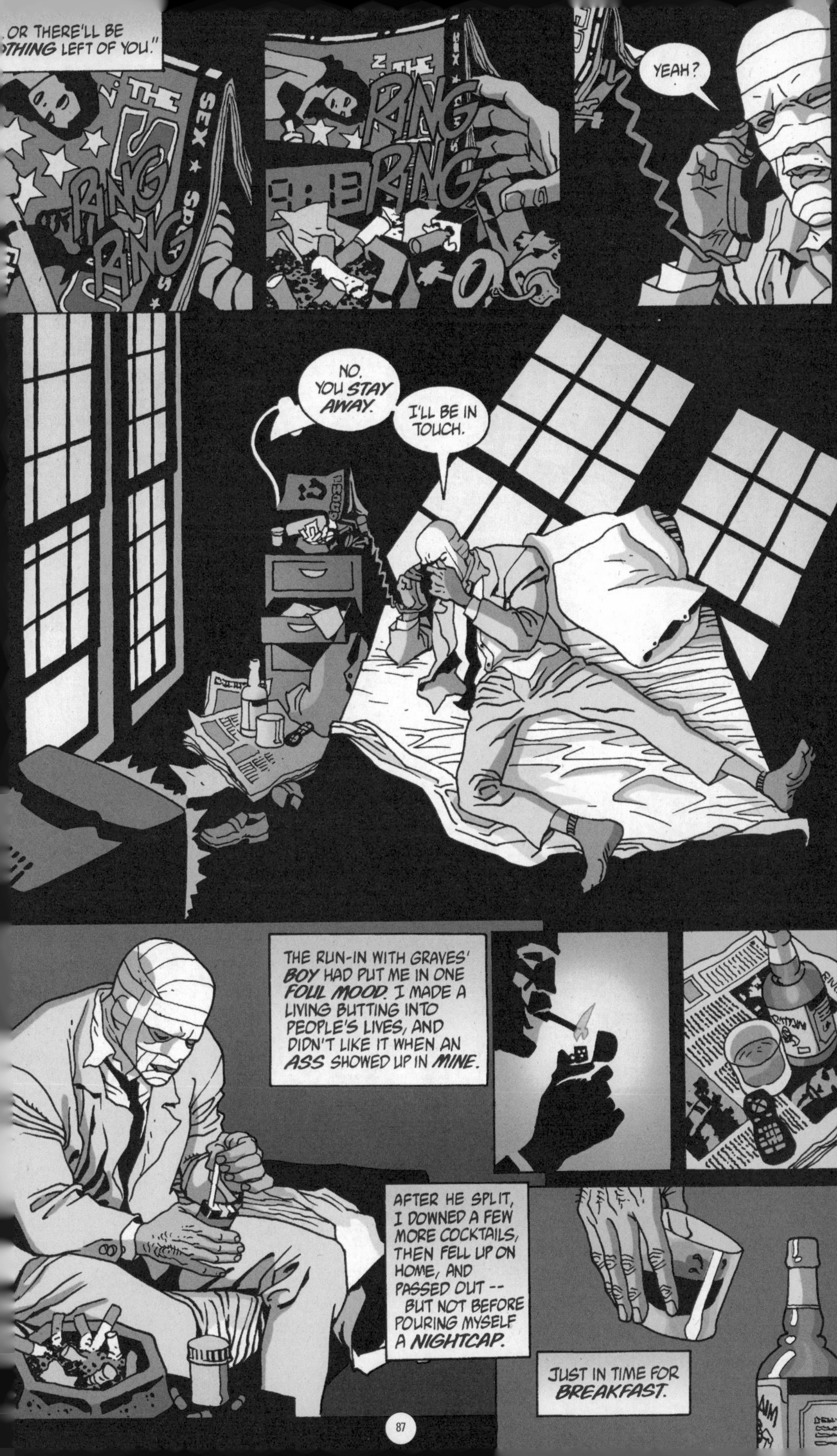

.OR THERE'LL BE
OTHING LEFT OF YOU."
RING RING
RING RING
YEAH?
NO. YOU STAY AWAY.
I'LL BE IN TOUCH.
THE RUN-IN WITH GRAVES' BOY HAD PUT ME IN ONE FOUL MOOD. I MADE A LIVING BUTTING INTO PEOPLE'S LIVES, AND DIDN'T LIKE IT WHEN AN ASS SHOWED UP IN MINE.
AFTER HE SPLIT, I DOWNED A FEW MORE COCKTAILS, THEN FELL UP ON HOME, AND PASSED OUT -- BUT NOT BEFORE POURING MYSELF A NIGHTCAP.
JUST IN TIME FOR BREAKFAST.

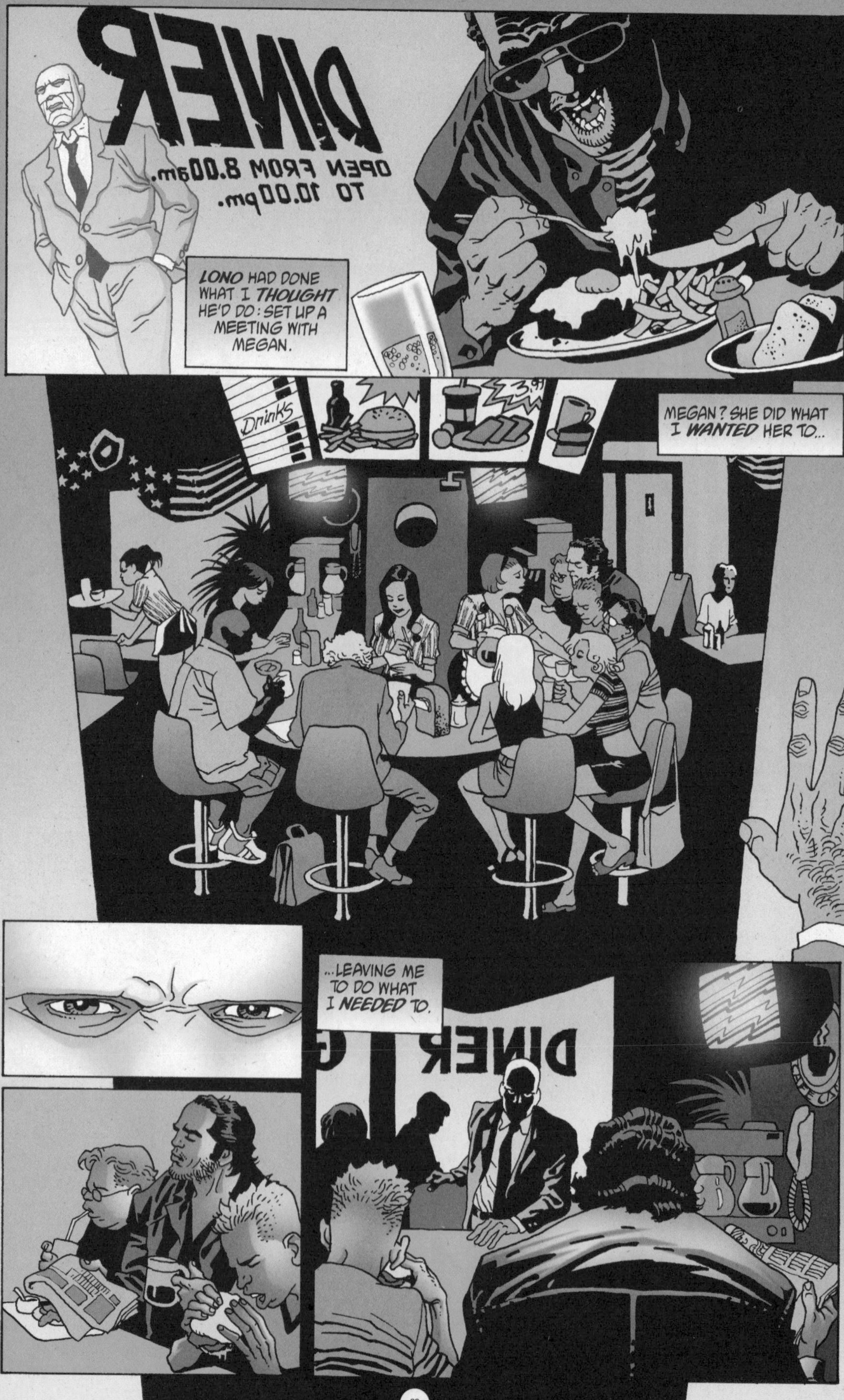
DINER
OPEN FROM 8.00am.
TO 10.00pm.
LONO HAD DONE WHAT I THOUGHT HE'D DO: SET UP A MEETING WITH MEGAN.
Drinks
MEGAN? SHE DID WHAT I WANTED HER TO...
...LEAVING ME TO DO WHAT I NEEDED TO.
DINER

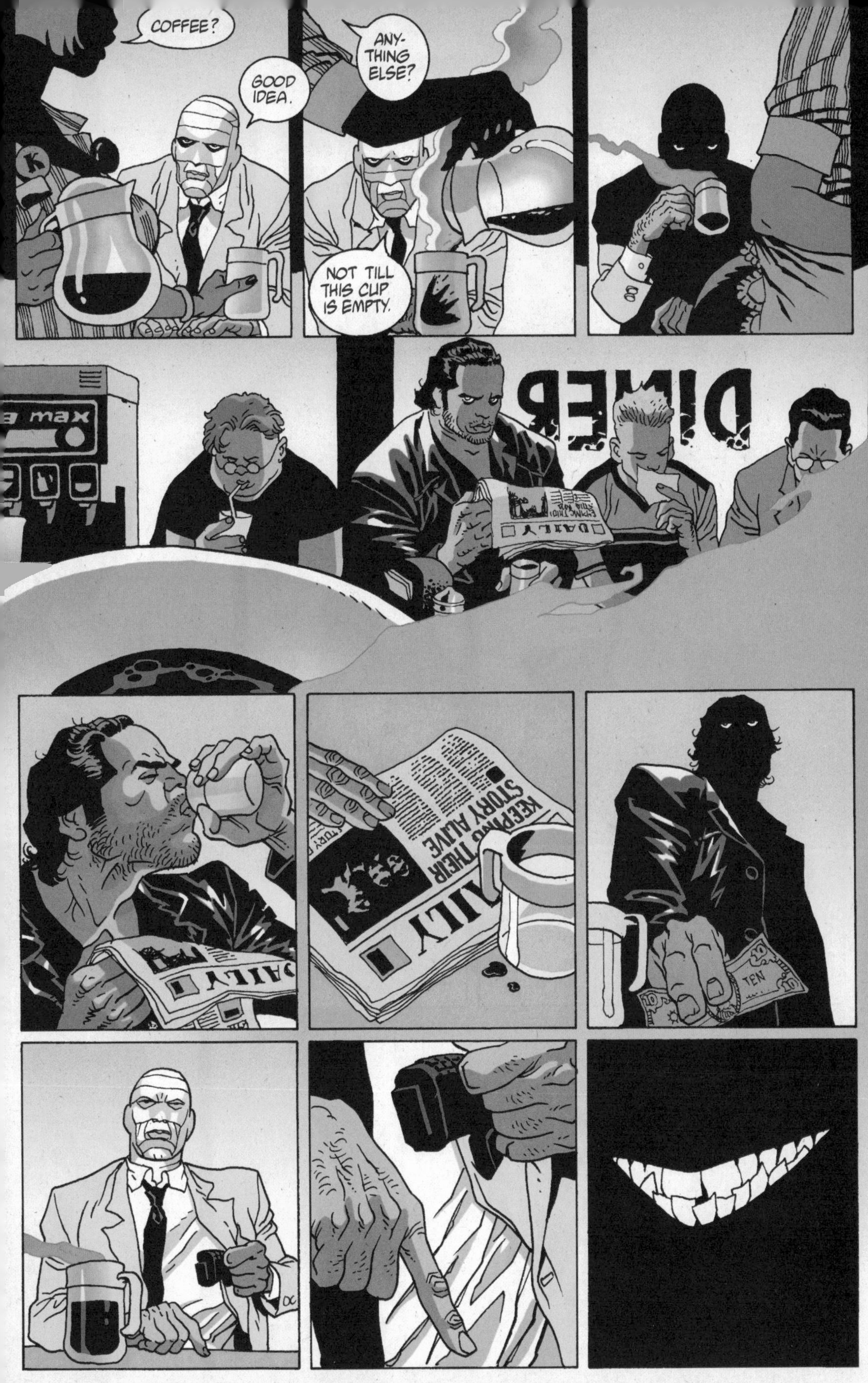
COFFEE?
GOOD IDEA.
ANY-THING ELSE?
NOT TILL THIS CUP IS EMPTY.
DAILY
KEEPING THEIR STORY ALIVE
TEN

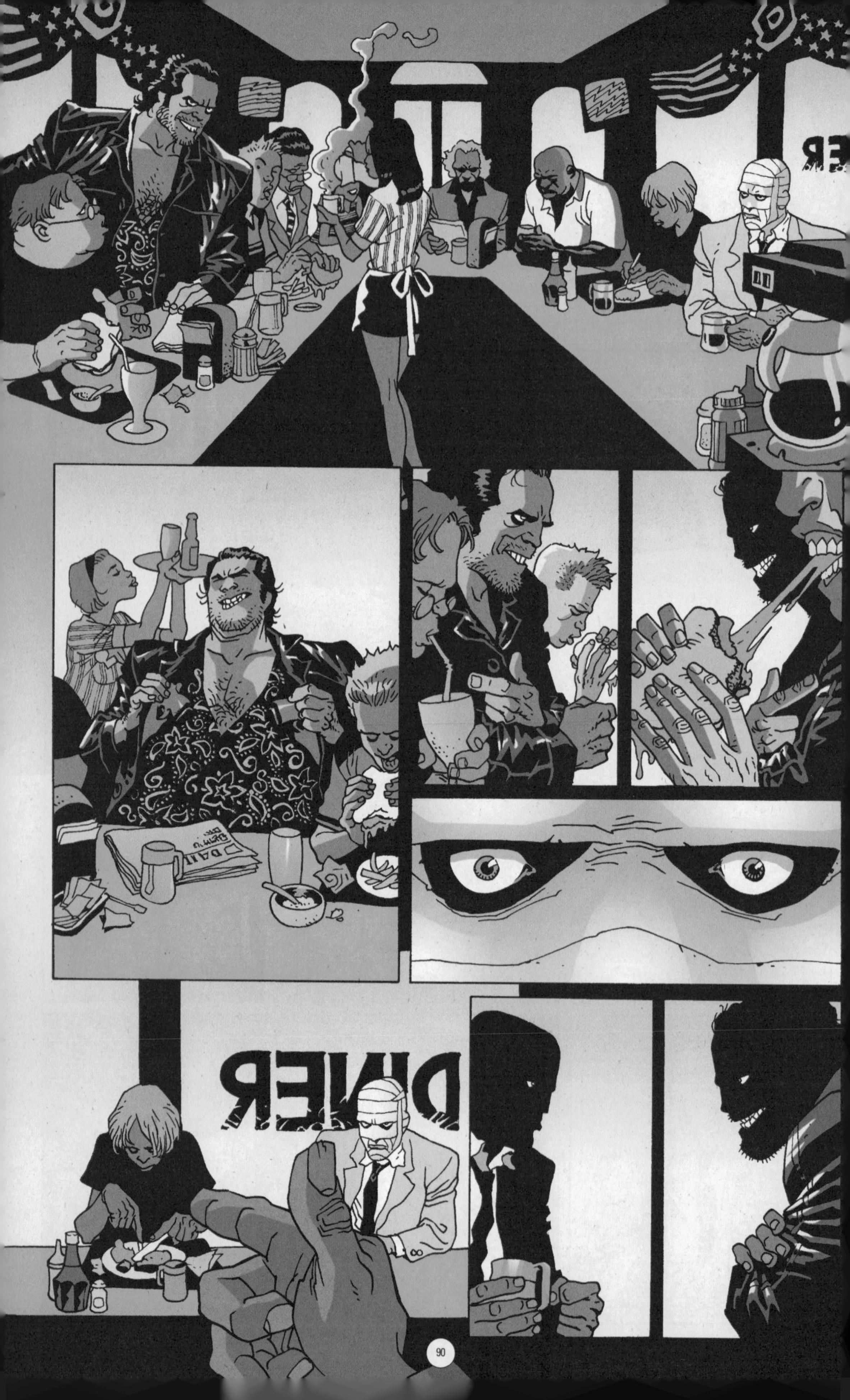
DINER

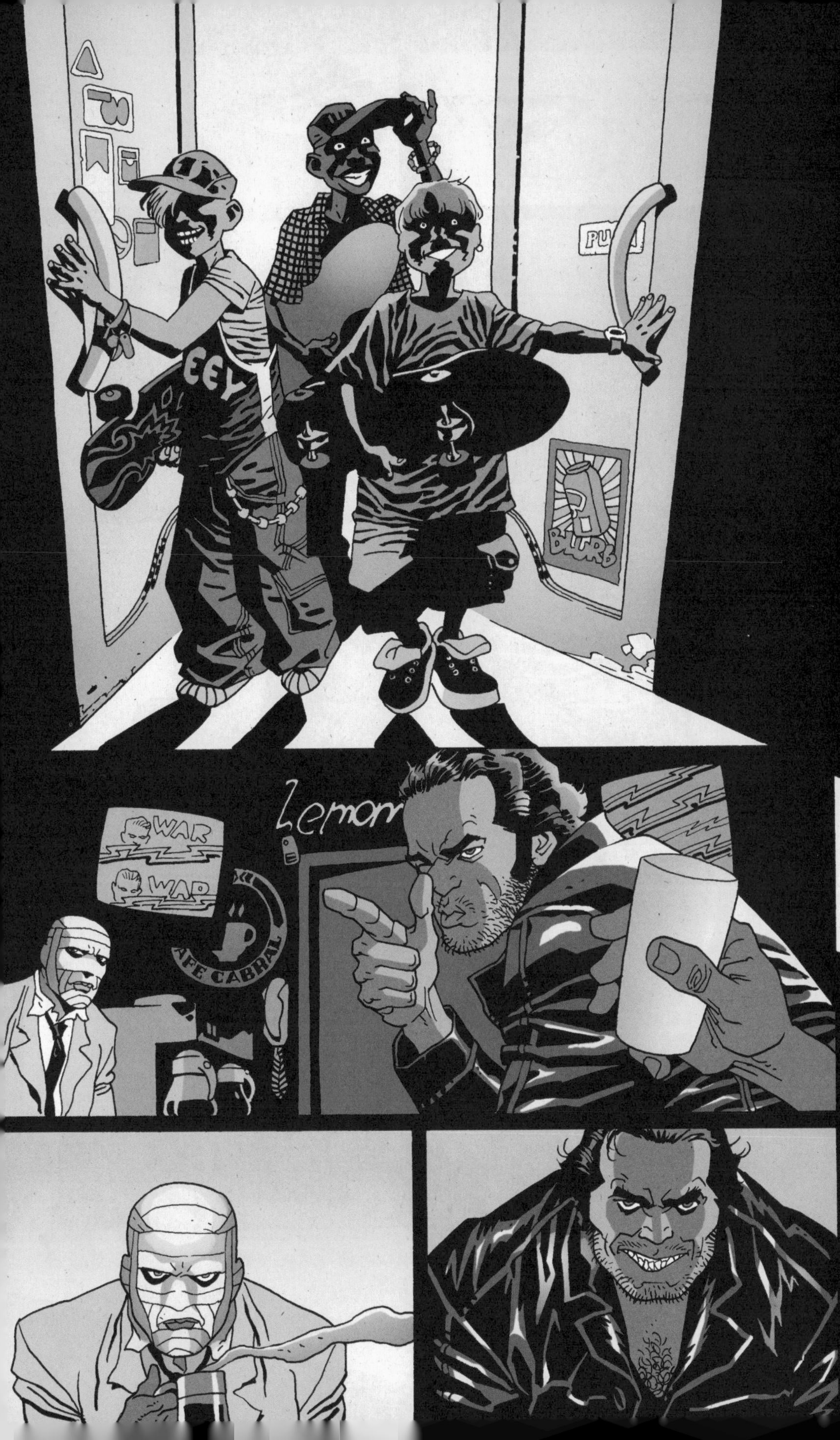
BLURB
WAR

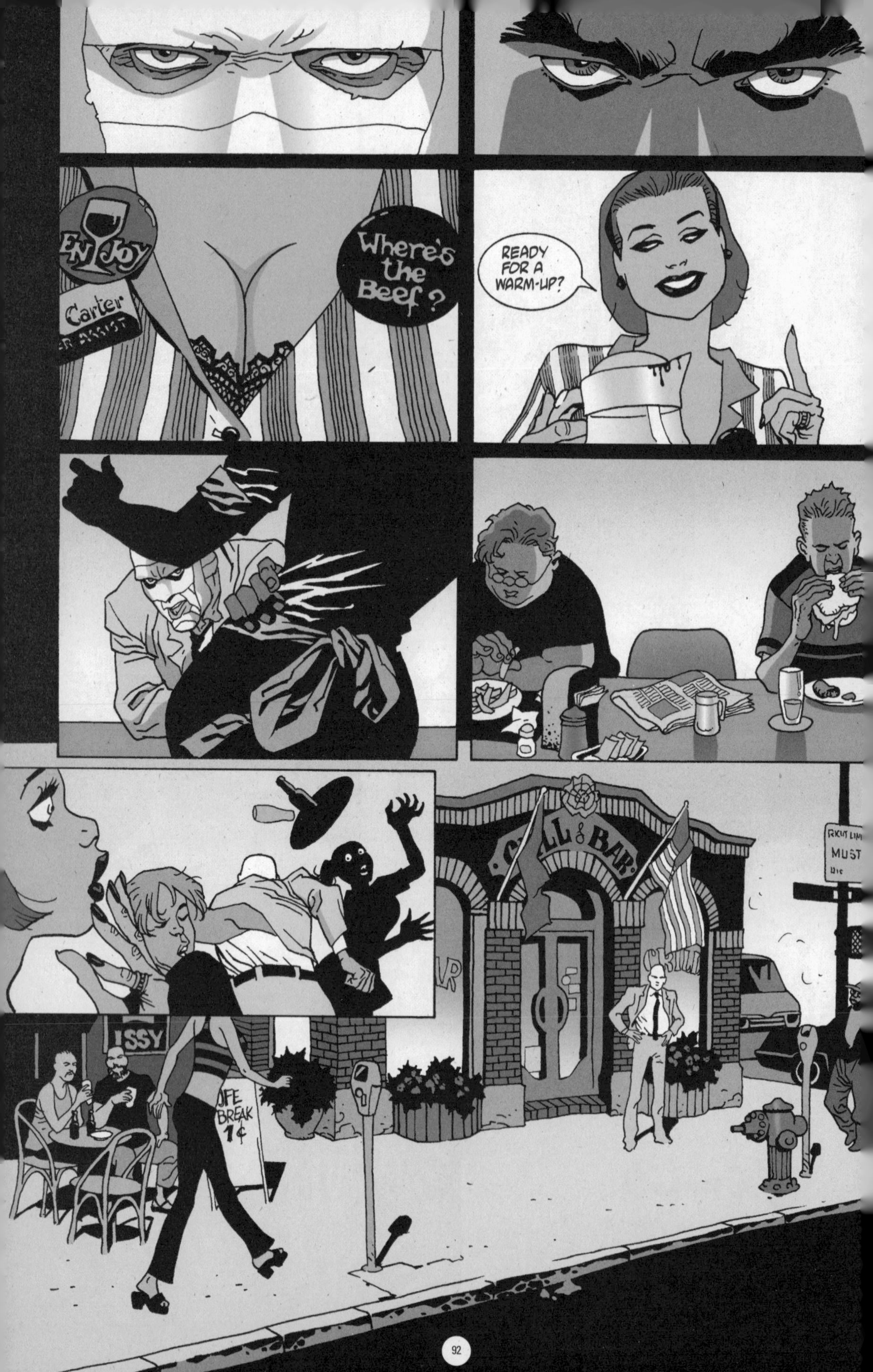

EN JOY
Where's the Beef?
Carter
READY FOR A WARM-UP?
GRILL & BAR
ISSY
BREAK 1¢
MUST

I WAS SWEATIN' *HARD.* THE *SLOW BURN* I WAS WORKIN' ON *FLARED UP* AFTER I BOTCHED THE PLAY ON LONO.

EVEN A *DUMB APE* LIKE THAT CAN PUT TWO AN' TWO TOGETHER, WHICH USUALLY ADDS UP TO *SIX FEET UNDER* FOR THE *DOUBLE-CROSSER.*

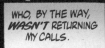

WHO, BY THE WAY, *WASN'T* RETURNING MY CALLS.

WAITING BY THE PHONE I POURED *FUEL* ON THE *FIRE,* AND BY THE TIME THE MOON CAME UP? I WAS *HOWLIN' DRUNK,* AN' *PISSED*--MOSTLY AT *MYSELF.*

I KNEW FOR *DAMN* SURE WHO LONO WAS *PISSED AT* TOO. THE DAY WAS SHOT TO *HELL*--

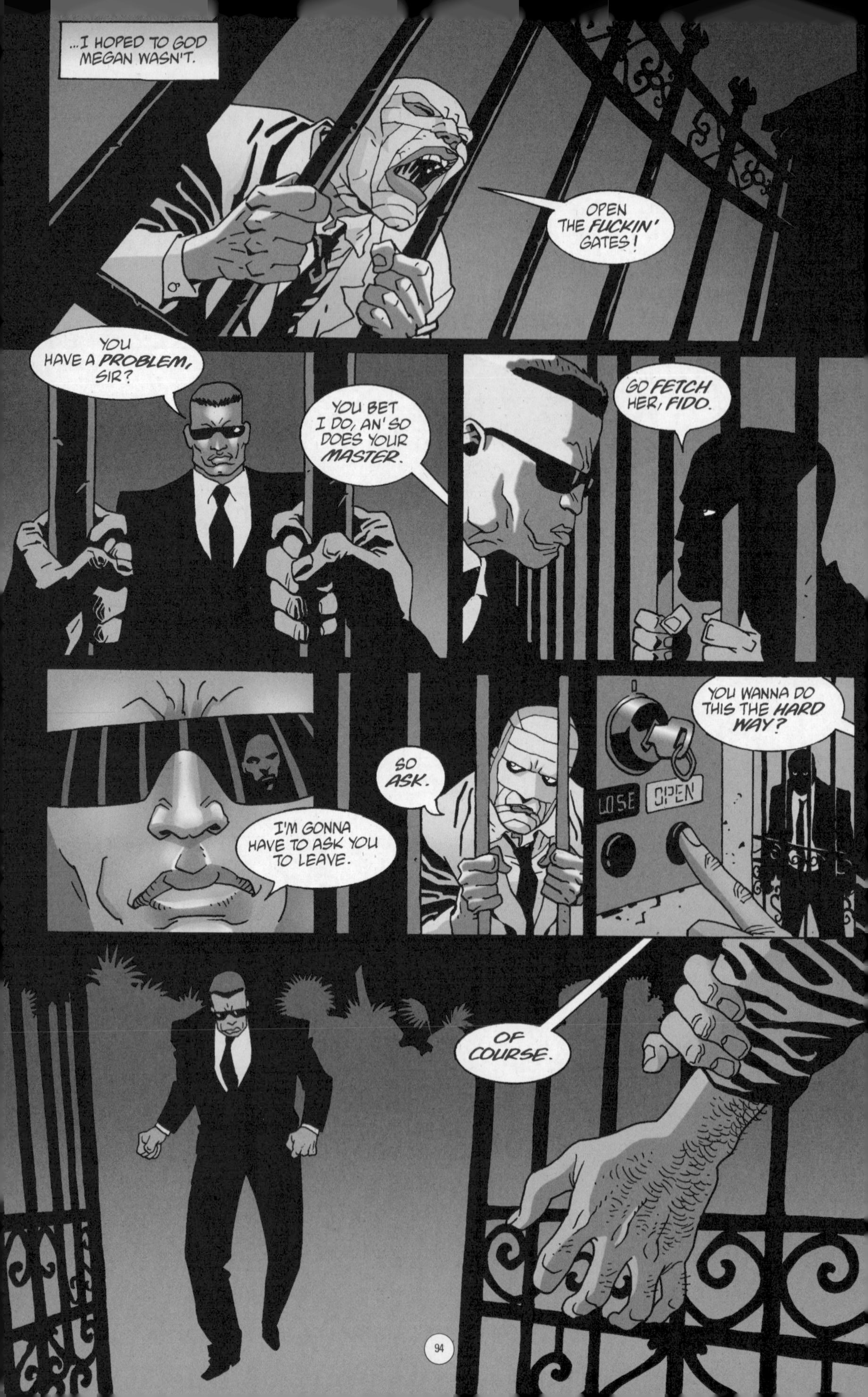
...I HOPED TO GOD MEGAN WASN'T.
OPEN THE FUCKIN' GATES!
YOU HAVE A PROBLEM, SIR?
YOU BET I DO, AN' SO DOES YOUR MASTER.
GO FETCH HER, FIDO.
I'M GONNA HAVE TO ASK YOU TO LEAVE.
SO ASK.
YOU WANNA DO THIS THE HARD WAY?
LOSE
OPEN
OF COURSE.

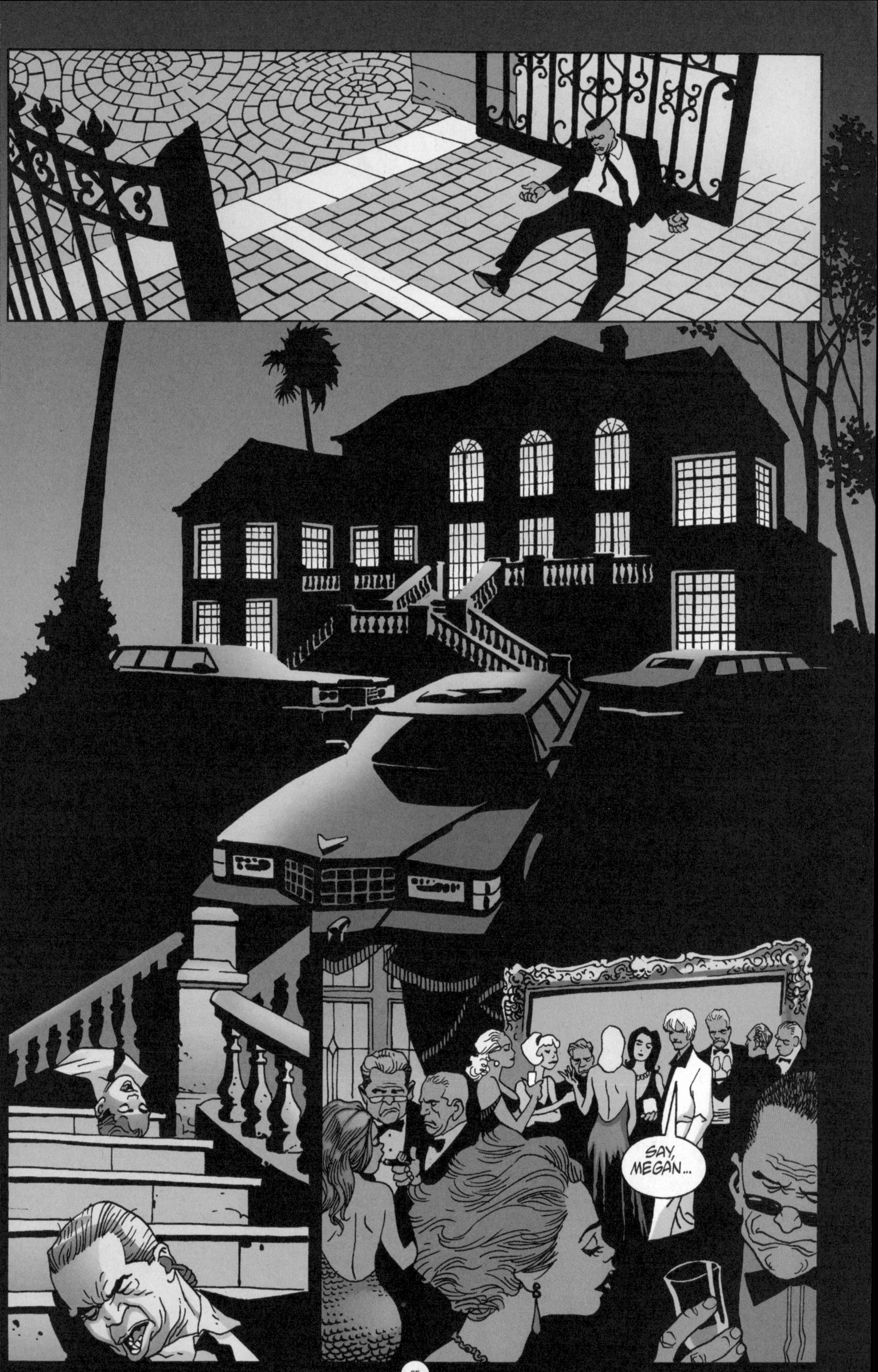
SAY, MEGAN...

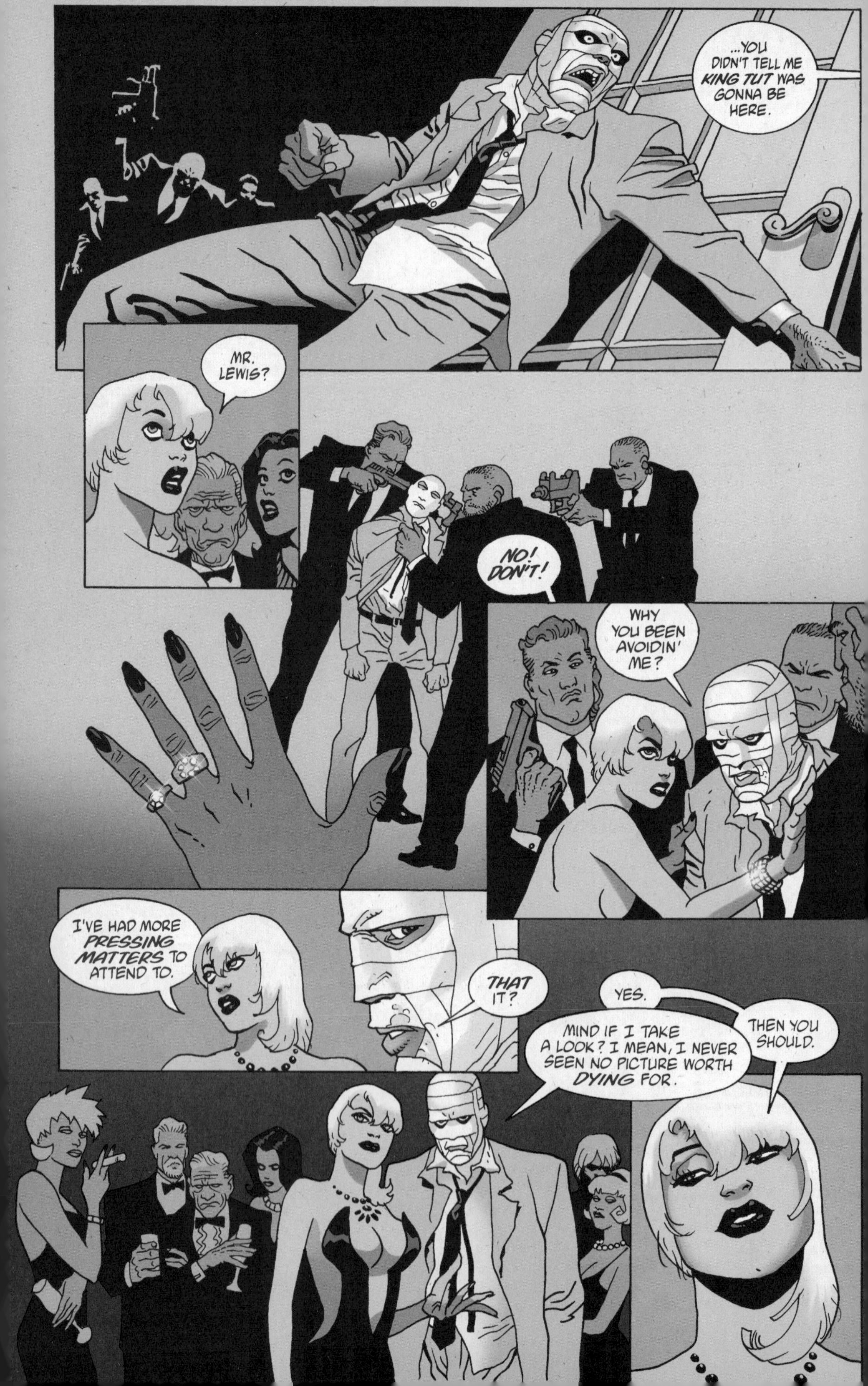
...YOU DIDN'T TELL ME KING TUT WAS GONNA BE HERE.
MR. LEWIS?
NO! DON'T!
WHY YOU BEEN AVOIDIN' ME?
I'VE HAD MORE PRESSING MATTERS TO ATTEND TO.
THAT IT?
YES.
THEN YOU SHOULD.
MIND IF I TAKE A LOOK? I MEAN, I NEVER SEEN NO PICTURE WORTH DYING FOR.

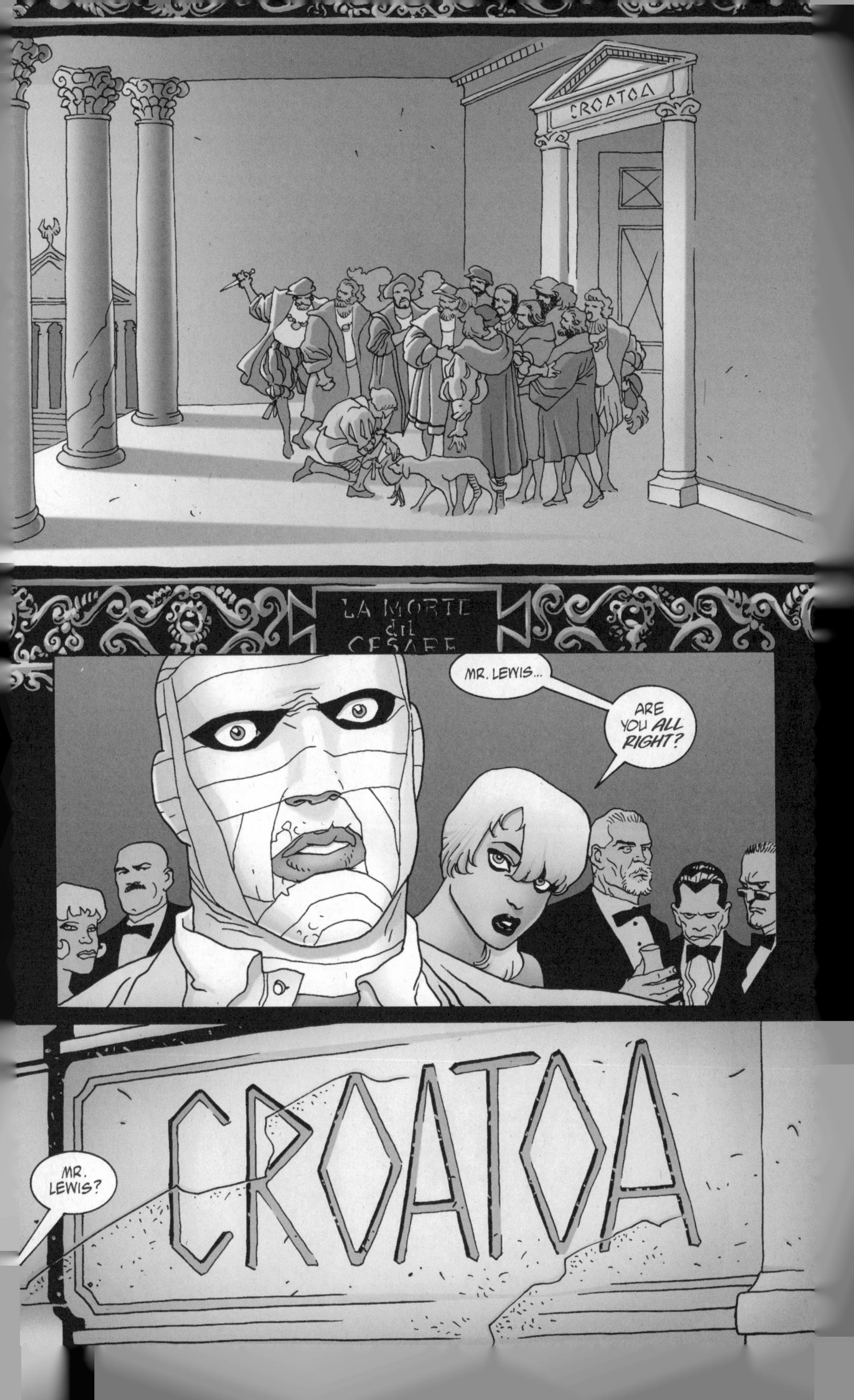
CROATOA
LA MORTE dil CESARE
MR. LEWIS...
ARE YOU *ALL RIGHT?*
CROATOA
MR. LEWIS?

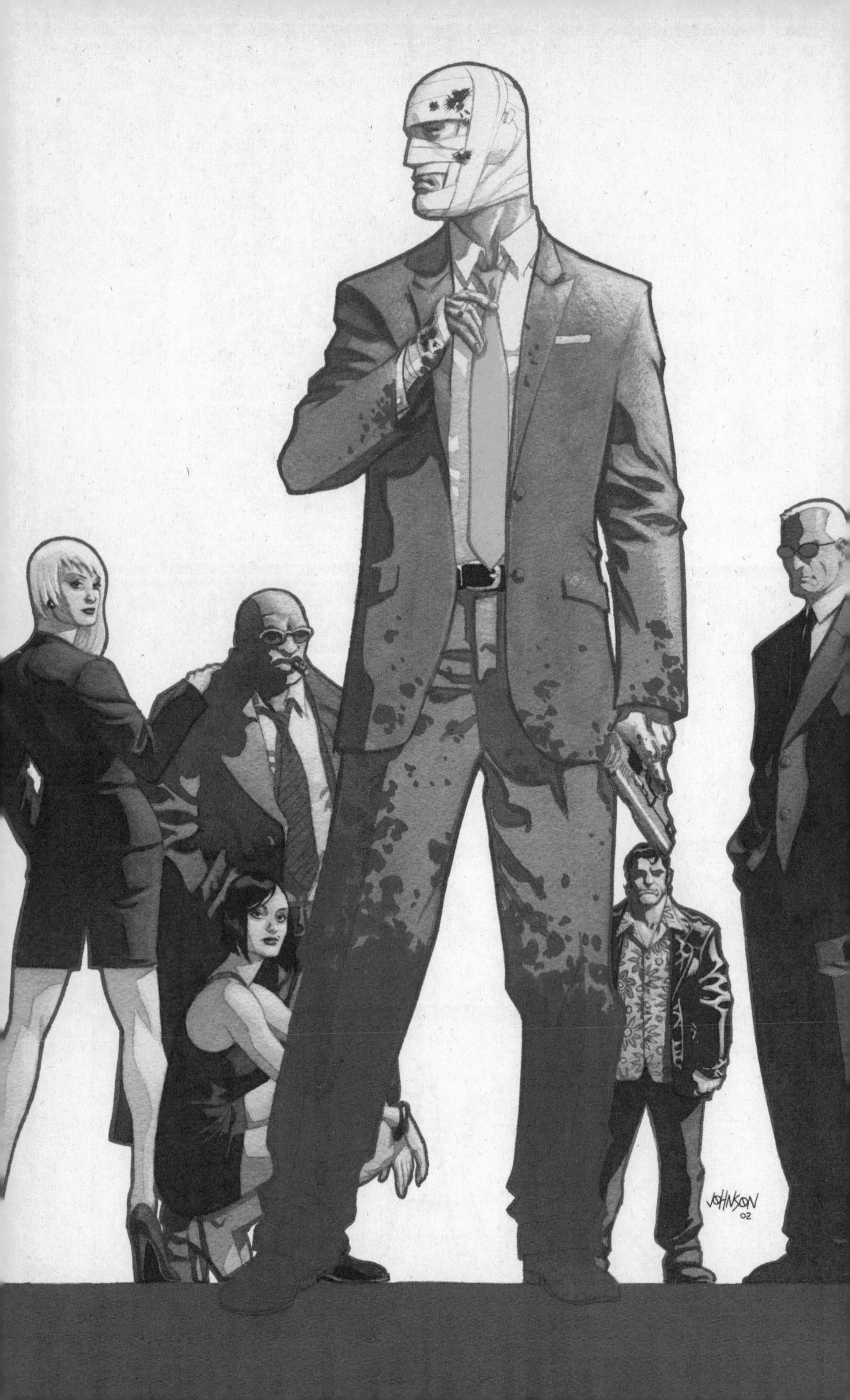
JOHNSON
02

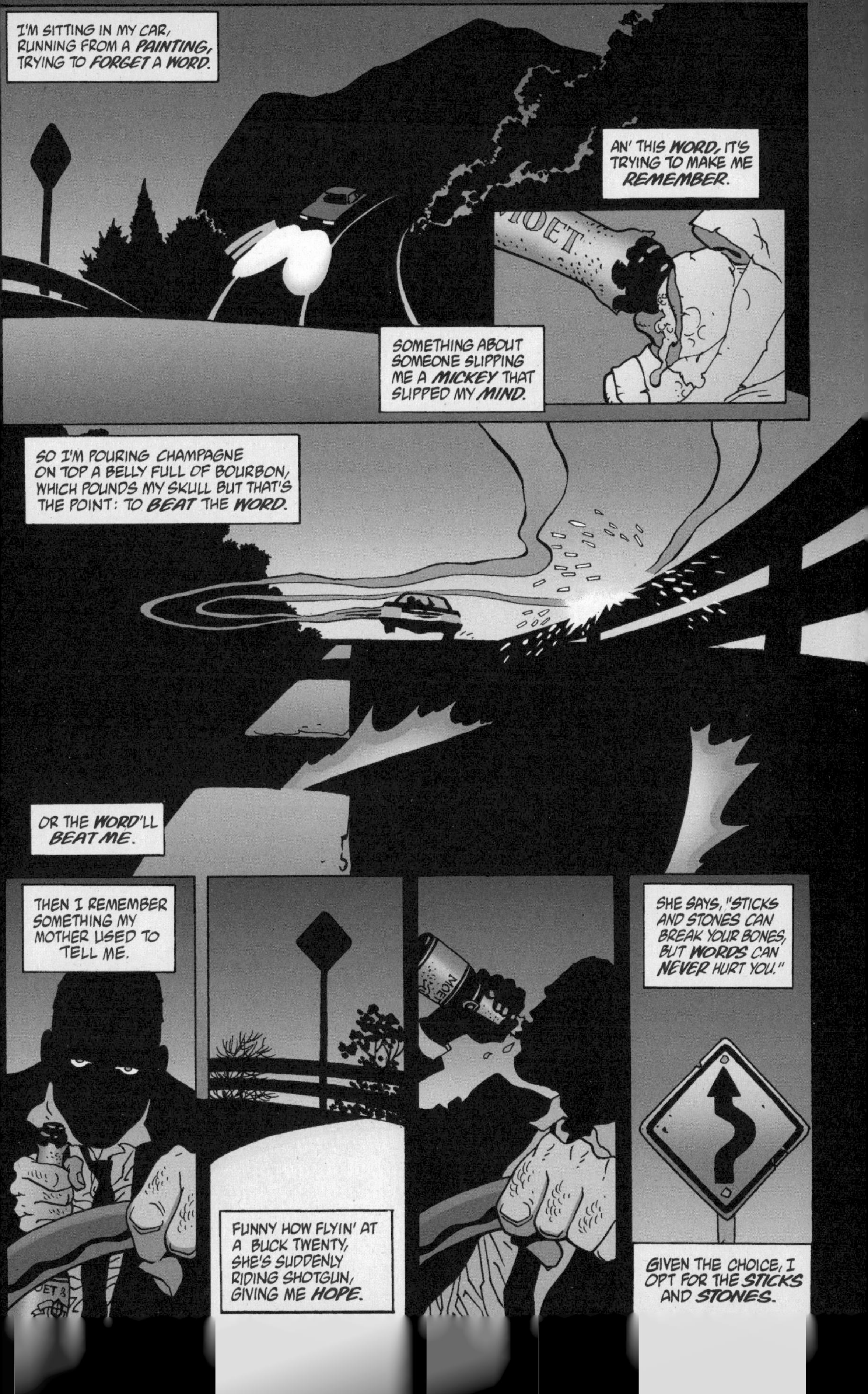
I'M SITTING IN MY CAR, RUNNING FROM A PAINTING, TRYING TO FORGET A WORD.
AN' THIS WORD, IT'S TRYING TO MAKE ME REMEMBER.
MOET
SOMETHING ABOUT SOMEONE SLIPPING ME A MICKEY THAT SLIPPED MY MIND.
SO I'M POURING CHAMPAGNE ON TOP A BELLY FULL OF BOURBON, WHICH POUNDS MY SKULL BUT THAT'S THE POINT: TO BEAT THE WORD.
OR THE WORD'LL BEAT ME.
THEN I REMEMBER SOMETHING MY MOTHER USED TO TELL ME.
FUNNY HOW FLYIN' AT A BUCK TWENTY, SHE'S SUDDENLY RIDING SHOTGUN, GIVING ME HOPE.
SHE SAYS, "STICKS AND STONES CAN BREAK YOUR BONES, BUT WORDS CAN NEVER HURT YOU."
GIVEN THE CHOICE, I OPT FOR THE STICKS AND STONES.

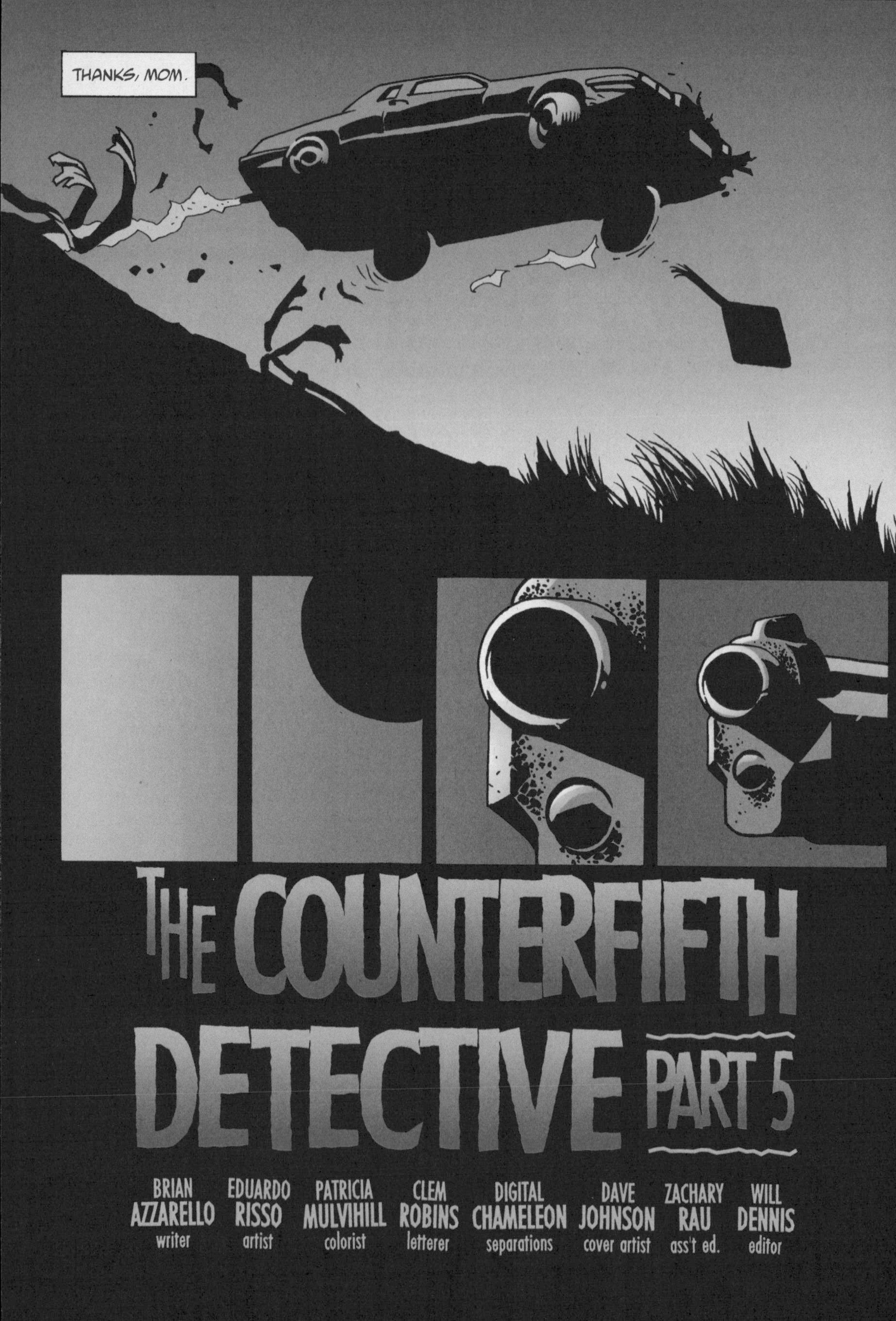
THANKS, MOM.
THE COUNTERFIFTH DETECTIVE PART 5
BRIAN AZZARELLO writer
EDUARDO RISSO artist
PATRICIA MULVIHILL colorist
CLEM ROBINS letterer
DIGITAL CHAMELEON separations
DAVE JOHNSON cover artist
ZACHARY RAU ass't ed.
WILL DENNIS editor

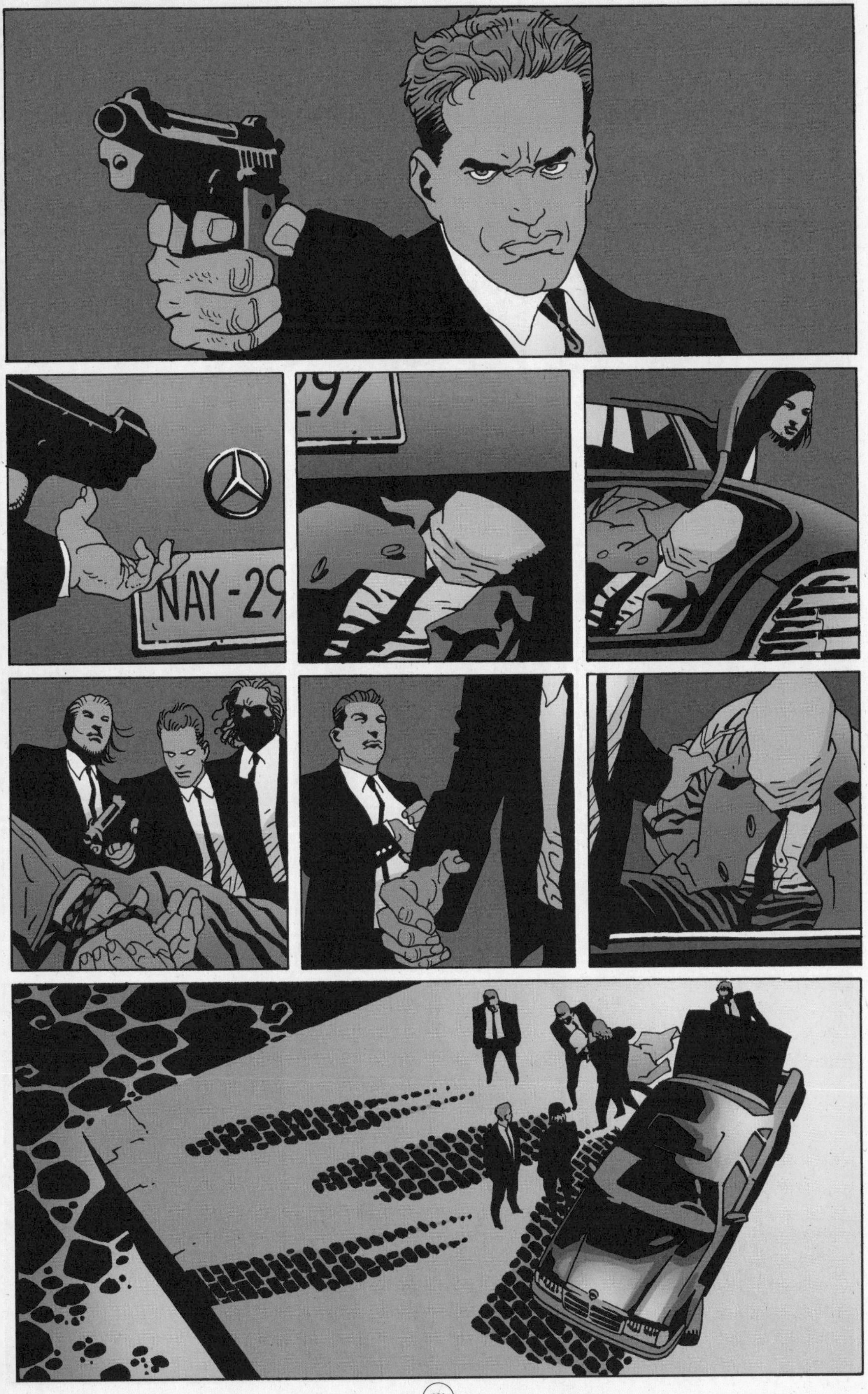
NAY -29
297

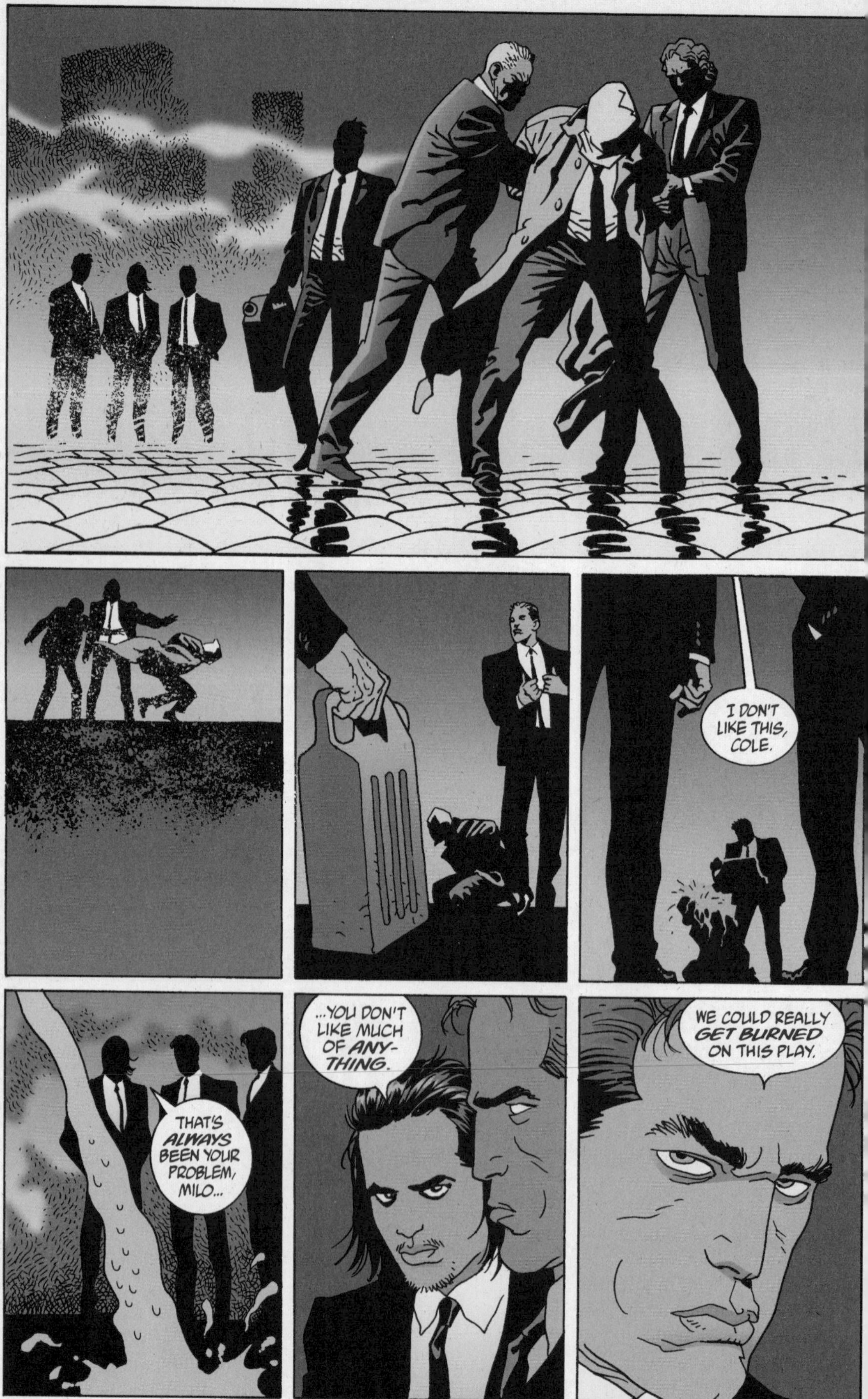
I DON'T LIKE THIS, COLE.
THAT'S *ALWAYS* BEEN YOUR PROBLEM, MILO...
...YOU DON'T LIKE MUCH OF *ANY-THING*.
WE COULD REALLY *GET BURNED* ON THIS PLAY.

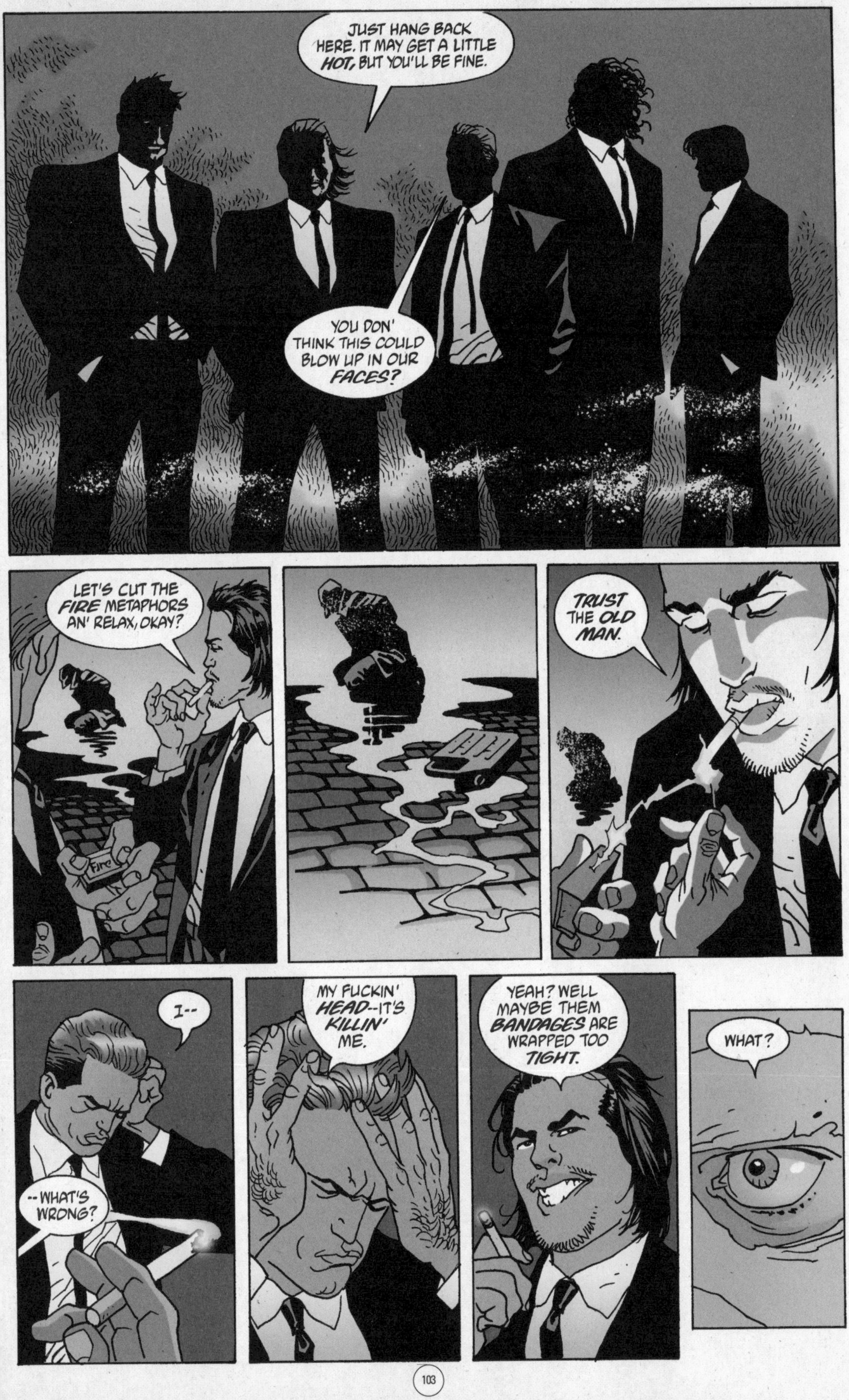
JUST HANG BACK HERE. IT MAY GET A LITTLE HOT, BUT YOU'LL BE FINE.
YOU DON' THINK THIS COULD BLOW UP IN OUR FACES?
LET'S CUT THE FIRE METAPHORS AN' RELAX, OKAY?
Fire
TRUST THE OLD MAN.
I--
--WHAT'S WRONG?
MY FUCKIN' HEAD--IT'S KILLIN' ME.
YEAH? WELL MAYBE THEM BANDAGES ARE WRAPPED TOO TIGHT.
WHAT?

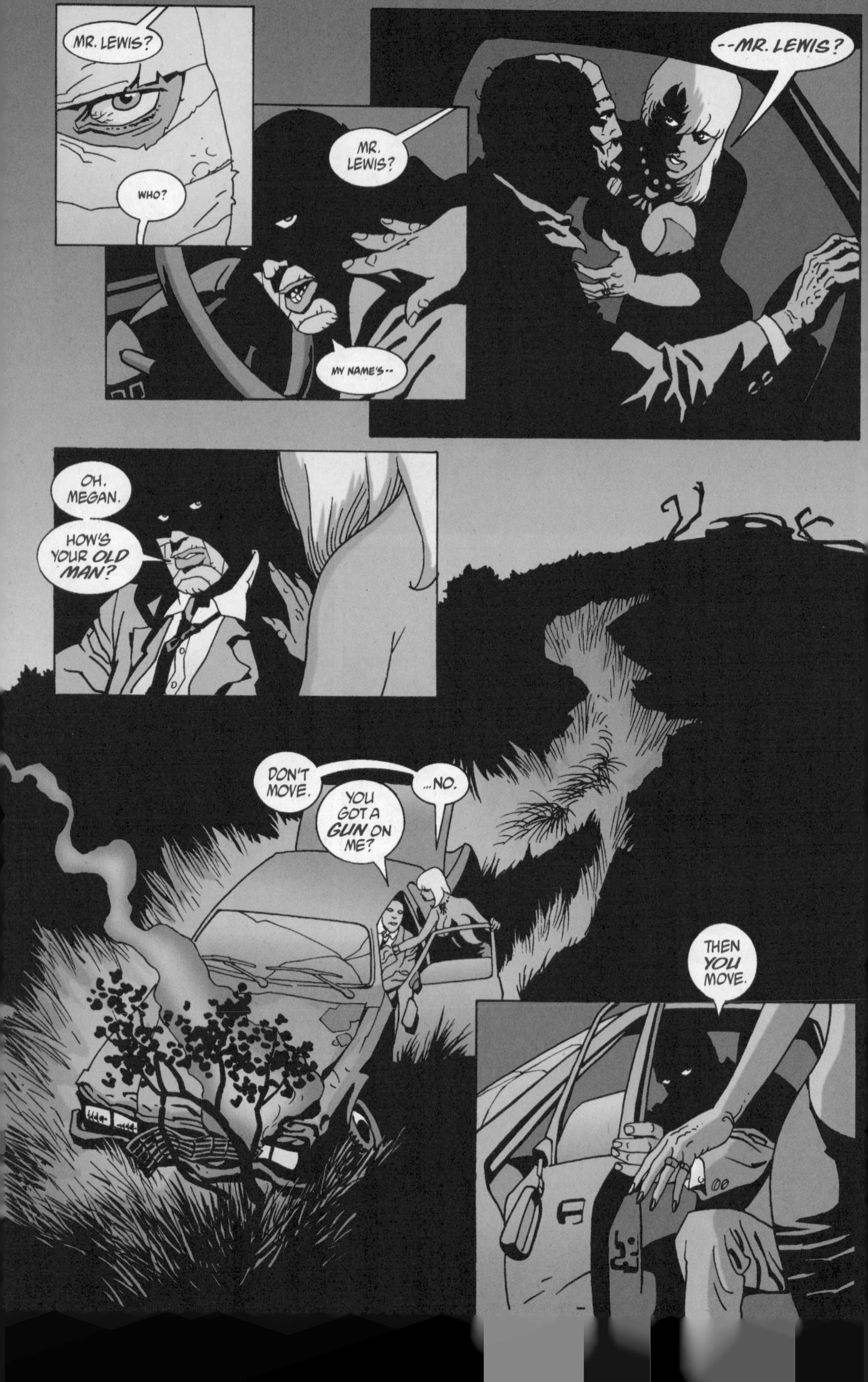

MR. LEWIS?
WHO?
MR. LEWIS?
MY NAME'S--
--MR. LEWIS?
OH. MEGAN.
HOW'S YOUR OLD MAN?
DON'T MOVE.
...NO.
YOU GOT A GUN ON ME?
THEN YOU MOVE.

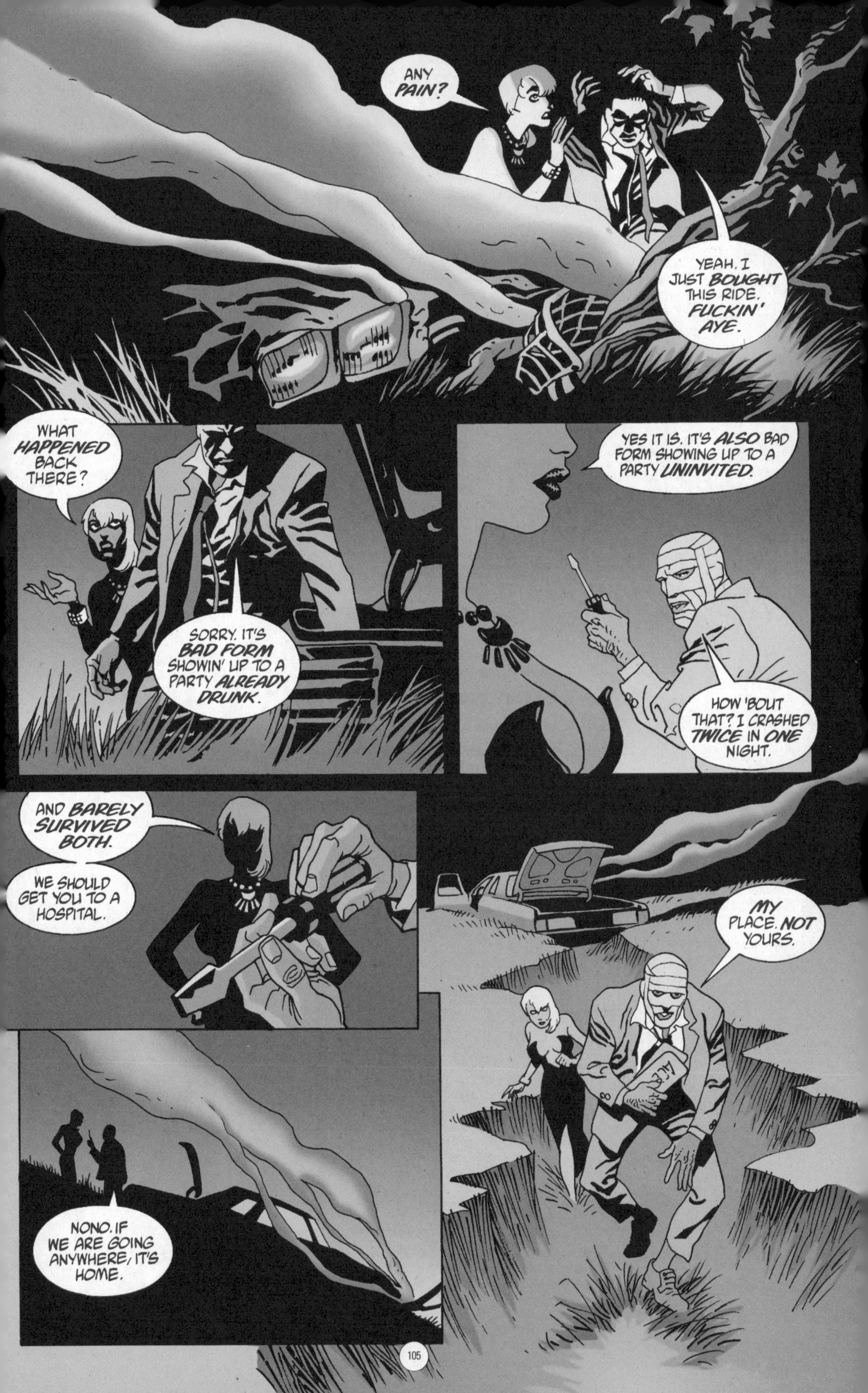

ANY PAIN?
YEAH. I JUST BOUGHT THIS RIDE. FUCKIN' AYE.
WHAT HAPPENED BACK THERE?
SORRY. IT'S BAD FORM SHOWIN' UP TO A PARTY ALREADY DRUNK.
YES IT IS. IT'S ALSO BAD FORM SHOWING UP TO A PARTY UNINVITED.
HOW 'BOUT THAT? I CRASHED TWICE IN ONE NIGHT.
AND BARELY SURVIVED BOTH.
WE SHOULD GET YOU TO A HOSPITAL.
NONO. IF WE ARE GOING ANYWHERE, IT'S HOME.
MY PLACE. NOT YOURS.

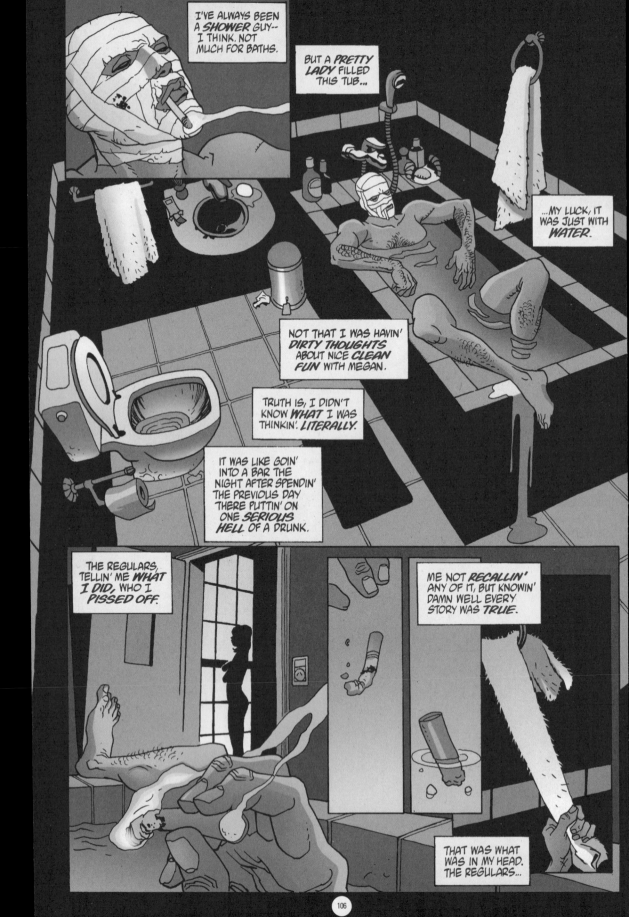

I'VE ALWAYS BEEN A *SHOWER* GUY-- I THINK. NOT MUCH FOR BATHS.

BUT A *PRETTY LADY* FILLED THIS TUB...

...MY LUCK, IT WAS JUST WITH *WATER.*

NOT THAT I WAS HAVIN' *DIRTY THOUGHTS* ABOUT NICE *CLEAN FUN* WITH MEGAN.

TRUTH IS, I DIDN'T KNOW *WHAT* I WAS THINKIN'. *LITERALLY.*

IT WAS LIKE GOIN' INTO A BAR THE NIGHT AFTER SPENDIN' THE PREVIOUS DAY THERE PUTTIN' ON ONE *SERIOUS HELL* OF A DRUNK.

THE REGULARS, TELLIN' ME *WHAT I DID,* WHO I *PISSED OFF.*

ME NOT *RECALLIN'* ANY OF IT, BUT KNOWIN' DAMN WELL EVERY STORY WAS *TRUE.*

THAT WAS WHAT WAS IN MY HEAD. THE REGULARS...

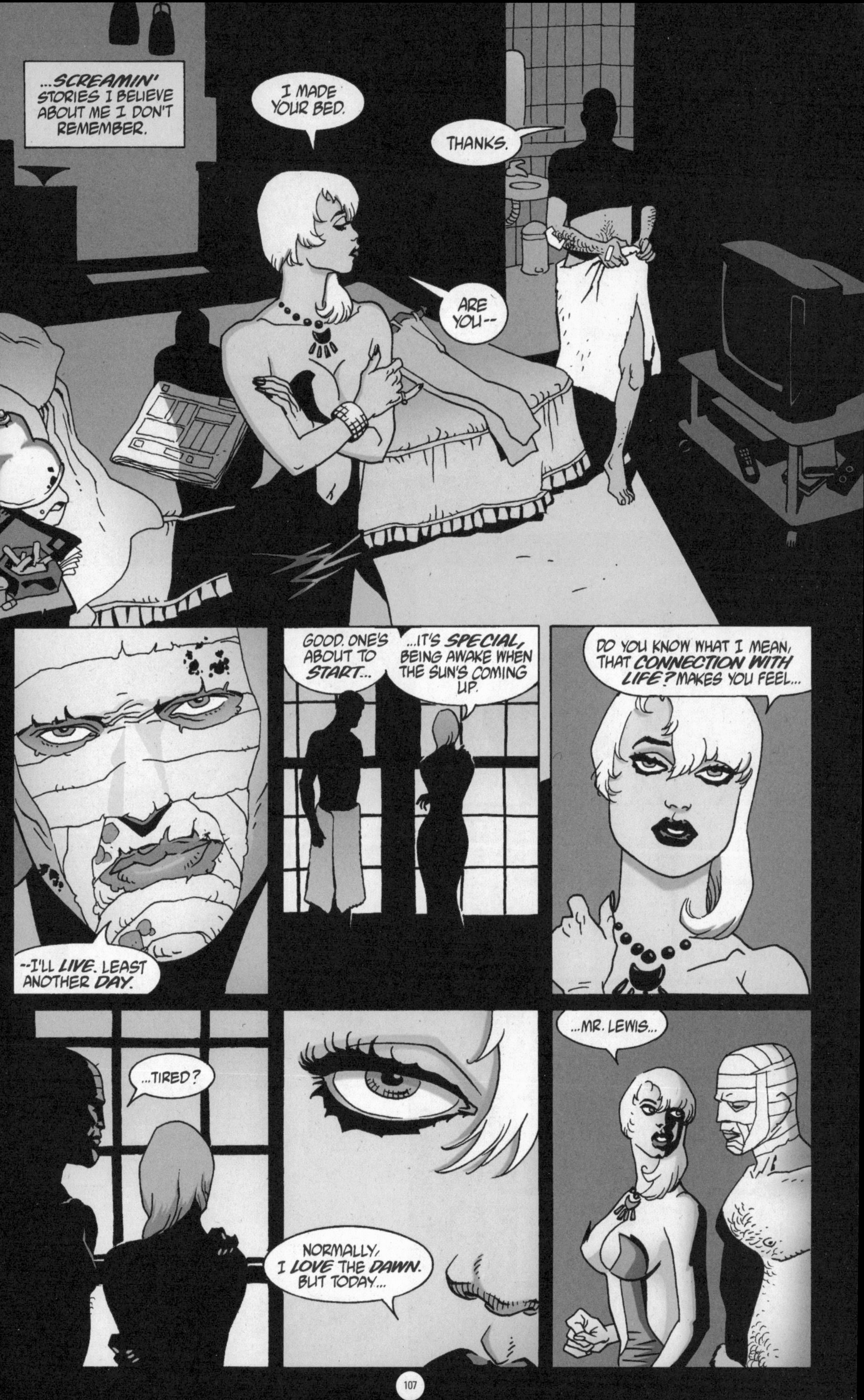
...SCREAMIN' STORIES I BELIEVE ABOUT ME I DON'T REMEMBER.
I MADE YOUR BED.
THANKS.
ARE YOU--
--I'LL LIVE. LEAST ANOTHER DAY.
GOOD. ONE'S ABOUT TO START...
...IT'S SPECIAL, BEING AWAKE WHEN THE SUN'S COMING UP.
DO YOU KNOW WHAT I MEAN, THAT CONNECTION WITH LIFE? MAKES YOU FEEL...
...TIRED?
NORMALLY, I LOVE THE DAWN. BUT TODAY...
...MR. LEWIS...

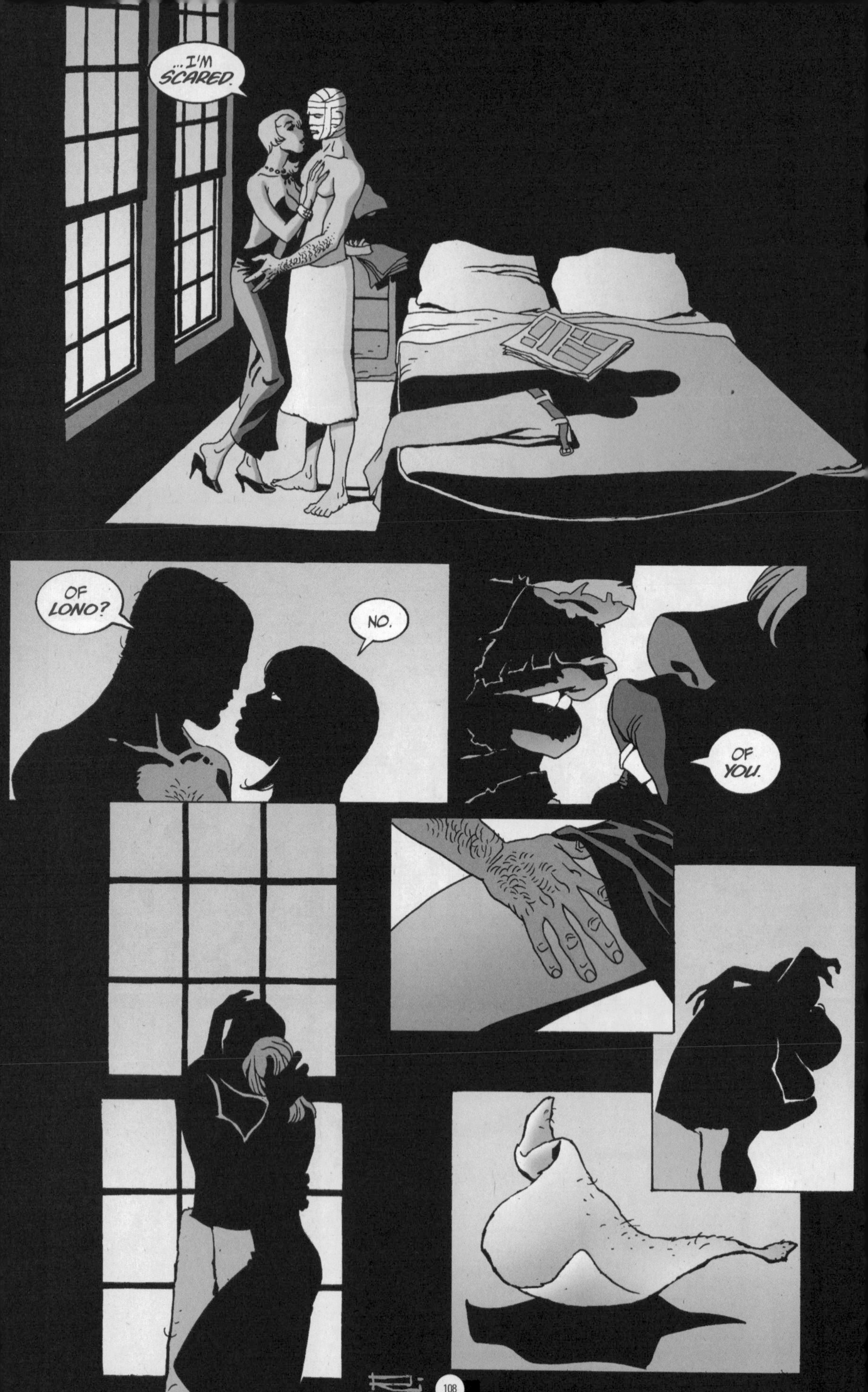
...I'M SCARED.
OF LONO?
NO.
OF YOU.

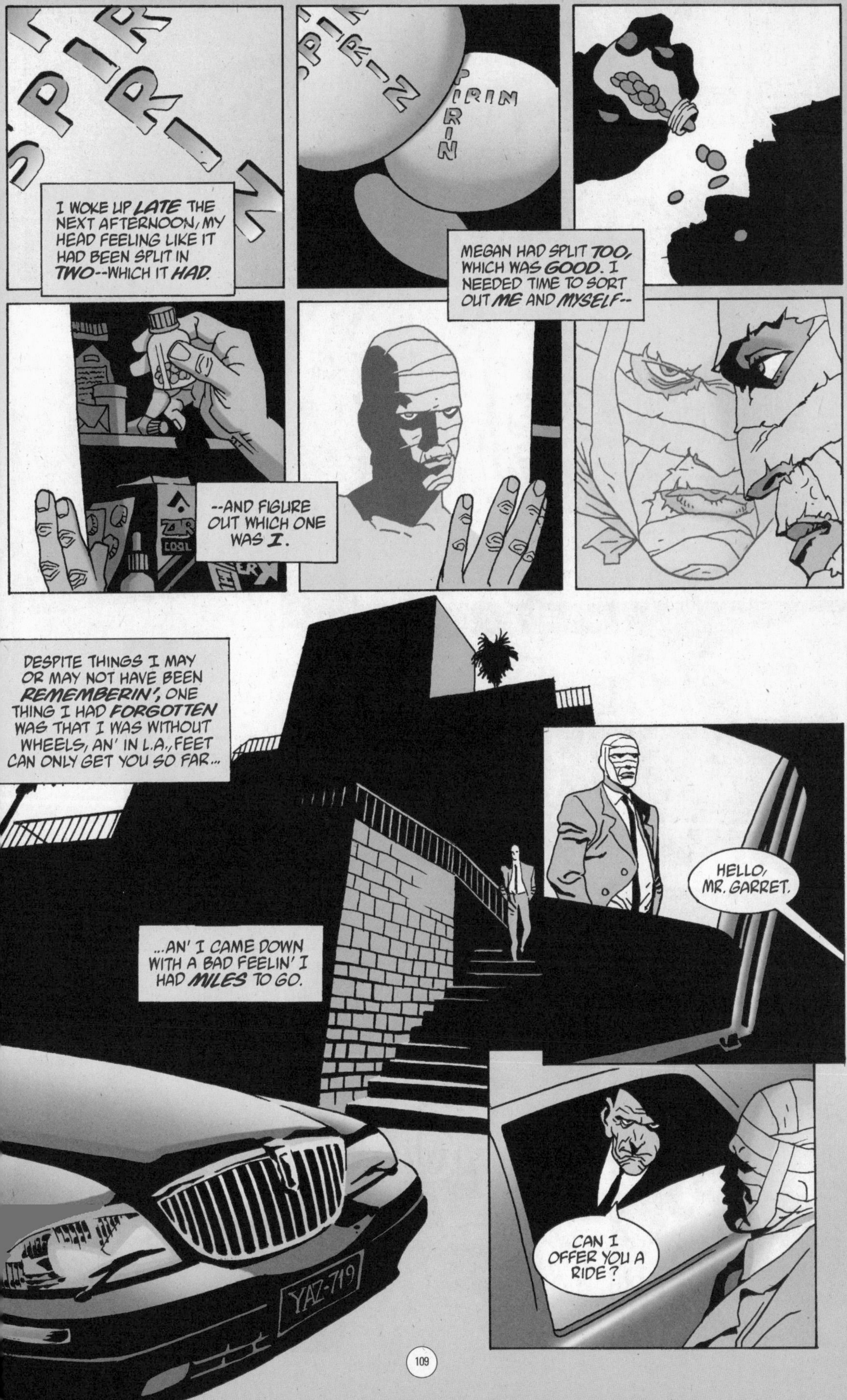
I WOKE UP LATE THE NEXT AFTERNOON, MY HEAD FEELING LIKE IT HAD BEEN SPLIT IN TWO--WHICH IT HAD.
MEGAN HAD SPLIT TOO, WHICH WAS GOOD. I NEEDED TIME TO SORT OUT ME AND MYSELF--
--AND FIGURE OUT WHICH ONE WAS I.
DESPITE THINGS I MAY OR MAY NOT HAVE BEEN REMEMBERIN', ONE THING I HAD FORGOTTEN WAS THAT I WAS WITHOUT WHEELS, AN' IN L.A., FEET CAN ONLY GET YOU SO FAR...
...AN' I CAME DOWN WITH A BAD FEELIN' I HAD MILES TO GO.
HELLO, MR. GARRET.
CAN I OFFER YOU A RIDE?
YAZ-719

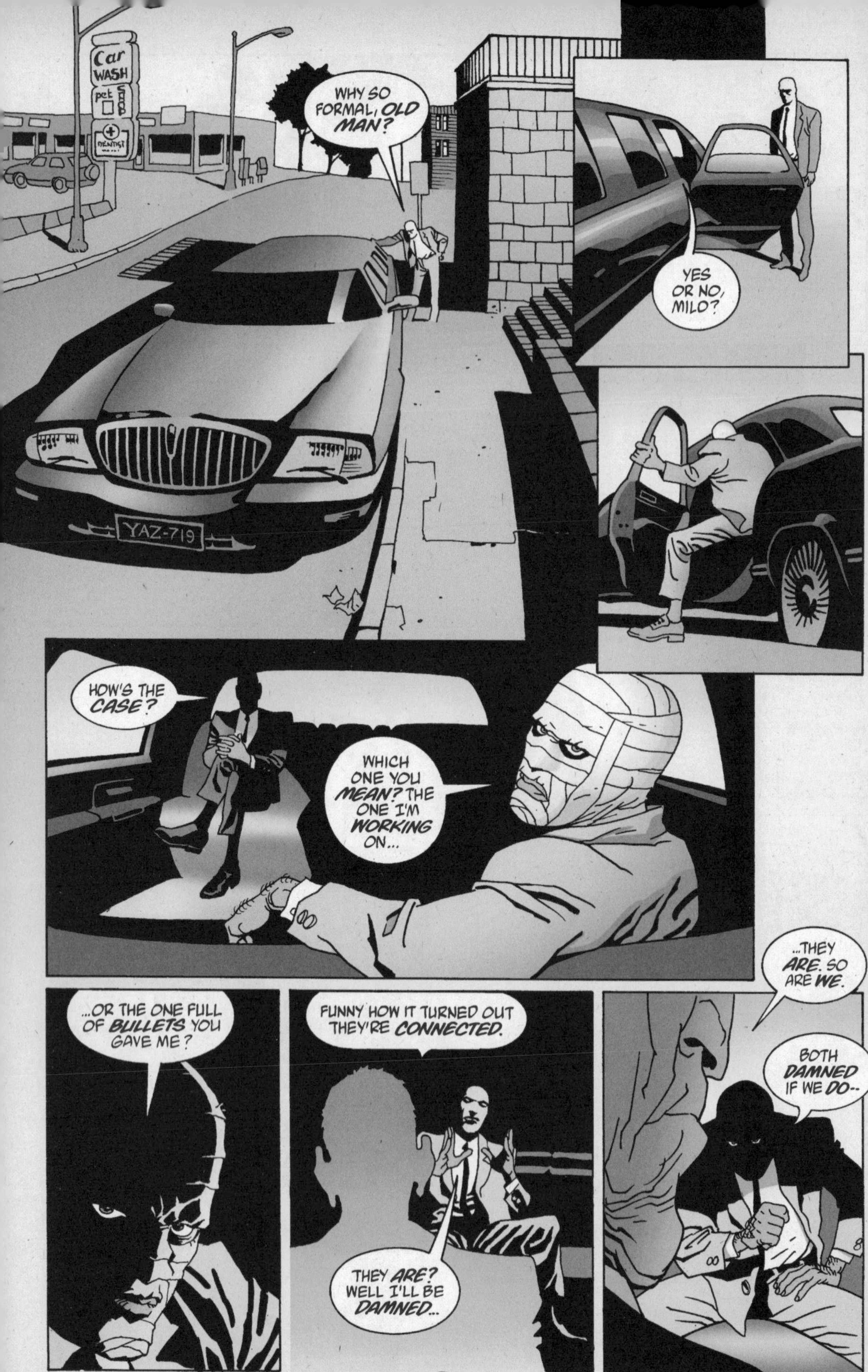

Car WASH
pet shop
DENTIST
WHY SO FORMAL, OLD MAN?
YAZ-719
YES OR NO, MILO?
HOW'S THE CASE?
WHICH ONE YOU MEAN? THE ONE I'M WORKING ON...
...OR THE ONE FULL OF BULLETS YOU GAVE ME?
FUNNY HOW IT TURNED OUT THEY'RE CONNECTED.
THEY ARE? WELL I'LL BE DAMNED...
...THEY ARE. SO ARE WE.
BOTH DAMNED IF WE DO--

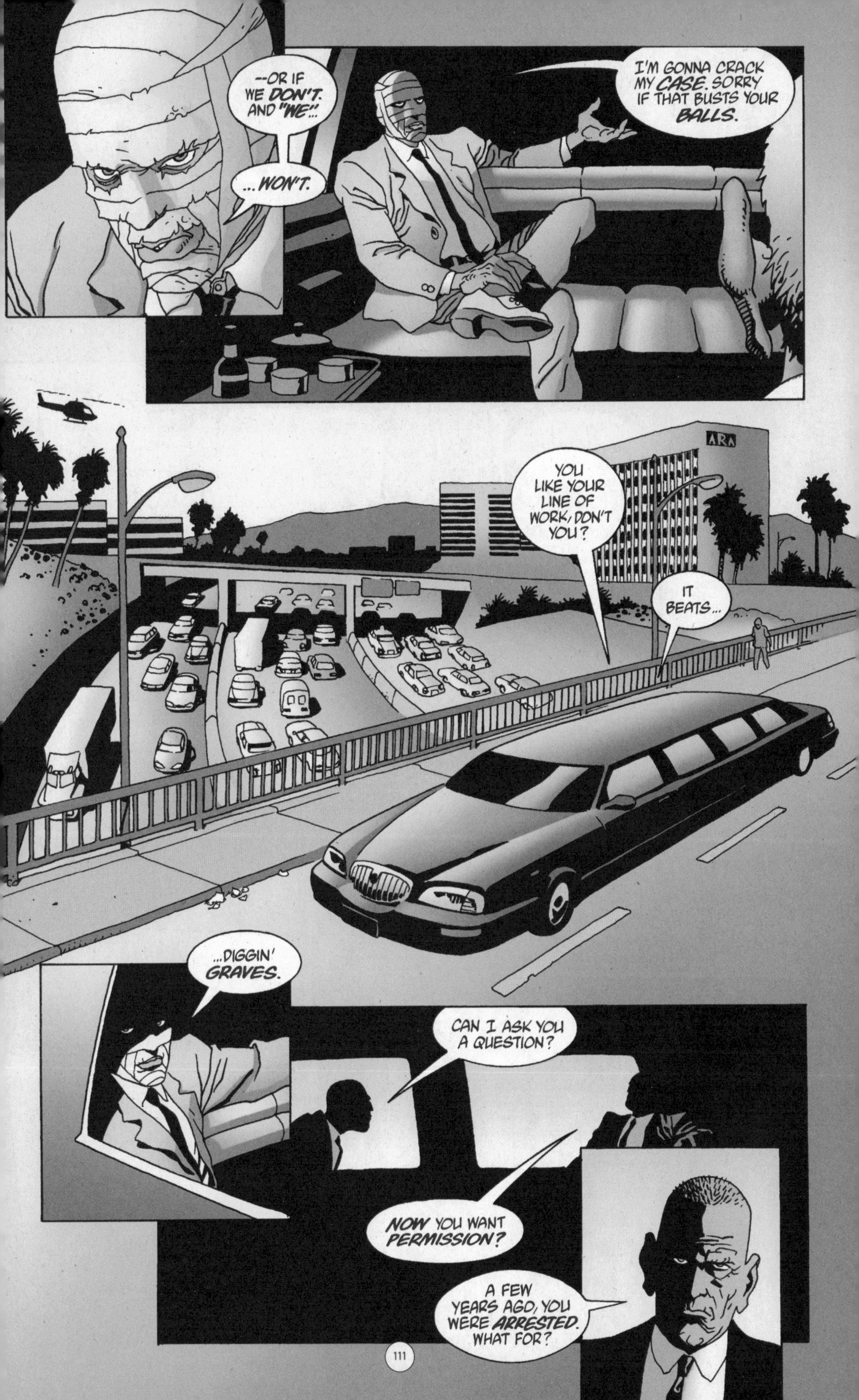
--OR IF WE DON'T. AND "WE"...
...WON'T.
I'M GONNA CRACK MY CASE. SORRY IF THAT BUSTS YOUR BALLS.
ARA
YOU LIKE YOUR LINE OF WORK, DON'T YOU?
IT BEATS...
...DIGGIN' GRAVES.
CAN I ASK YOU A QUESTION?
NOW YOU WANT PERMISSION?
A FEW YEARS AGO, YOU WERE ARRESTED. WHAT FOR?

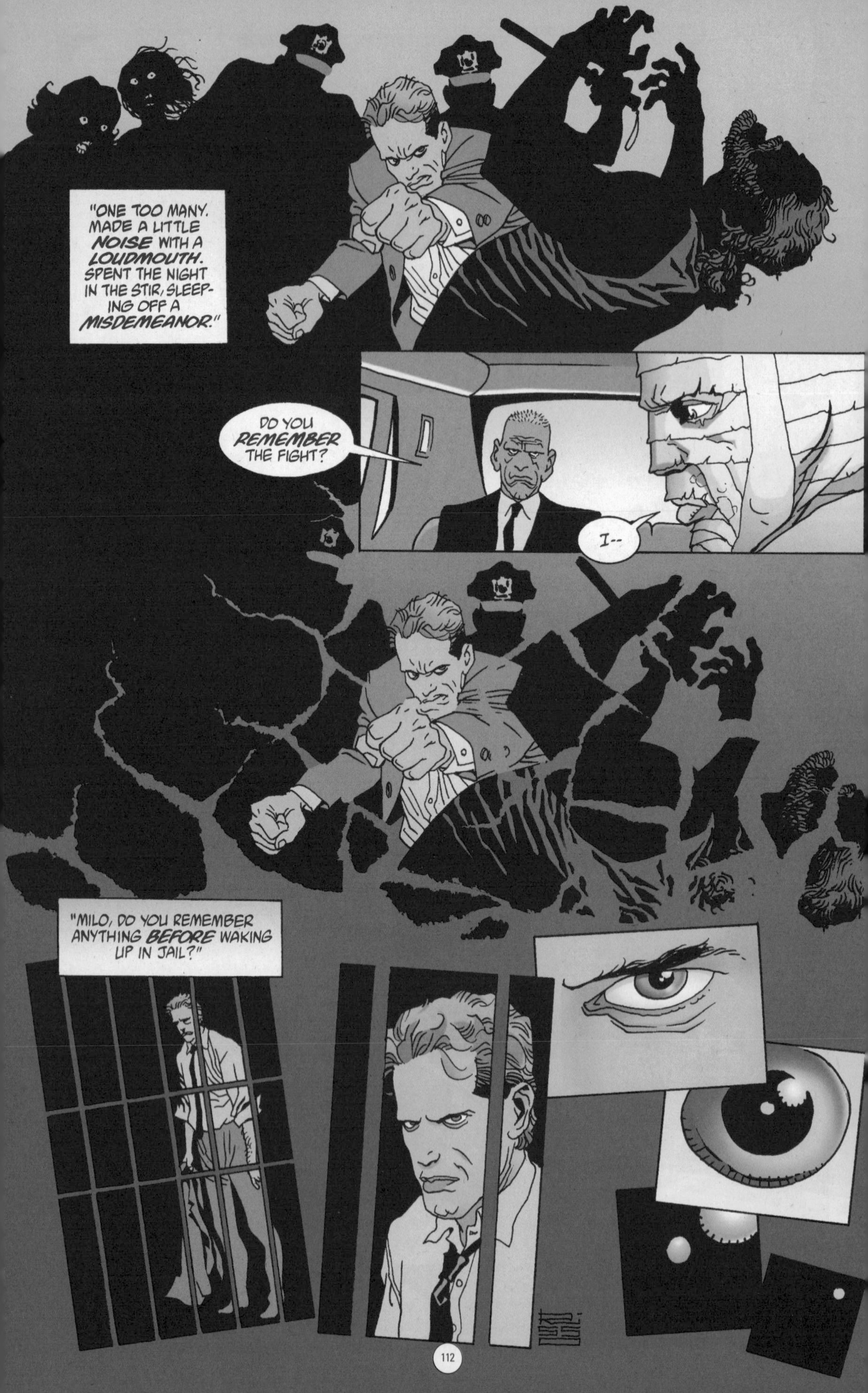
"ONE TOO MANY. MADE A LITTLE NOISE WITH A LOUDMOUTH. SPENT THE NIGHT IN THE STIR, SLEEPING OFF A MISDEMEANOR."
DO YOU REMEMBER THE FIGHT?
I--
"MILO, DO YOU REMEMBER ANYTHING BEFORE WAKING UP IN JAIL?"

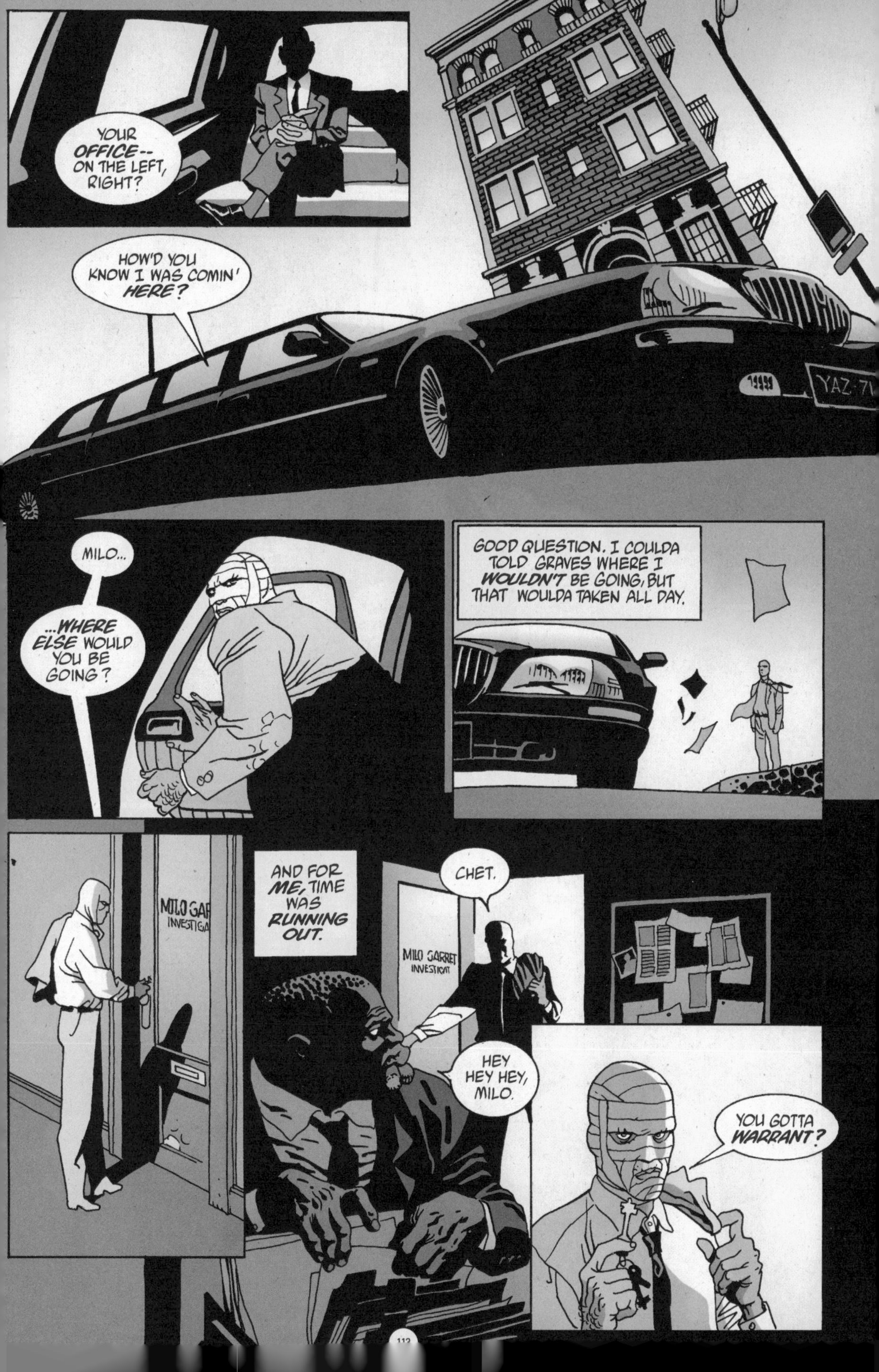
YOUR OFFICE-- ON THE LEFT, RIGHT?
HOW'D YOU KNOW I WAS COMIN' HERE?
YAZ-7
MILO...
...WHERE ELSE WOULD YOU BE GOING?
GOOD QUESTION. I COULDA TOLD GRAVES WHERE I WOULDN'T BE GOING, BUT THAT WOULDA TAKEN ALL DAY.
MILO GARR INVESTIGA
AND FOR ME, TIME WAS RUNNING OUT.
CHET.
MILO GARRET INVESTIGAT
HEY HEY HEY, MILO.
YOU GOTTA WARRANT?

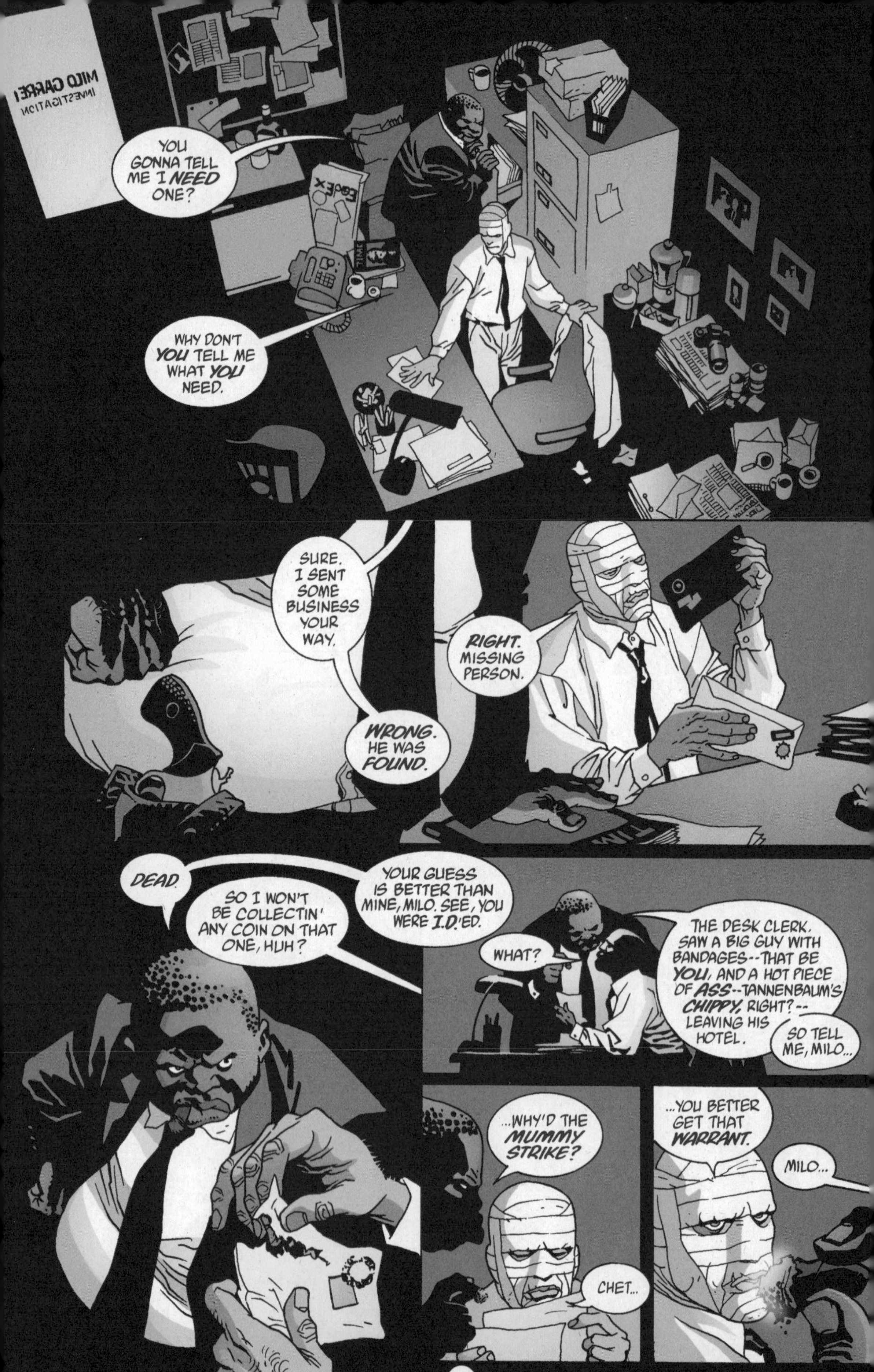
MILO GARRET
INVESTIGATION
YOU GONNA TELL ME I NEED ONE?
WHY DON'T YOU TELL ME WHAT YOU NEED.
SURE. I SENT SOME BUSINESS YOUR WAY.
RIGHT. MISSING PERSON.
WRONG. HE WAS FOUND.
DEAD.
SO I WON'T BE COLLECTIN' ANY COIN ON THAT ONE, HUH?
YOUR GUESS IS BETTER THAN MINE, MILO. SEE, YOU WERE I.D.'ED.
WHAT?
THE DESK CLERK. SAW A BIG GUY WITH BANDAGES--THAT BE YOU, AND A HOT PIECE OF ASS--TANNENBAUM'S CHIPPY, RIGHT?--LEAVING HIS HOTEL.
SO TELL ME, MILO...
...WHY'D THE MUMMY STRIKE?
CHET...
...YOU BETTER GET THAT WARRANT.
MILO...

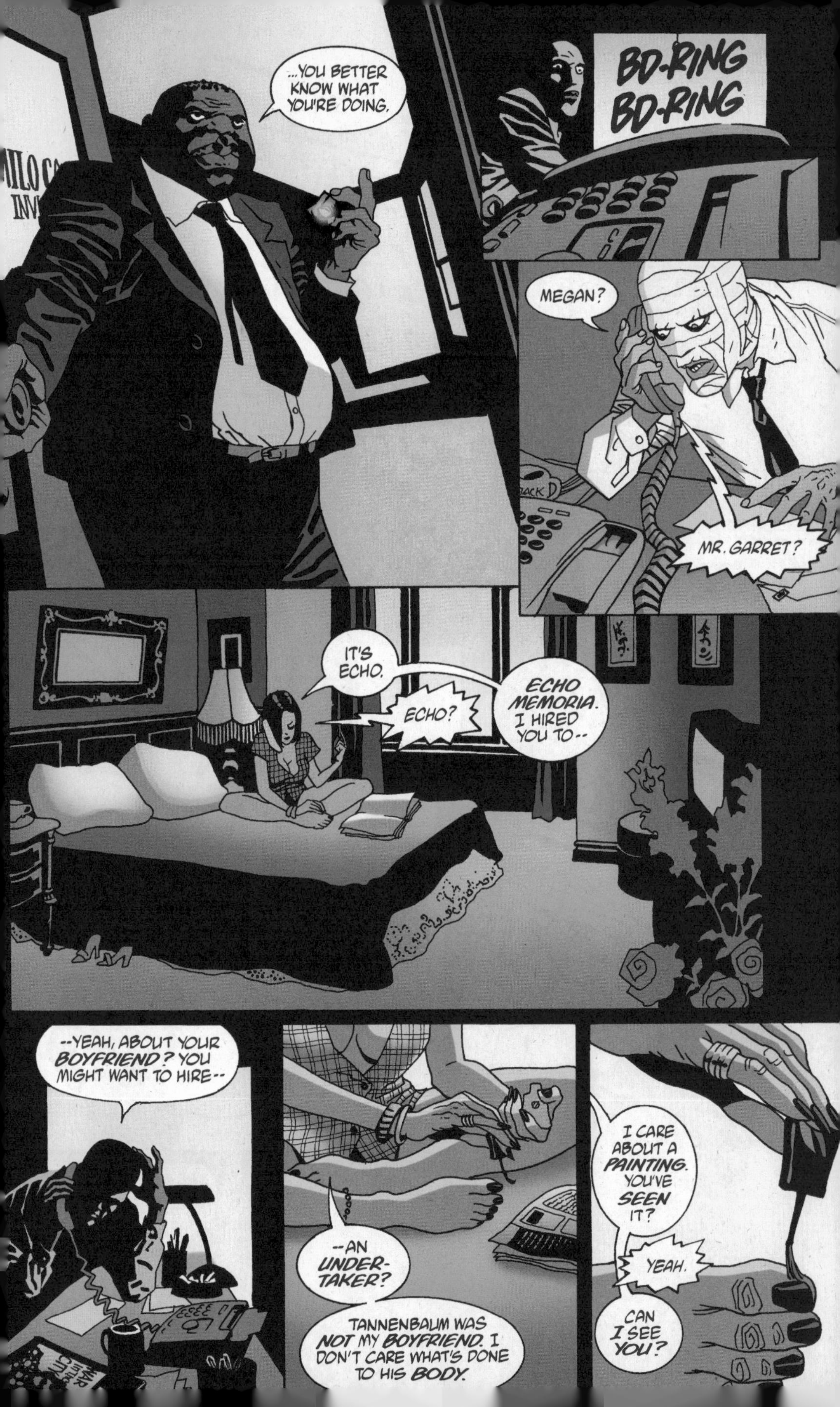
...YOU BETTER KNOW WHAT YOU'RE DOING.
BD-RING BD-RING
MEGAN?
MR. GARRET?
IT'S ECHO.
ECHO?
ECHO MEMORIA. I HIRED YOU TO--
--YEAH, ABOUT YOUR BOYFRIEND? YOU MIGHT WANT TO HIRE--
--AN UNDER-TAKER?
TANNENBAUM WAS NOT MY BOYFRIEND. I DON'T CARE WHAT'S DONE TO HIS BODY.
I CARE ABOUT A PAINTING. YOU'VE SEEN IT?
YEAH.
CAN I SEE YOU?

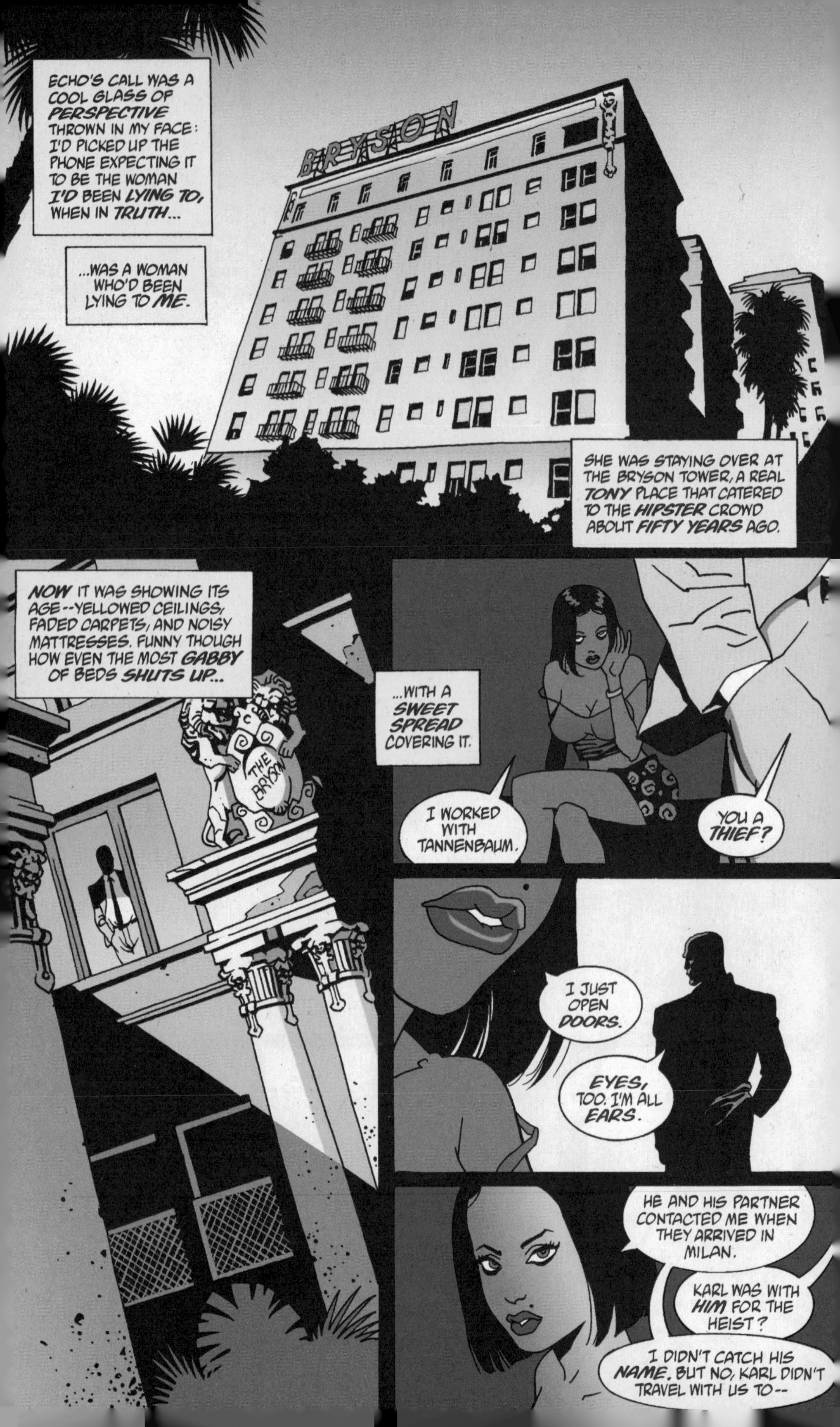
ECHO'S CALL WAS A COOL GLASS OF PERSPECTIVE THROWN IN MY FACE: I'D PICKED UP THE PHONE EXPECTING IT TO BE THE WOMAN I'D BEEN LYING TO, WHEN IN TRUTH...
...WAS A WOMAN WHO'D BEEN LYING TO ME.
BRYSON
SHE WAS STAYING OVER AT THE BRYSON TOWER, A REAL TONY PLACE THAT CATERED TO THE HIPSTER CROWD ABOUT FIFTY YEARS AGO.
NOW IT WAS SHOWING ITS AGE--YELLOWED CEILINGS, FADED CARPETS, AND NOISY MATTRESSES. FUNNY THOUGH HOW EVEN THE MOST GABBY OF BEDS SHUTS UP...
THE BRYSON
...WITH A SWEET SPREAD COVERING IT.
I WORKED WITH TANNENBAUM.
YOU A THIEF?
I JUST OPEN DOORS.
EYES, TOO. I'M ALL EARS.
HE AND HIS PARTNER CONTACTED ME WHEN THEY ARRIVED IN MILAN.
KARL WAS WITH HIM FOR THE HEIST?
I DIDN'T CATCH HIS NAME. BUT NO, KARL DIDN'T TRAVEL WITH US TO--

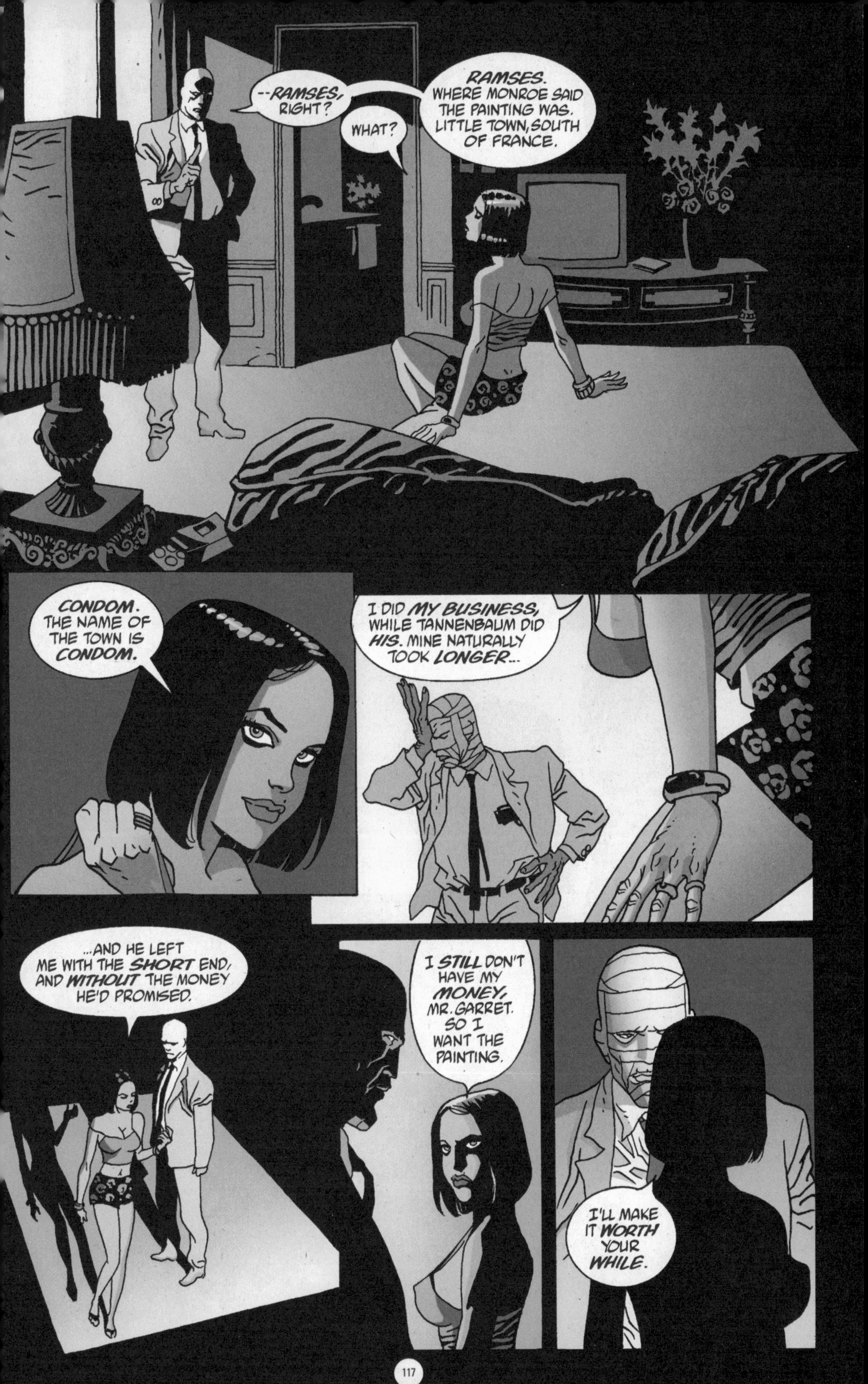
--RAMSES, RIGHT?
RAMSES. WHERE MONROE SAID THE PAINTING WAS. LITTLE TOWN, SOUTH OF FRANCE.
WHAT?
CONDOM. THE NAME OF THE TOWN IS CONDOM.
I DID MY BUSINESS, WHILE TANNENBAUM DID HIS. MINE NATURALLY TOOK LONGER...
...AND HE LEFT ME WITH THE SHORT END, AND WITHOUT THE MONEY HE'D PROMISED.
I STILL DON'T HAVE MY MONEY, MR. GARRET. SO I WANT THE PAINTING.
I'LL MAKE IT WORTH YOUR WHILE.

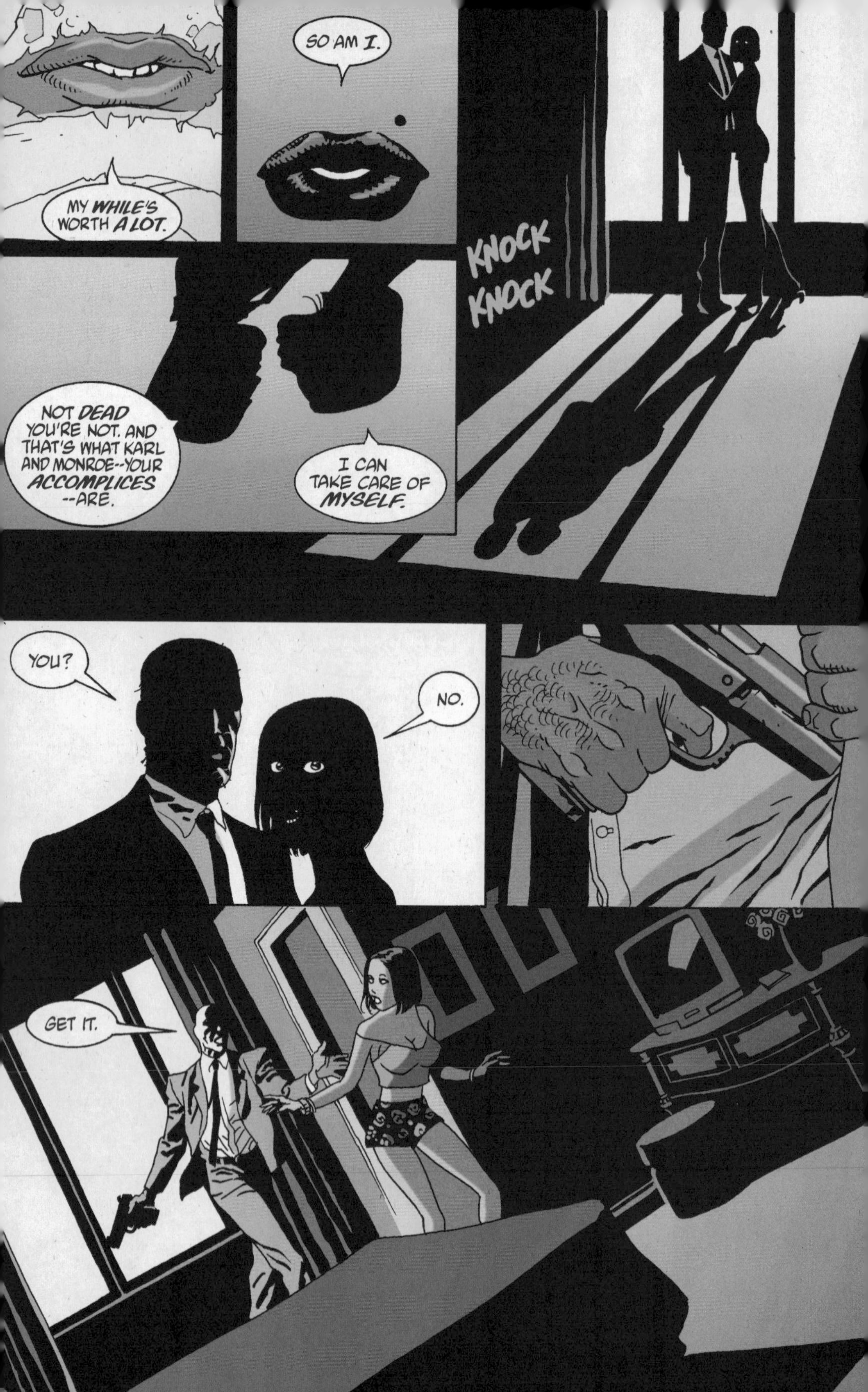
MY WHILE'S WORTH A LOT.
SO AM I.
KNOCK KNOCK
NOT DEAD YOU'RE NOT. AND THAT'S WHAT KARL AND MONROE--YOUR ACCOMPLICES --ARE.
I CAN TAKE CARE OF MYSELF.
YOU?
NO.
GET IT.

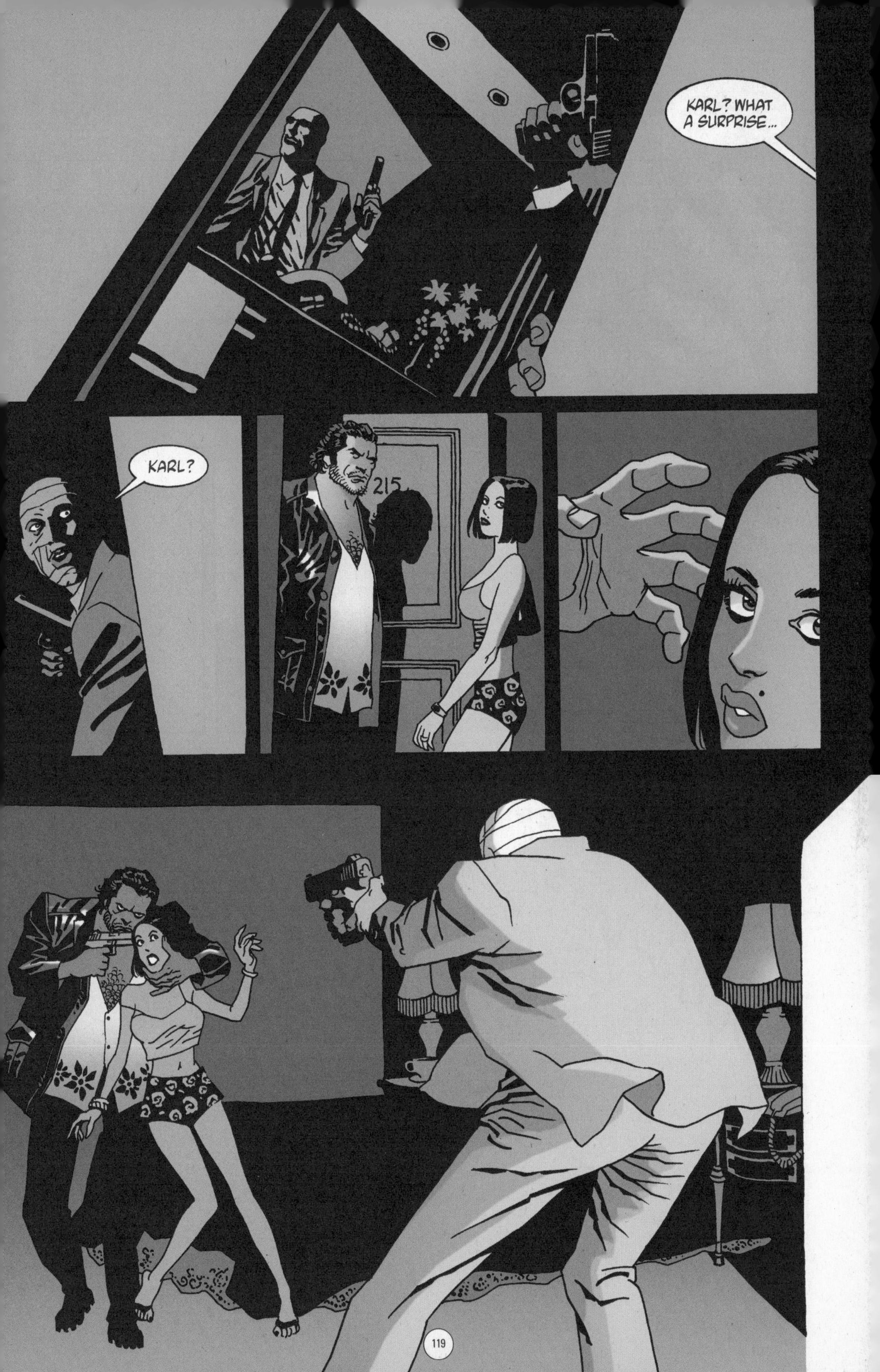
KARL? WHAT A SURPRISE...
KARL?

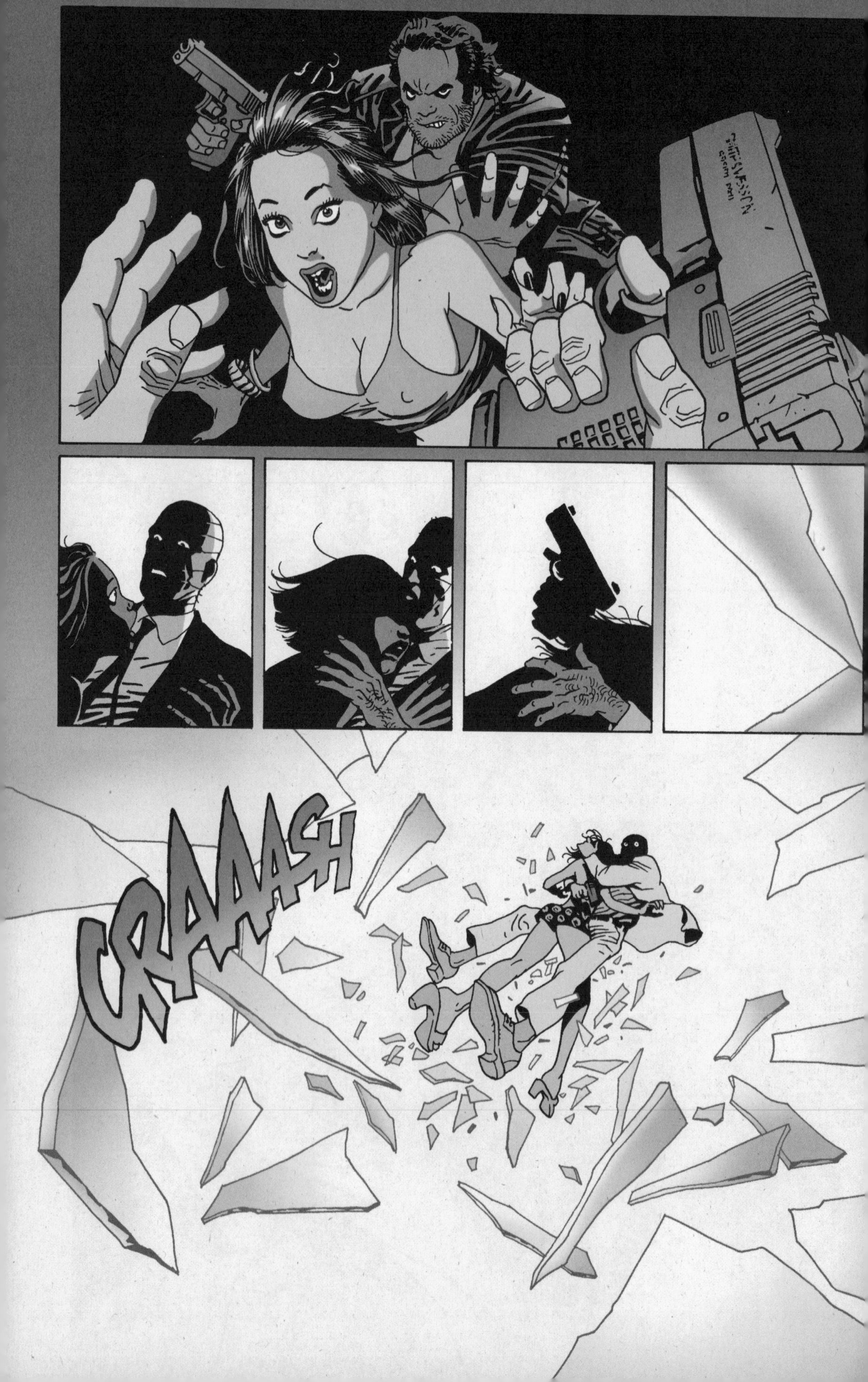
CRAAASH

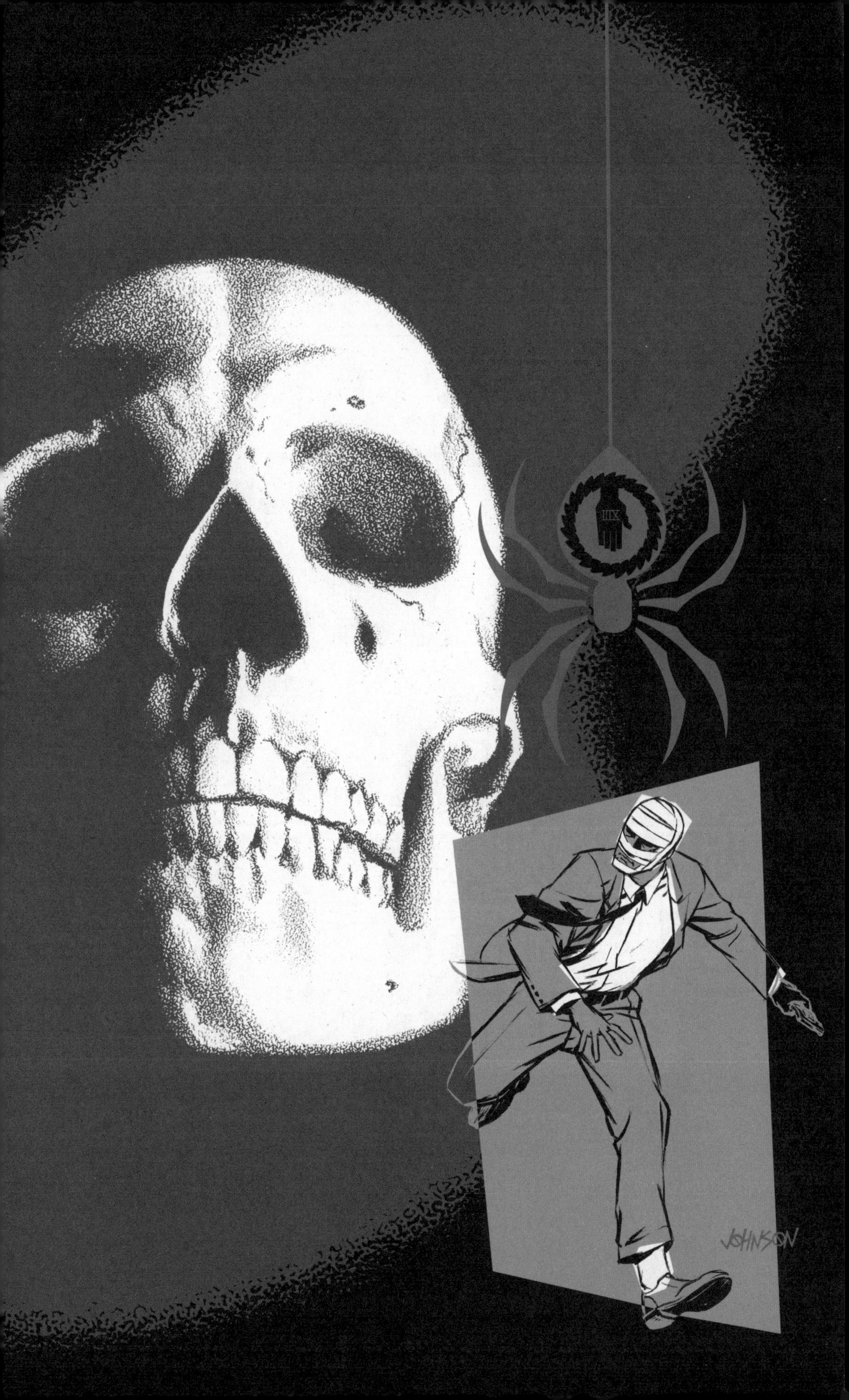
JOHNSON

FRESH, CLEAN SHEETS.

ALONG WITH THE ACHES AN' BRUISES IN ME AN' ON ME, CLEAN SHEETS WAS WHAT I WAS FEELIN' NEXT TO ME.

MEANING I WASN'T ANYWHERE NEAR MY OWN CRIB.

NO, I HAD TAKEN A TWO-STORY TUMBLE OUT A WINDOW AND RIGHT INTO A HOSPITAL BED.

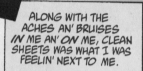

SANTA MONICA MASO HOSPITAL

TWO STORIES. ONE FALL.

MY LIFE.

THE COUNTERFIFTH DETECTIVE
CONCLUSION

BRIAN
AZZARELLO
writer

EDUARDO
RISSO
artist

PATRICIA
MULVIHILL
colorist

CLEM
ROBINS
letterer

DIGITAL
CHAMELEON
separations

DAVE
JOHNSON
cover artist

ZACHARY
RAU
ass't ed.

WILL
DENNIS
editor

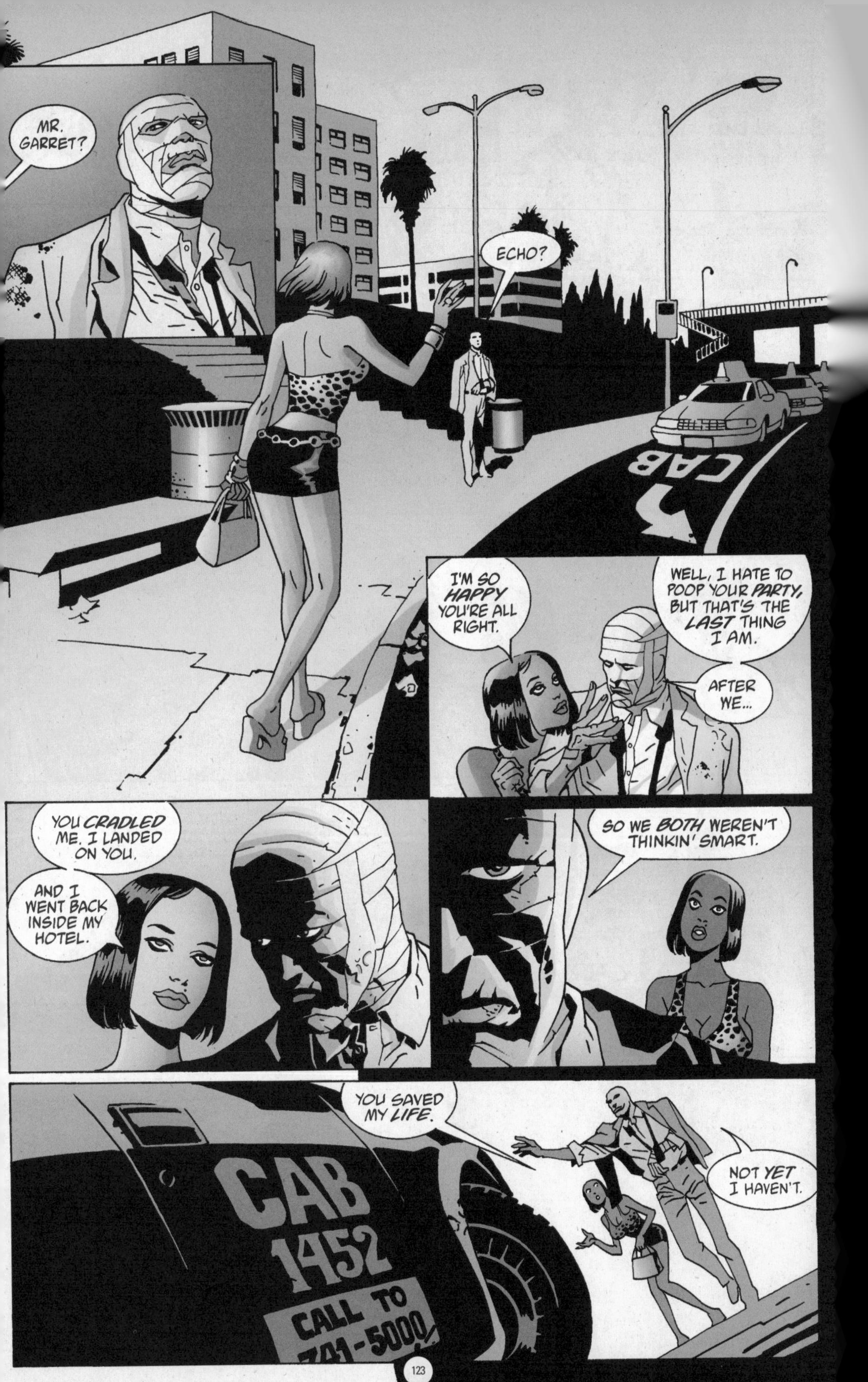
MR. GARRET?
ECHO?
I'M SO HAPPY YOU'RE ALL RIGHT.
WELL, I HATE TO POOP YOUR PARTY, BUT THAT'S THE LAST THING I AM.
AFTER WE...
YOU CRADLED ME. I LANDED ON YOU.
AND I WENT BACK INSIDE MY HOTEL.
SO WE BOTH WEREN'T THINKIN' SMART.
CAB
CAB 1452
CALL TO 741-5000
YOU SAVED MY LIFE.
NOT YET I HAVEN'T.

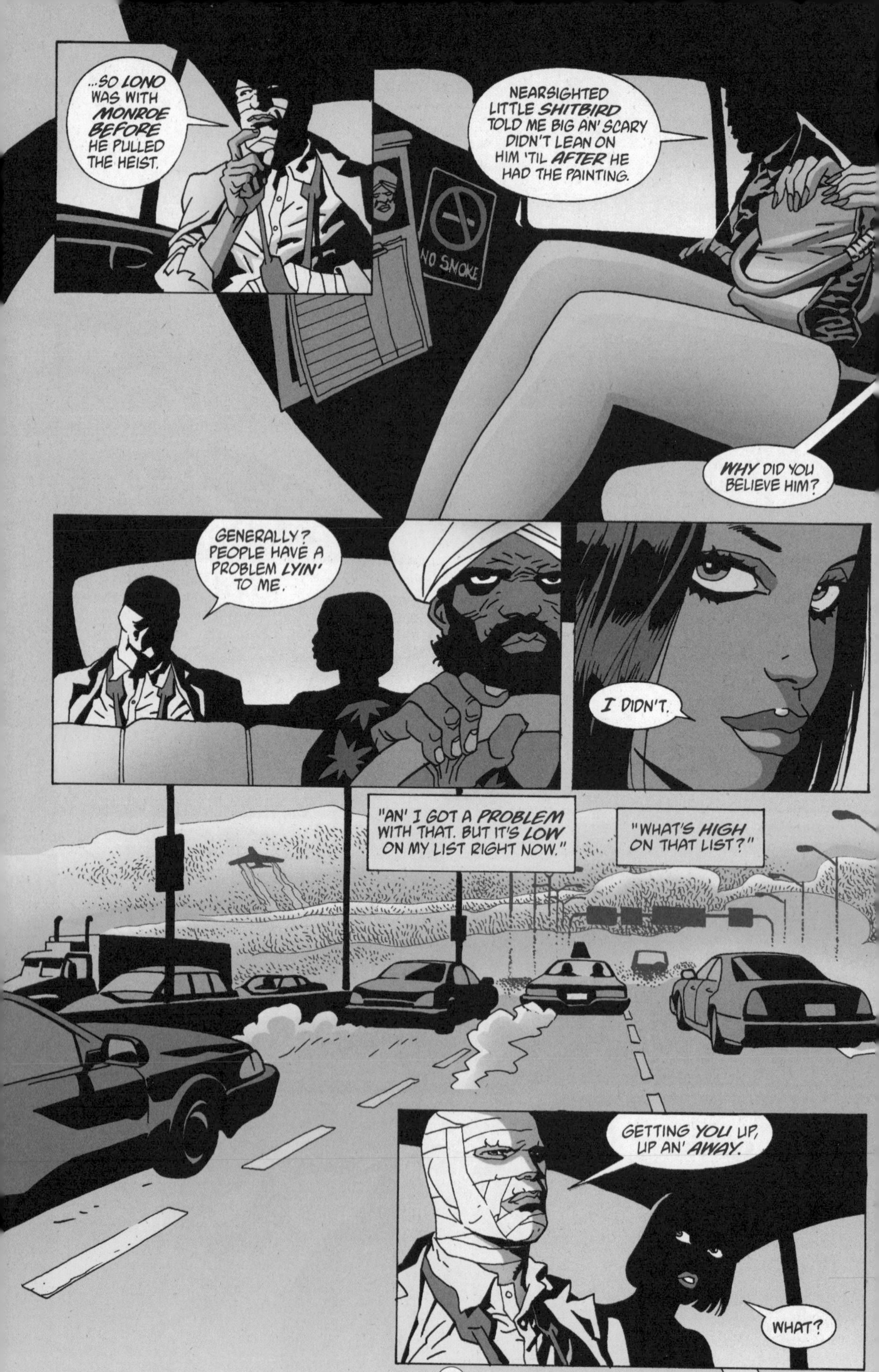
...SO LONO WAS WITH MONROE BEFORE HE PULLED THE HEIST.
NEARSIGHTED LITTLE SHITBIRD TOLD ME BIG AN' SCARY DIDN'T LEAN ON HIM 'TIL AFTER HE HAD THE PAINTING.
NO SMOKE
WHY DID YOU BELIEVE HIM?
GENERALLY? PEOPLE HAVE A PROBLEM LYIN' TO ME.
I DIDN'T.
"AN' I GOT A PROBLEM WITH THAT. BUT IT'S LOW ON MY LIST RIGHT NOW."
"WHAT'S HIGH ON THAT LIST?"
GETTING YOU UP, UP AN' AWAY.
WHAT?

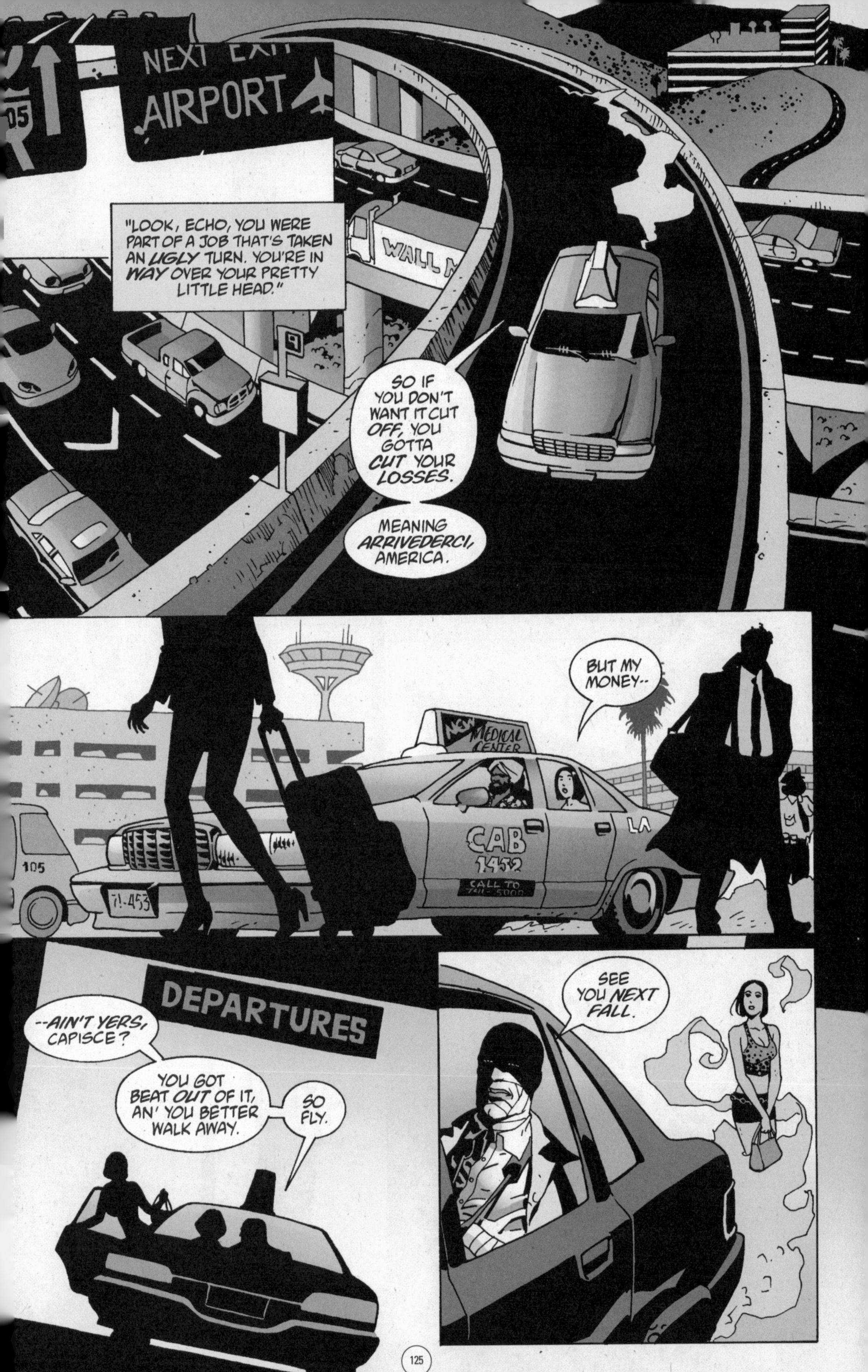
NEXT EXIT
AIRPORT
105
"LOOK, ECHO, YOU WERE PART OF A JOB THAT'S TAKEN AN UGLY TURN. YOU'RE IN WAY OVER YOUR PRETTY LITTLE HEAD."
WALL M
SO IF YOU DON'T WANT IT CUT OFF, YOU GOTTA CUT YOUR LOSSES.
MEANING ARRIVEDERCI, AMERICA.
BUT MY MONEY--
NEW MEDICAL CENTER
CAB 1452
CALL TO
LA
105
DEPARTURES
--AIN'T YERS, CAPISCE?
YOU GOT BEAT OUT OF IT, AN' YOU BETTER WALK AWAY.
SO FLY.
SEE YOU NEXT FALL.

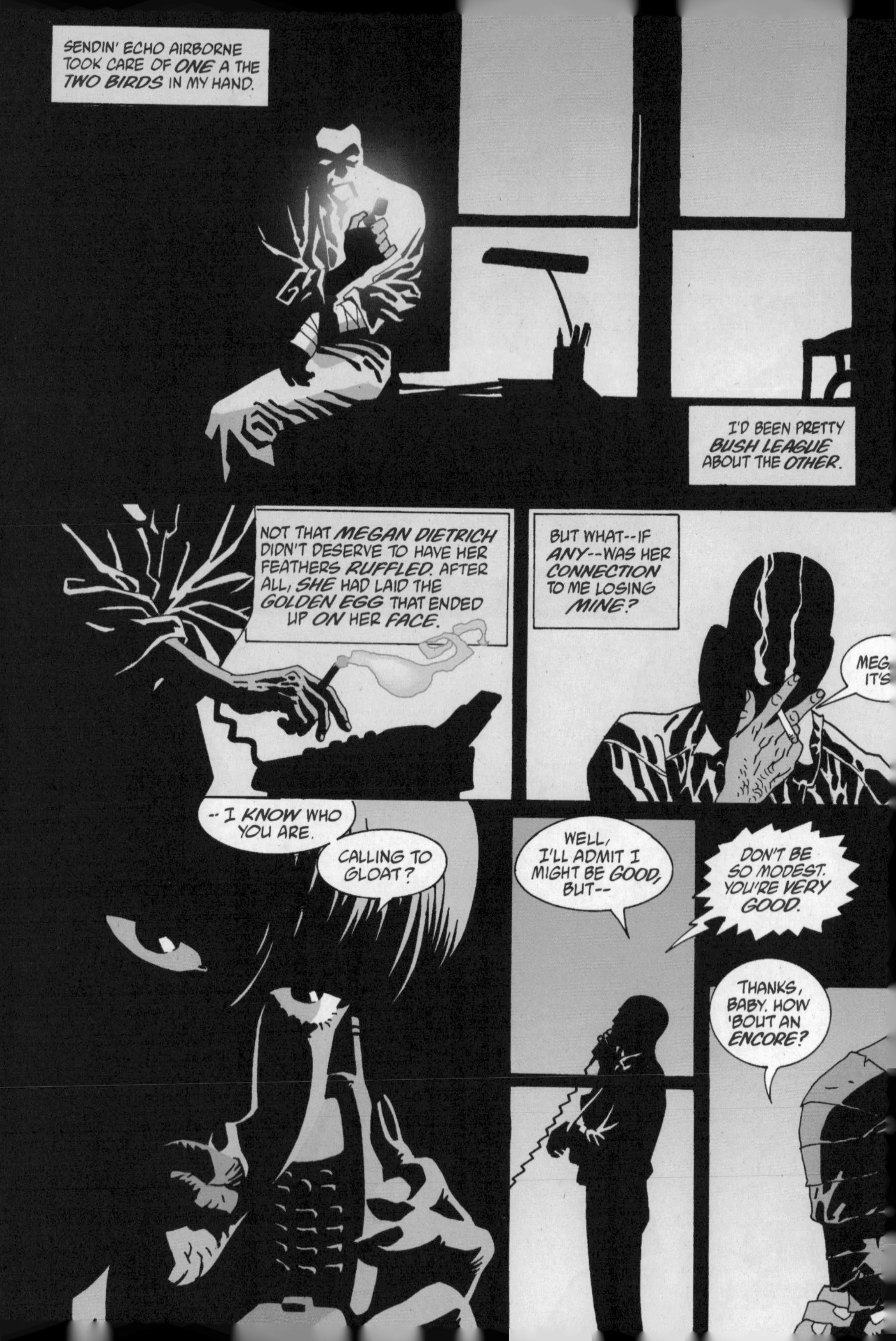
SENDIN' ECHO AIRBORNE TOOK CARE OF ONE A THE TWO BIRDS IN MY HAND.
I'D BEEN PRETTY BUSH LEAGUE ABOUT THE OTHER.
NOT THAT MEGAN DIETRICH DIDN'T DESERVE TO HAVE HER FEATHERS RUFFLED. AFTER ALL, SHE HAD LAID THE GOLDEN EGG THAT ENDED UP ON HER FACE.
BUT WHAT--IF ANY--WAS HER CONNECTION TO ME LOSING MINE?
-- I KNOW WHO YOU ARE.
CALLING TO GLOAT?
WELL, I'LL ADMIT I MIGHT BE GOOD, BUT--
DON'T BE SO MODEST. YOU'RE VERY GOOD.
THANKS, BABY. HOW 'BOUT AN ENCORE?

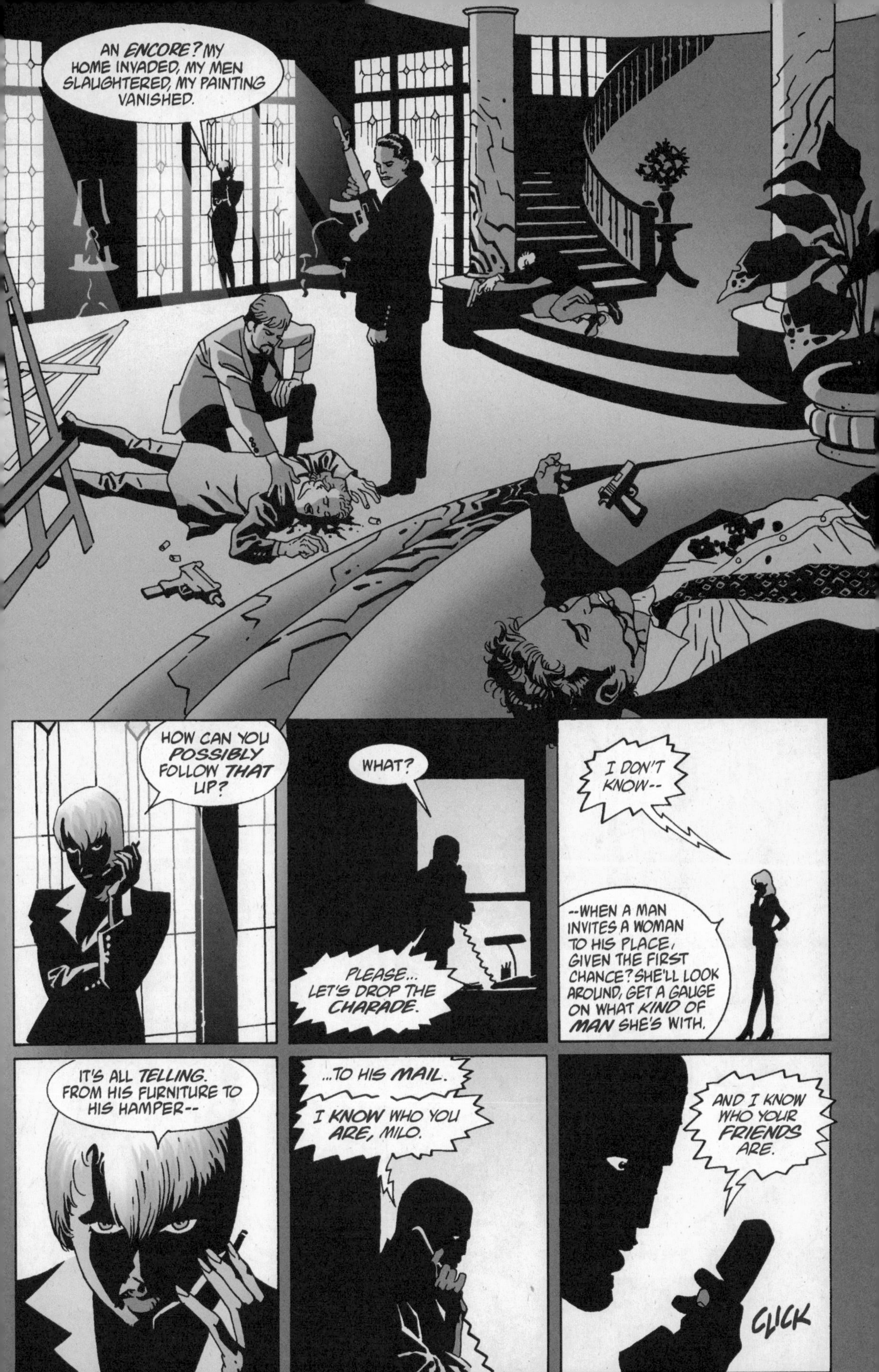
AN ENCORE? MY HOME INVADED, MY MEN SLAUGHTERED, MY PAINTING VANISHED.
HOW CAN YOU POSSIBLY FOLLOW THAT UP?
WHAT?
PLEASE... LET'S DROP THE CHARADE.
I DON'T KNOW--
--WHEN A MAN INVITES A WOMAN TO HIS PLACE, GIVEN THE FIRST CHANCE? SHE'LL LOOK AROUND, GET A GAUGE ON WHAT KIND OF MAN SHE'S WITH.
IT'S ALL TELLING. FROM HIS FURNITURE TO HIS HAMPER--
...TO HIS MAIL.
I KNOW WHO YOU ARE, MILO.
AND I KNOW WHO YOUR FRIENDS ARE.
CLICK

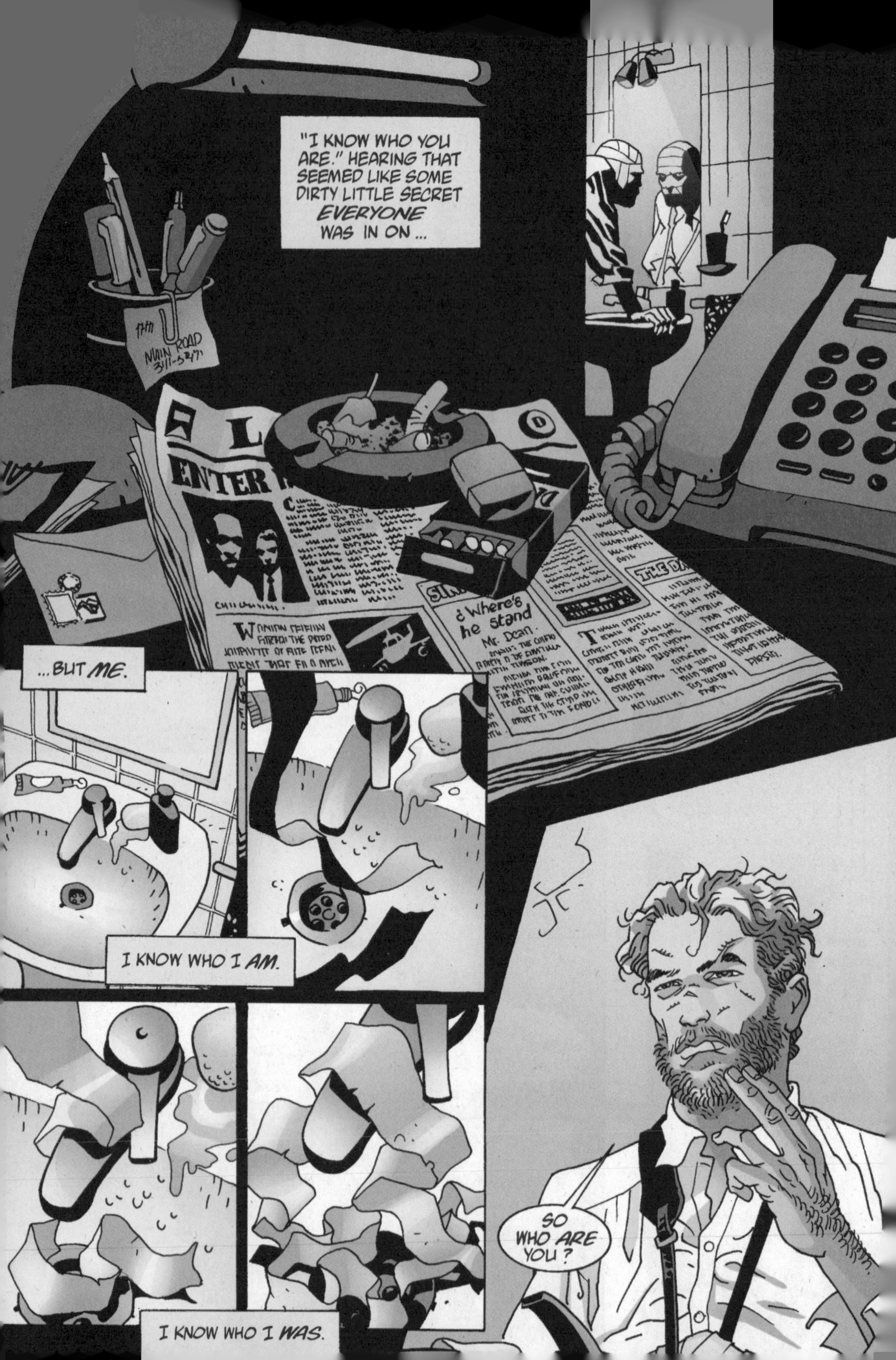
"I KNOW WHO YOU ARE." HEARING THAT SEEMED LIKE SOME DIRTY LITTLE SECRET EVERYONE WAS IN ON...
...BUT ME.
I KNOW WHO I AM.
I KNOW WHO I WAS.
SO WHO ARE YOU?

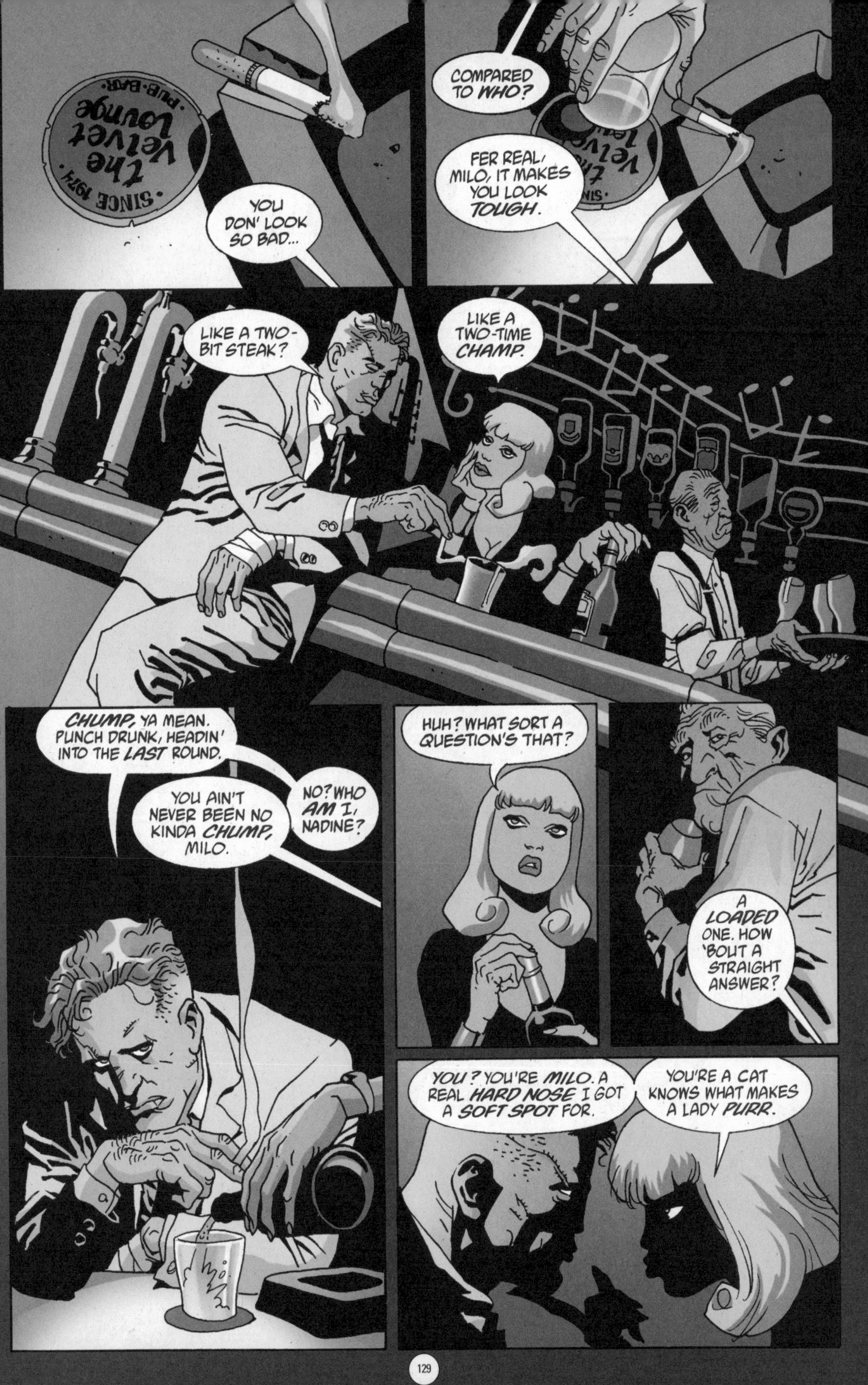
SINCE 1974
the velvet lounge
PUB·BAR
YOU DON' LOOK SO BAD...
COMPARED TO WHO?
FER REAL, MILO, IT MAKES YOU LOOK TOUGH.
LIKE A TWO-BIT STEAK?
LIKE A TWO-TIME CHAMP.
CHUMP, YA MEAN. PUNCH DRUNK, HEADIN' INTO THE LAST ROUND.
YOU AIN'T NEVER BEEN NO KINDA CHUMP, MILO.
NO? WHO AM I, NADINE?
HUH? WHAT SORT A QUESTION'S THAT?
A LOADED ONE. HOW 'BOUT A STRAIGHT ANSWER?
YOU? YOU'RE MILO. A REAL HARD NOSE I GOT A SOFT SPOT FOR.
YOU'RE A CAT KNOWS WHAT MAKES A LADY PURR.

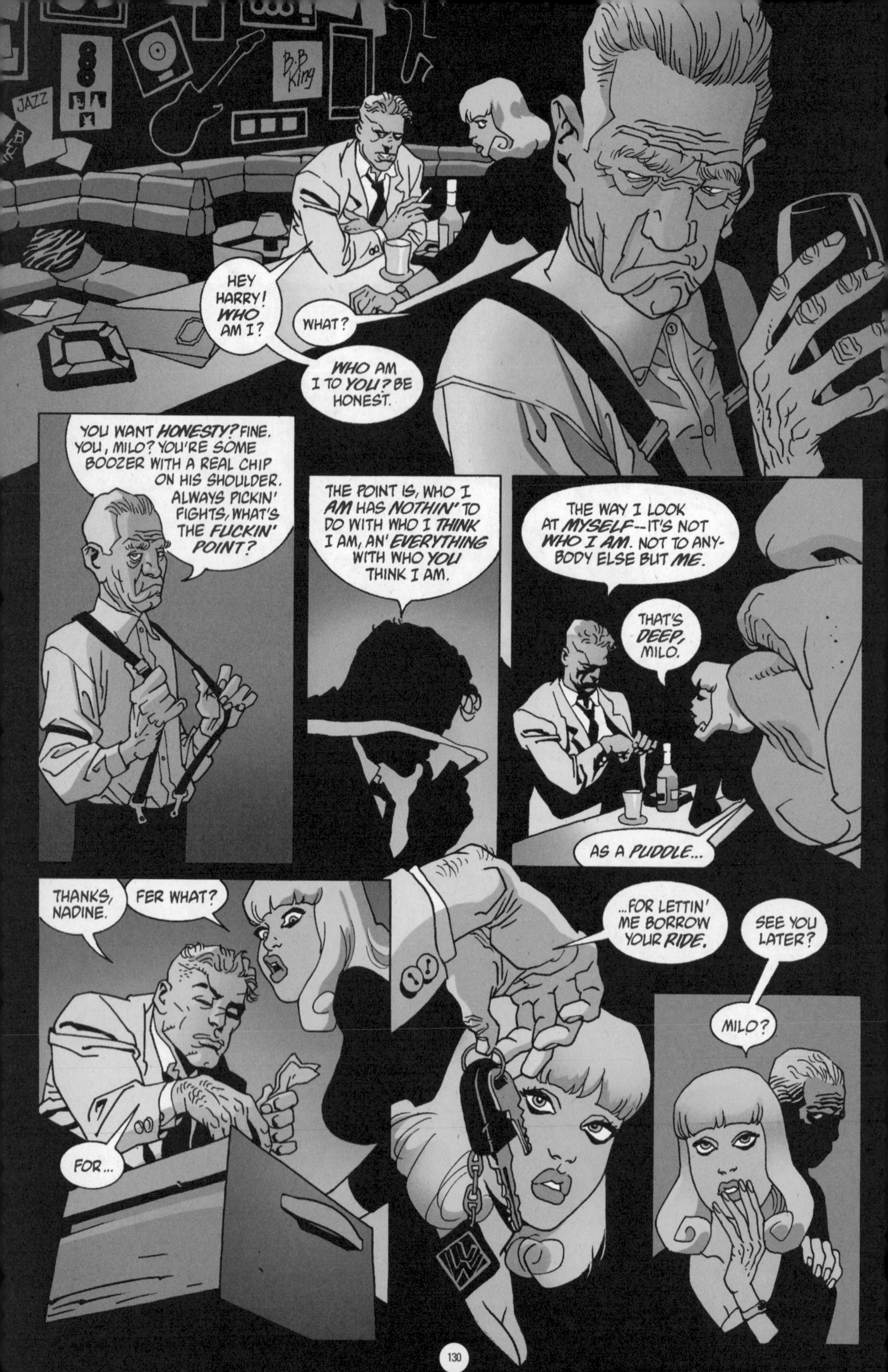
B.B King
JAZZ
HEY HARRY! WHO AM I?
WHAT?
WHO AM I TO YOU? BE HONEST.
YOU WANT HONESTY? FINE. YOU, MILO? YOU'RE SOME BOOZER WITH A REAL CHIP ON HIS SHOULDER. ALWAYS PICKIN' FIGHTS, WHAT'S THE FUCKIN' POINT?
THE POINT IS, WHO I AM HAS NOTHIN' TO DO WITH WHO I THINK I AM, AN' EVERYTHING WITH WHO YOU THINK I AM.
THE WAY I LOOK AT MYSELF--IT'S NOT WHO I AM. NOT TO ANY-BODY ELSE BUT ME.
THAT'S DEEP, MILO.
AS A PUDDLE...
THANKS, NADINE.
FER WHAT?
FOR...
...FOR LETTIN' ME BORROW YOUR RIDE.
SEE YOU LATER?
MILO?

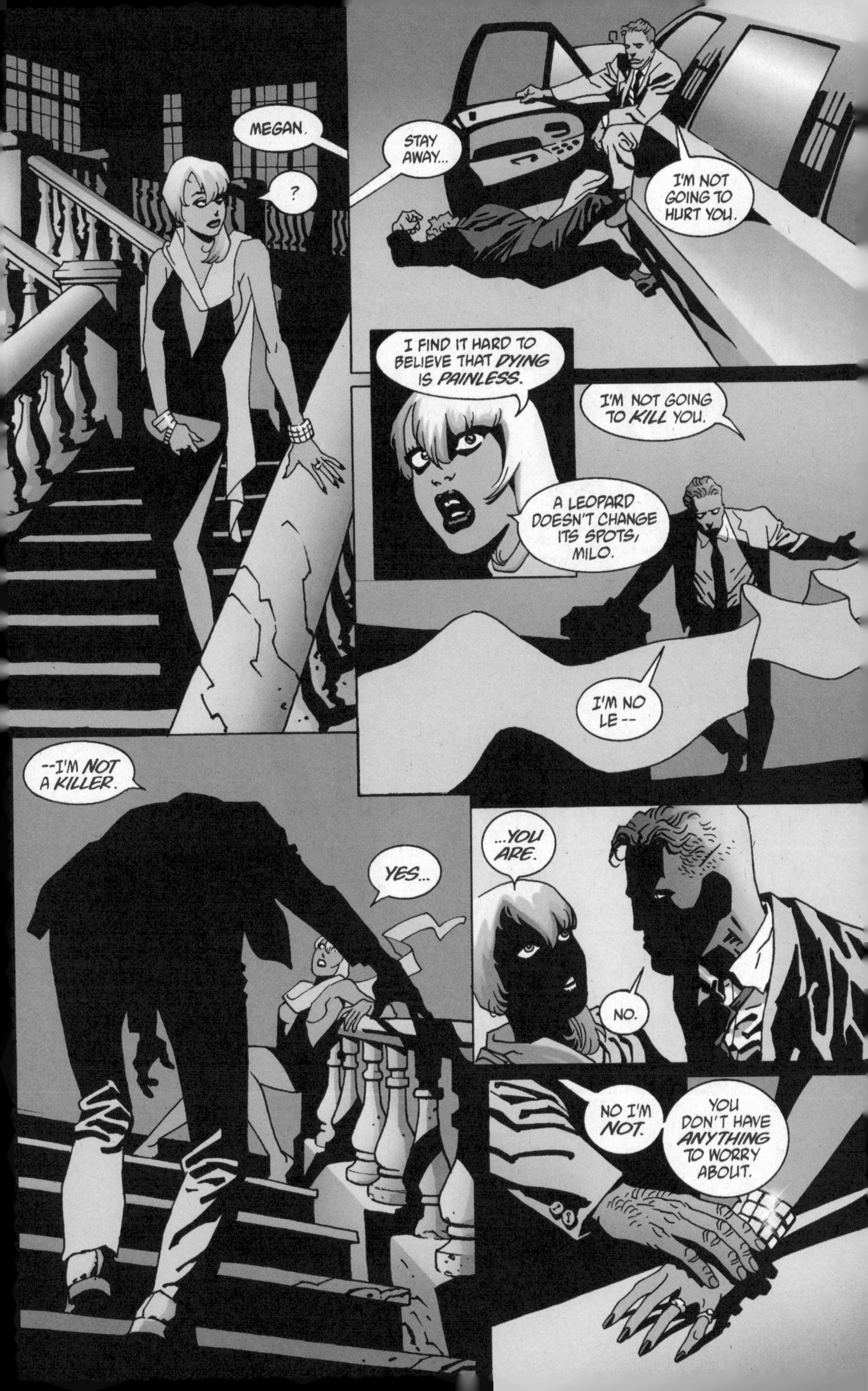
MEGAN.
?
STAY AWAY...
I'M NOT GOING TO HURT YOU.
I FIND IT HARD TO BELIEVE THAT DYING IS PAINLESS.
I'M NOT GOING TO KILL YOU.
A LEOPARD DOESN'T CHANGE ITS SPOTS, MILO.
I'M NO LE--
--I'M NOT A KILLER.
YES...
...YOU ARE.
NO.
NO I'M NOT.
YOU DON'T HAVE ANYTHING TO WORRY ABOUT.

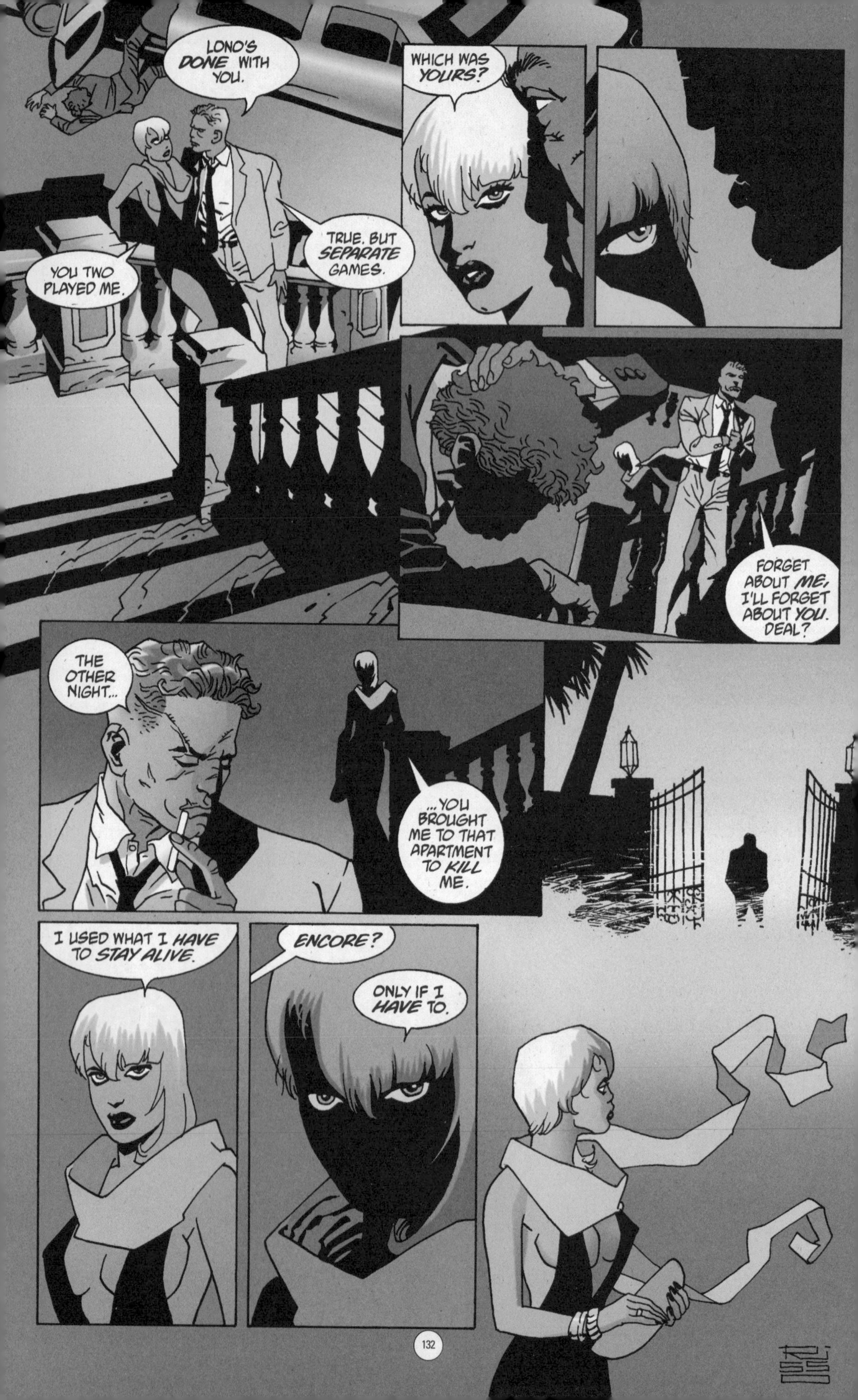
LONO'S DONE WITH YOU.
YOU TWO PLAYED ME.
TRUE. BUT SEPARATE GAMES.
WHICH WAS YOURS?
FORGET ABOUT ME, I'LL FORGET ABOUT YOU. DEAL?
THE OTHER NIGHT...
...YOU BROUGHT ME TO THAT APARTMENT TO KILL ME.
I USED WHAT I HAVE TO STAY ALIVE.
ENCORE?
ONLY IF I HAVE TO.

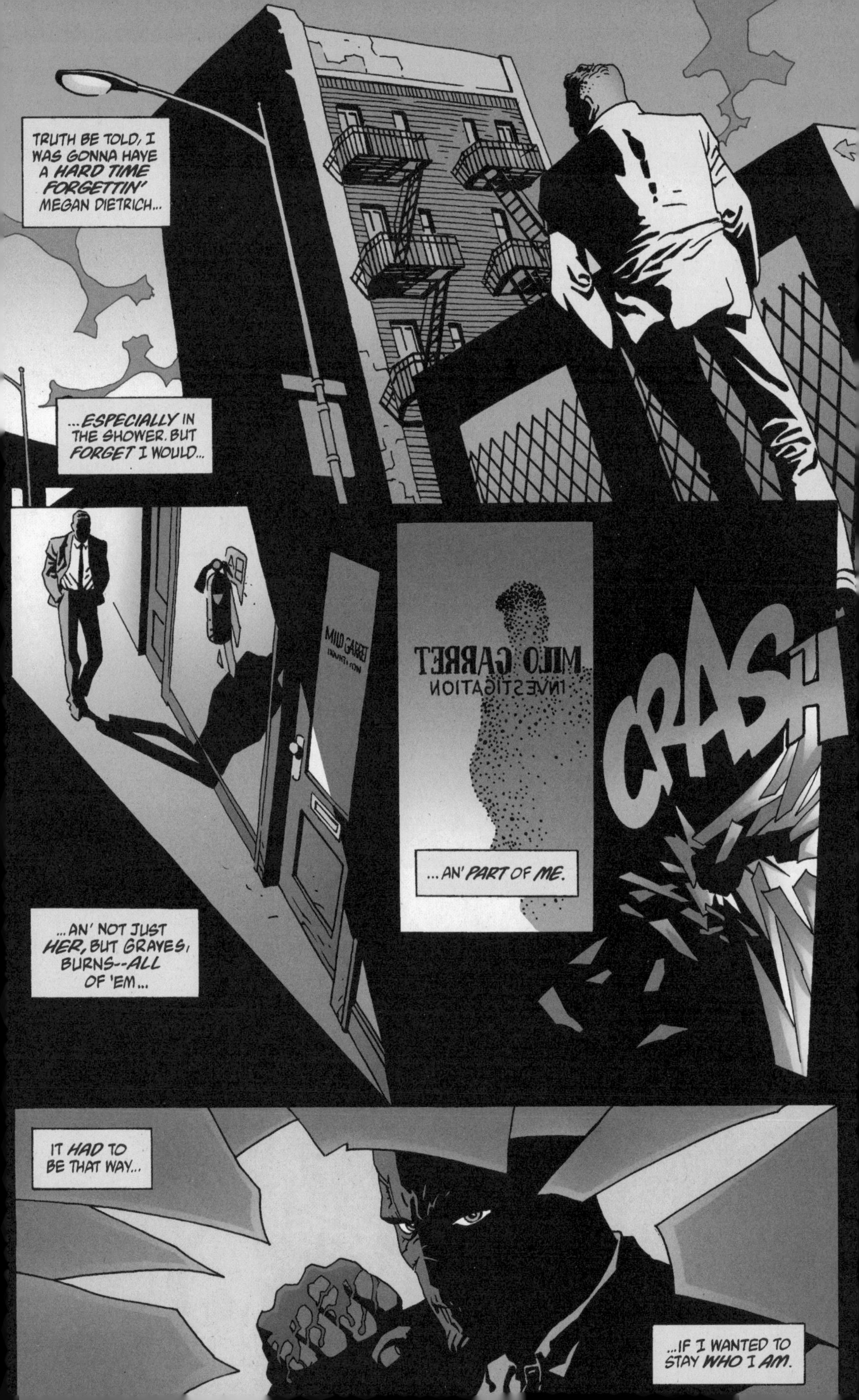
TRUTH BE TOLD, I WAS GONNA HAVE A *HARD TIME FORGETTIN'* MEGAN DIETRICH...
...*ESPECIALLY* IN THE SHOWER. BUT *FORGET* I WOULD...
...AN' NOT JUST *HER,* BUT GRAVES, BURNS--*ALL* OF 'EM...
MILO GARRET INVESTIGATION
...AN' *PART* OF *ME.*
CRASH
IT *HAD* TO BE THAT WAY...
...IF I WANTED TO STAY *WHO I AM.*

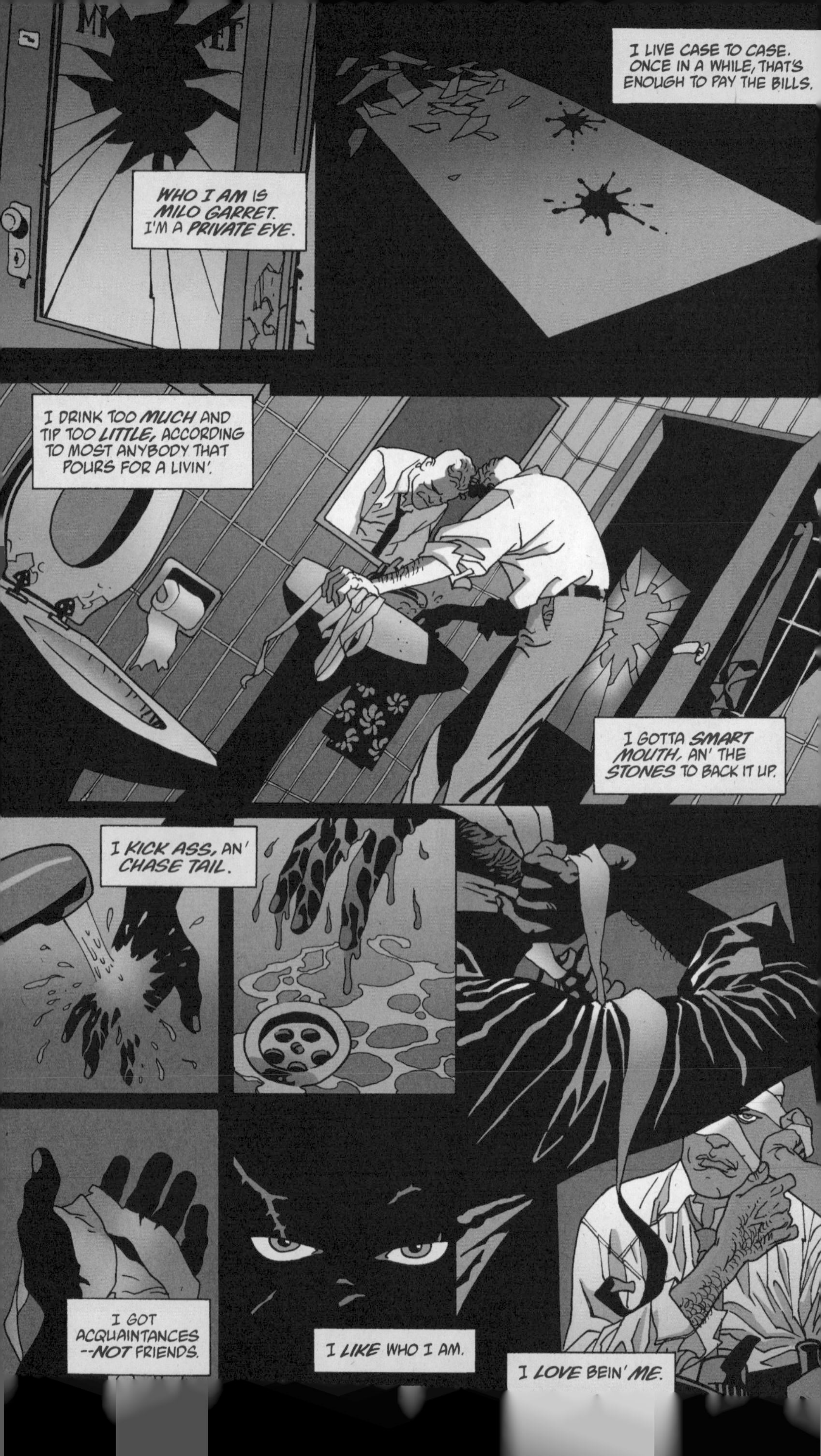

WHO I AM IS MILO GARRET. I'M A PRIVATE EYE.
I LIVE CASE TO CASE. ONCE IN A WHILE, THAT'S ENOUGH TO PAY THE BILLS.
I DRINK TOO MUCH AND TIP TOO LITTLE, ACCORDING TO MOST ANYBODY THAT POURS FOR A LIVIN'.
I GOTTA SMART MOUTH, AN' THE STONES TO BACK IT UP.
I KICK ASS, AN' CHASE TAIL.
I GOT ACQUAINTANCES --NOT FRIENDS.
I LIKE WHO I AM.
I LOVE BEIN' ME.

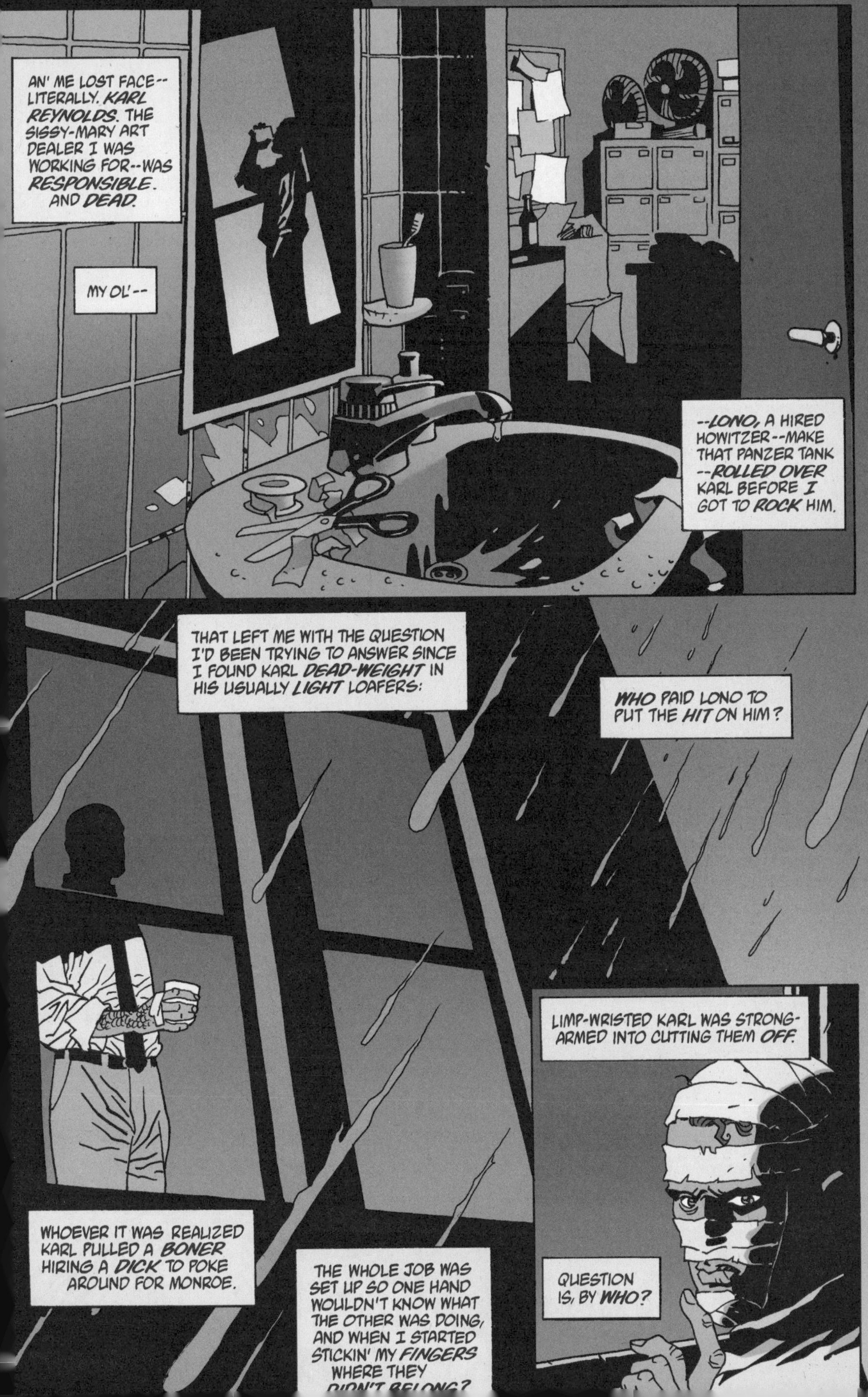
AN' ME LOST FACE-- LITERALLY. KARL REYNOLDS. THE SISSY-MARY ART DEALER I WAS WORKING FOR--WAS RESPONSIBLE. AND DEAD.
MY OL'--
--LONO, A HIRED HOWITZER--MAKE THAT PANZER TANK --ROLLED OVER KARL BEFORE I GOT TO ROCK HIM.
THAT LEFT ME WITH THE QUESTION I'D BEEN TRYING TO ANSWER SINCE I FOUND KARL DEAD-WEIGHT IN HIS USUALLY LIGHT LOAFERS:
WHO PAID LONO TO PUT THE HIT ON HIM?
LIMP-WRISTED KARL WAS STRONG-ARMED INTO CUTTING THEM OFF.
WHOEVER IT WAS REALIZED KARL PULLED A BONER HIRING A DICK TO POKE AROUND FOR MONROE.
THE WHOLE JOB WAS SET UP SO ONE HAND WOULDN'T KNOW WHAT THE OTHER WAS DOING, AND WHEN I STARTED STICKIN' MY FINGERS WHERE THEY
QUESTION IS, BY WHO?

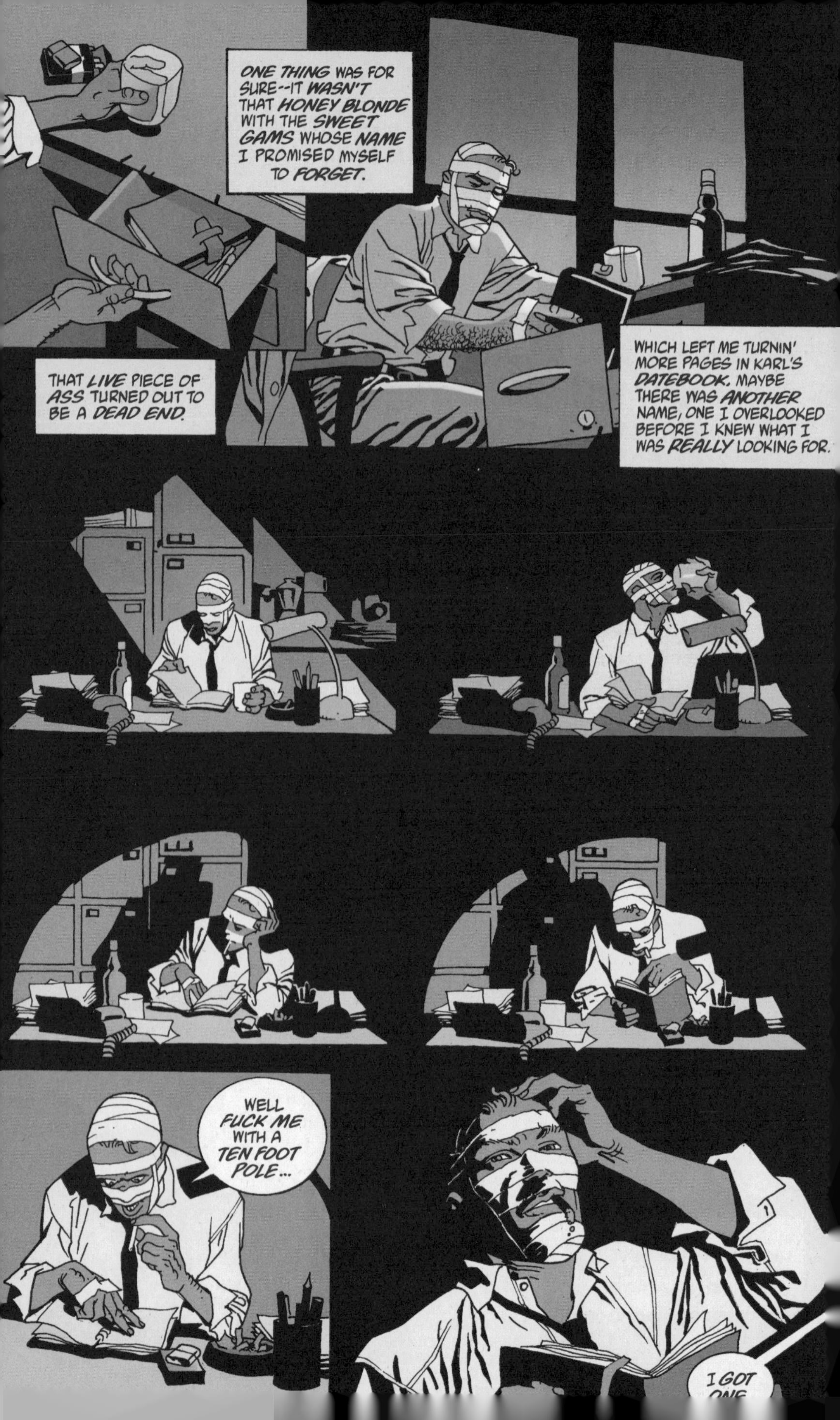
ONE THING WAS FOR SURE--IT WASN'T THAT HONEY BLONDE WITH THE SWEET GAMS WHOSE NAME I PROMISED MYSELF TO FORGET.
THAT LIVE PIECE OF ASS TURNED OUT TO BE A DEAD END.
WHICH LEFT ME TURNIN' MORE PAGES IN KARL'S DATEBOOK. MAYBE THERE WAS ANOTHER NAME, ONE I OVERLOOKED BEFORE I KNEW WHAT I WAS REALLY LOOKING FOR.
WELL FUCK ME WITH A TEN FOOT POLE...
I GOT

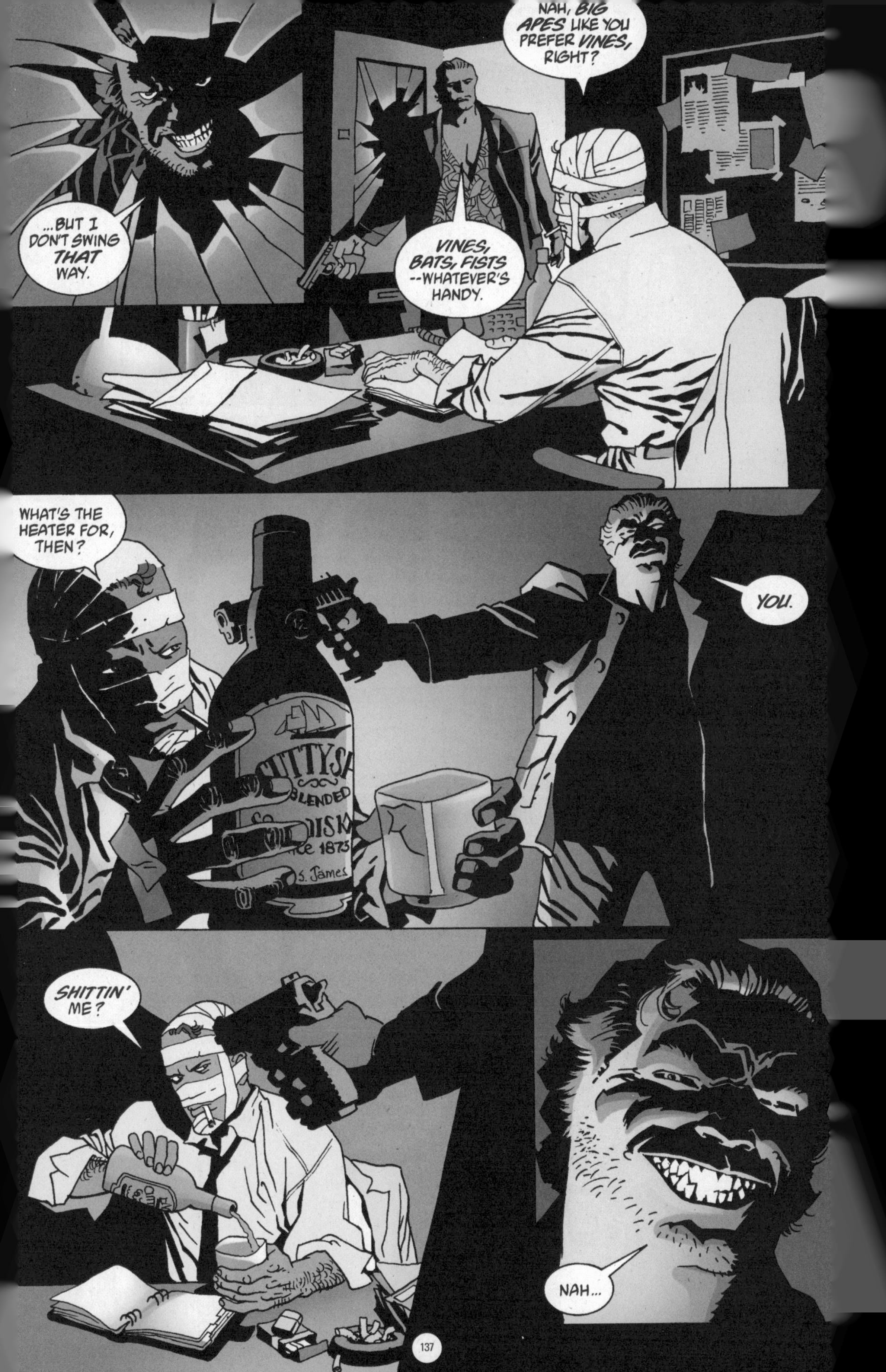
...BUT I DON'T SWING THAT WAY.
NAH, BIG APES LIKE YOU PREFER VINES, RIGHT?
VINES, BATS, FISTS --WHATEVER'S HANDY.
WHAT'S THE HEATER FOR, THEN?
YOU.
CUTTY SARK
BLENDED
S. James
SHITTIN' ME?
NAH...

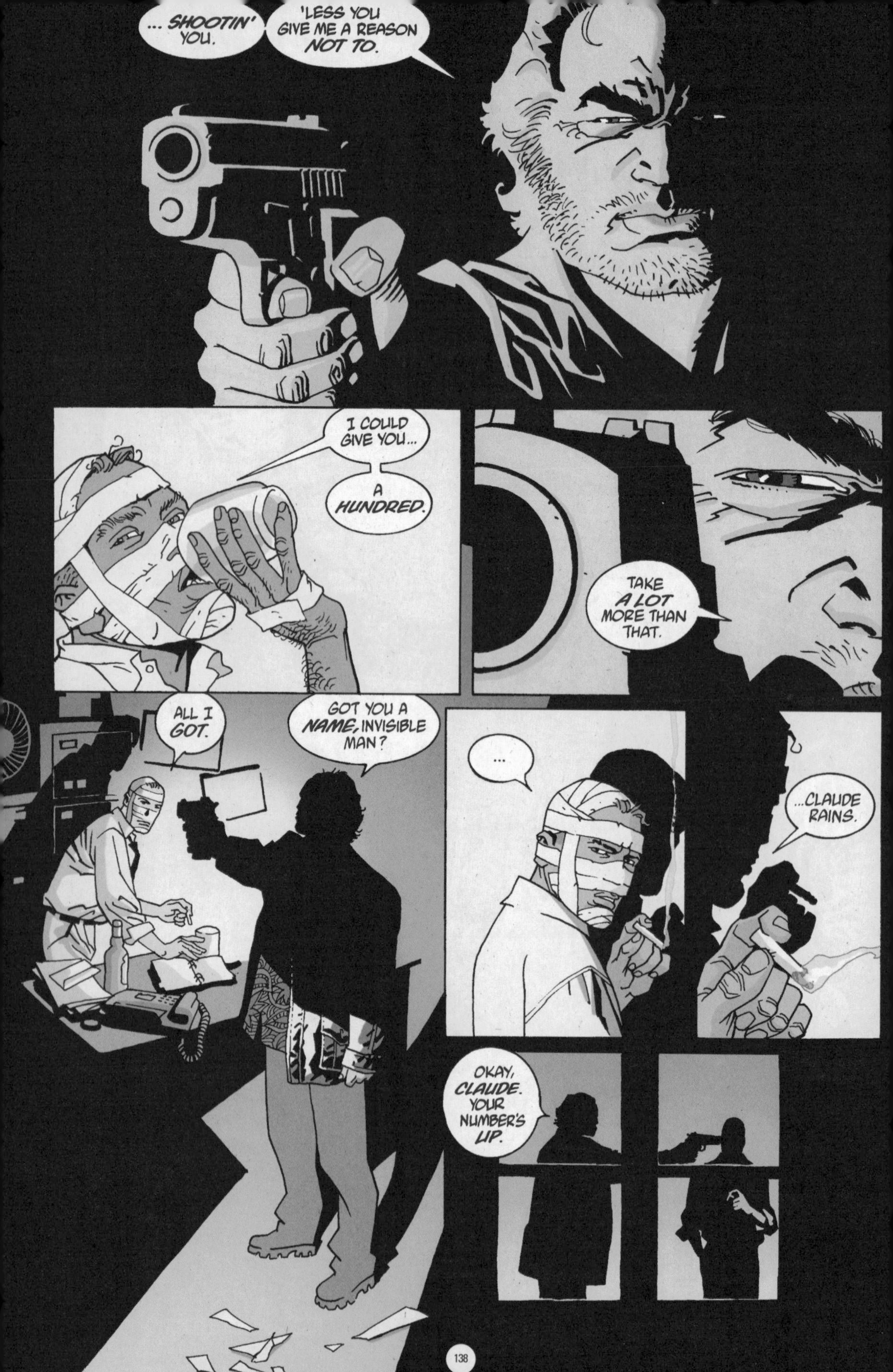

... SHOOTIN' YOU.
'LESS YOU GIVE ME A REASON NOT TO.
I COULD GIVE YOU...
A HUNDRED.
TAKE A LOT MORE THAN THAT.
ALL I GOT.
GOT YOU A NAME, INVISIBLE MAN?
...
...CLAUDE RAINS.
OKAY, CLAUDE. YOUR NUMBER'S UP.

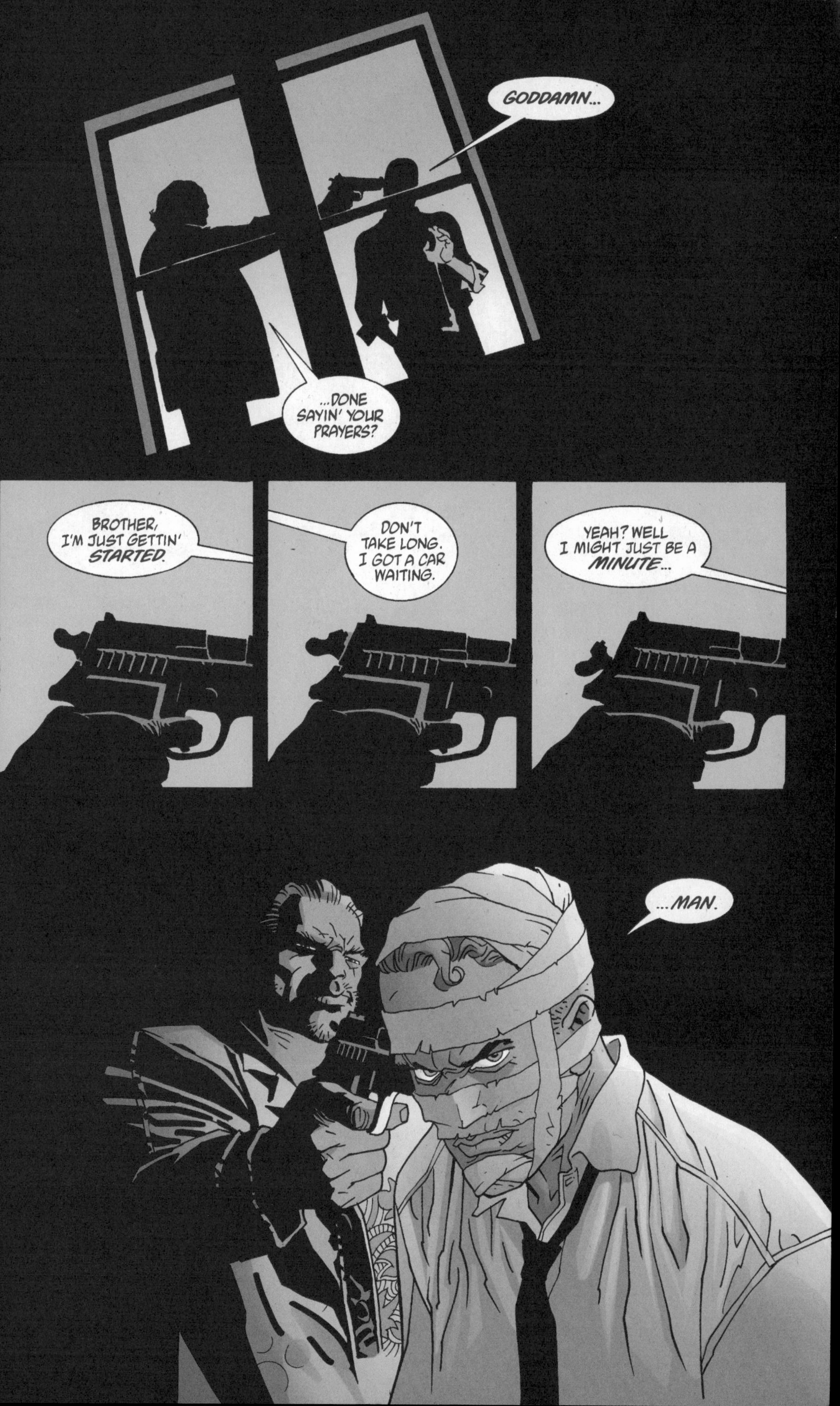
GODDAMN...
...DONE SAYIN' YOUR PRAYERS?
BROTHER, I'M JUST GETTIN' STARTED.
DON'T TAKE LONG. I GOT A CAR WAITING.
YEAH? WELL I MIGHT JUST BE A MINUTE...
...MAN.

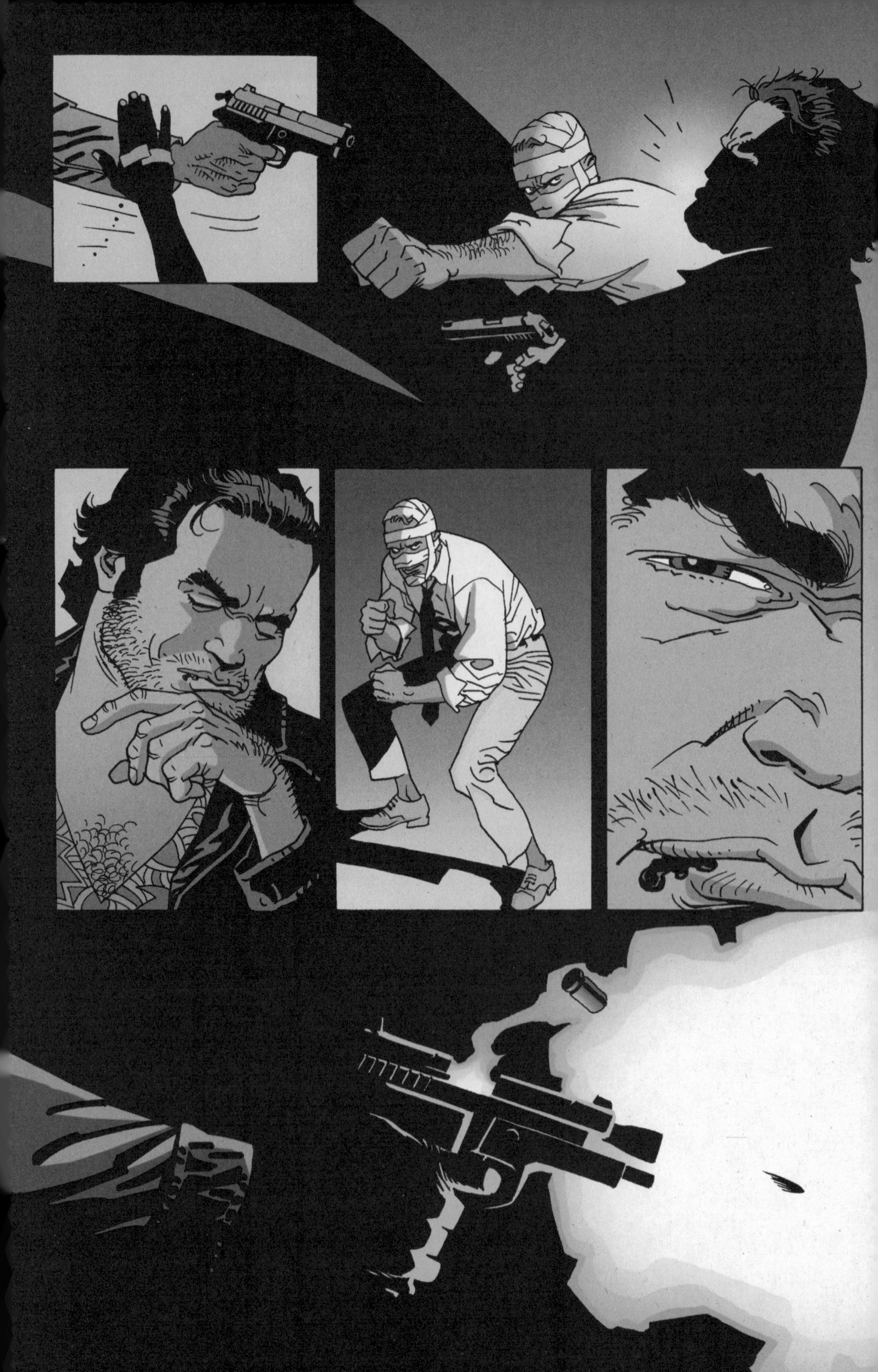

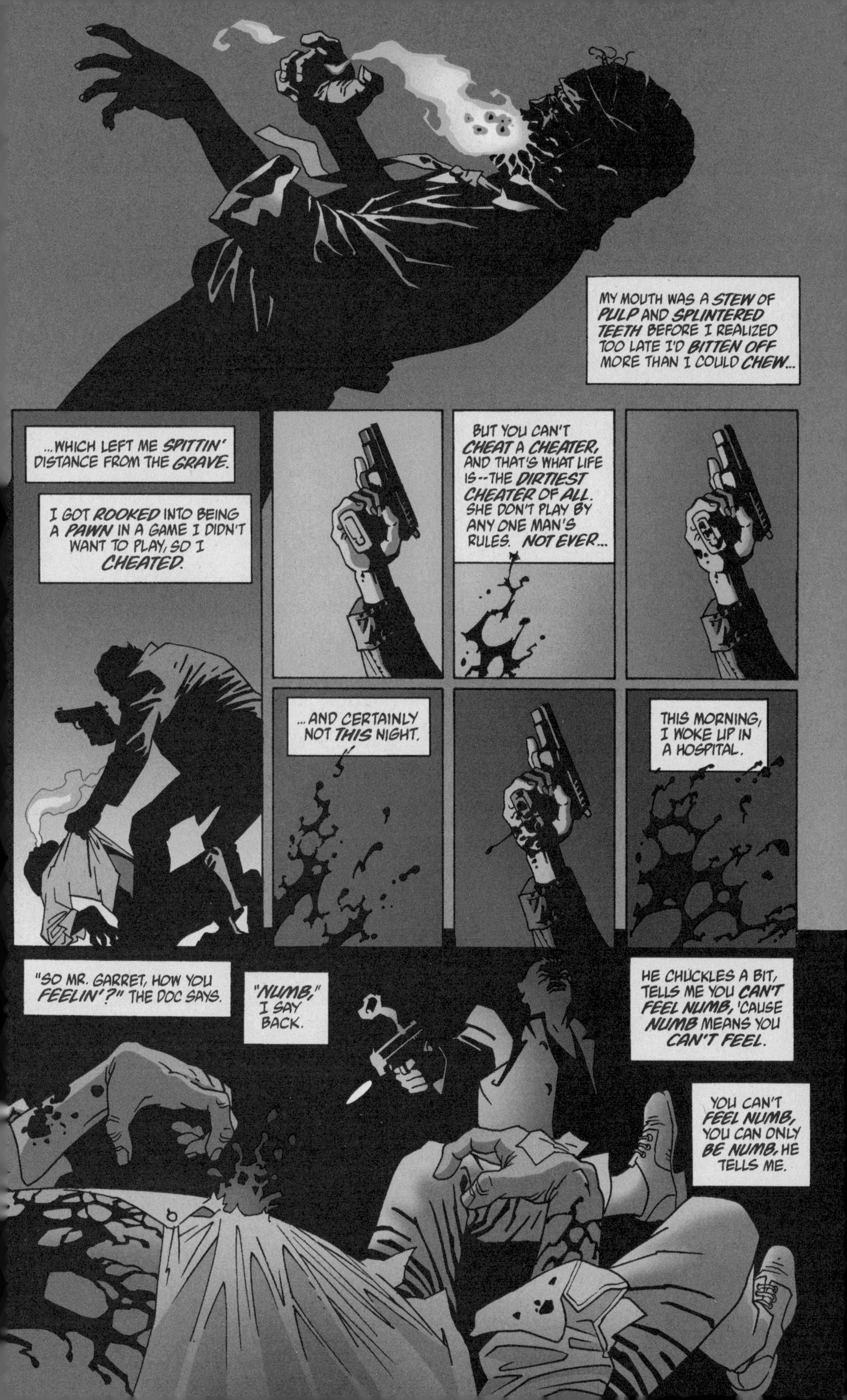
MY MOUTH WAS A STEW OF PULP AND SPLINTERED TEETH BEFORE I REALIZED TOO LATE I'D BITTEN OFF MORE THAN I COULD CHEW...
...WHICH LEFT ME SPITTIN' DISTANCE FROM THE GRAVE.
I GOT ROOKED INTO BEING A PAWN IN A GAME I DIDN'T WANT TO PLAY, SO I CHEATED.
BUT YOU CAN'T CHEAT A CHEATER, AND THAT'S WHAT LIFE IS--THE DIRTIEST CHEATER OF ALL. SHE DON'T PLAY BY ANY ONE MAN'S RULES. NOT EVER...
...AND CERTAINLY NOT THIS NIGHT.
THIS MORNING, I WOKE UP IN A HOSPITAL.
"SO MR. GARRET, HOW YOU FEELIN'?" THE DOC SAYS.
"NUMB," I SAY BACK.
HE CHUCKLES A BIT, TELLS ME YOU CAN'T FEEL NUMB, 'CAUSE NUMB MEANS YOU CAN'T FEEL.
YOU CAN'T FEEL NUMB, YOU CAN ONLY BE NUMB, HE TELLS ME.

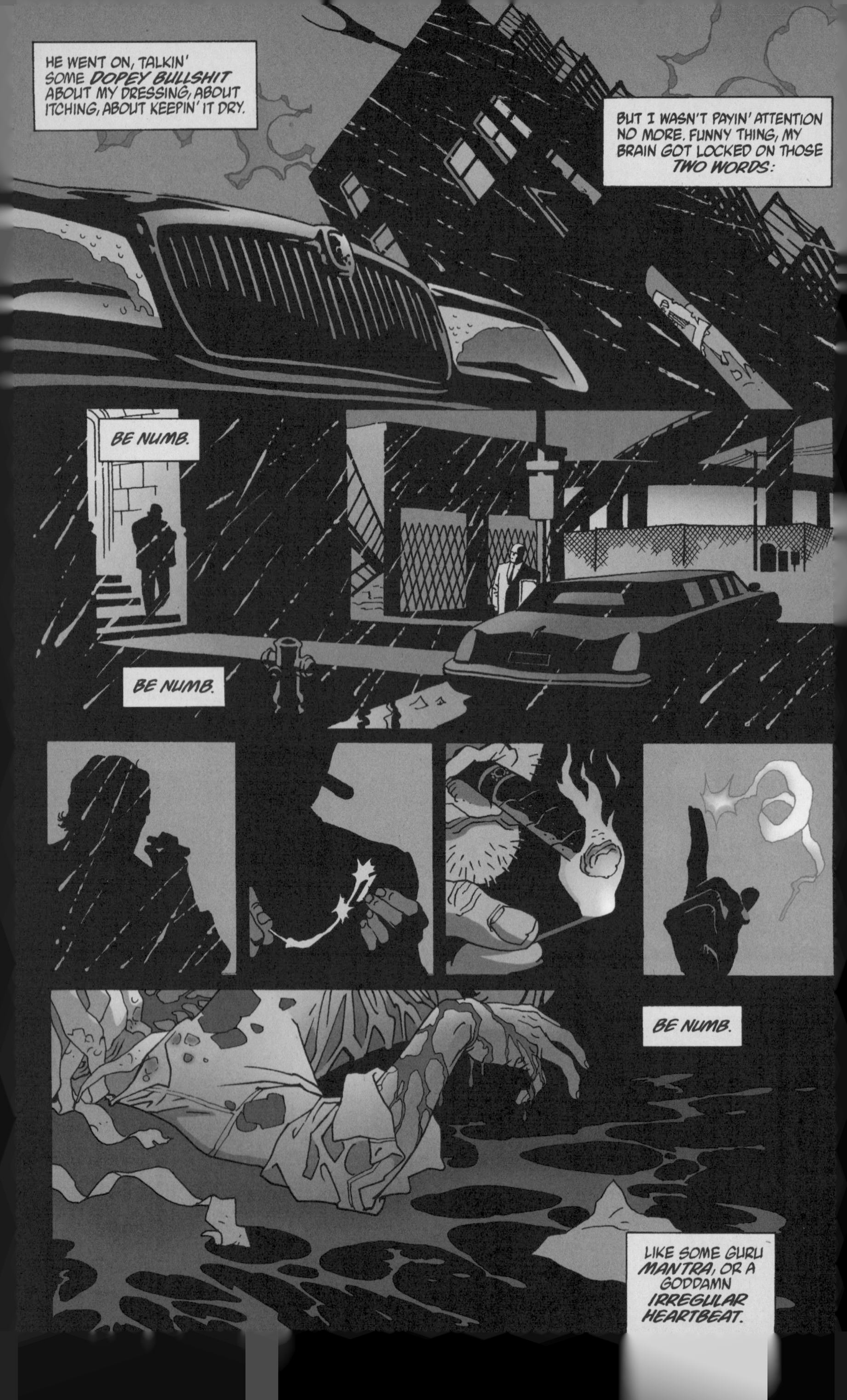
HE WENT ON, TALKIN' SOME DOPEY BULLSHIT ABOUT MY DRESSING, ABOUT ITCHING, ABOUT KEEPIN' IT DRY.
BUT I WASN'T PAYIN' ATTENTION NO MORE. FUNNY THING, MY BRAIN GOT LOCKED ON THOSE TWO WORDS:
BE NUMB.
BE NUMB.
BE NUMB.
LIKE SOME GURU MANTRA, OR A GODDAMN IRREGULAR HEARTBEAT.

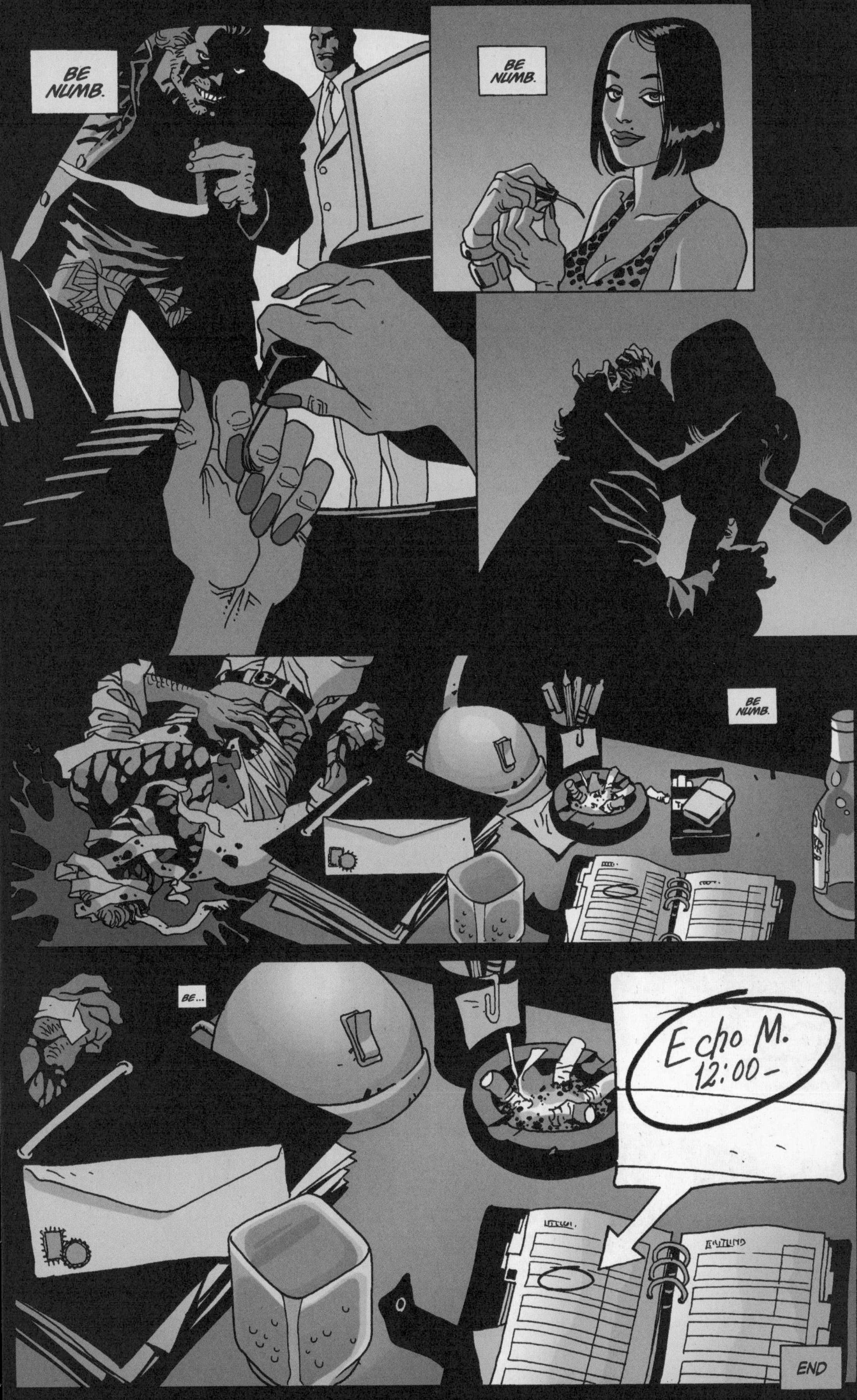
BE NUMB.
BE NUMB.
BE NUMB.
BE...
Echo M.
12:00 -
END